D0195841

PICABO

PICABO

NOTHING TO HIDE

PICABO STREET

WITH DANA WHITE

Contemporary Books

Chicago New York San Francisco Lisbon London Madrid Mexico City
Milan New Delhi San Juan Seoul Singapore Sydney Toronto

Library of Congress Cataloging-in-Publication Data

Street, Picabo, 1971–
  Picabo : nothing to hide / Picabo Street with Dana White.
   p. cm.
  ISBN 0-07-138312-3
   1. Street, Picabo, 1971– . 2. Skiers—United
States—Biography. I. White, Dana. II. Title.

  GV854.2.S843 A3 2002
  796.93′5′092—dc21
  [B]   2001047585

Contemporary Books

A Division of The McGraw·Hill Companies

Copyright © 2002 by Picabo Street. All rights reserved. Printed in the United States of America. Except as permitted under the United States Copyright Act of 1976, no part of this publication may be reproduced or distributed in any form or by any means, or stored in a database or retrieval system, without the prior written permission of the publisher.

1 2 3 4 5 6 7 8 9 0 LBM/LBM 0 9 8 7 6 5 4 3 2 1

ISBN 0-07-138312-3

This book was set in Sabon
Printed and bound by Lake Book Manufacturing

McGraw-Hill books are available at special quantity discounts to use as premiums and sales promotions, or for use in corporate training programs. For more information, please write to the Director of Special Sales, Professional Publishing, McGraw-Hill, Two Penn Plaza, New York, NY 10121-2298. Or contact your local bookstore.

This book is printed on acid-free paper.

To my mother for always teaching me, for being my best friend, and for giving me what little patience I do possess.

To my dad for the competitive and disciplined nature that has carried me to countless successes.

To my brother for pushing and protecting me. I love you, buddy.

To my sister-in-law, Lauren, for friendship and support.

To Jess for teaching me how to be a kind person.
I love you, friendy.

To Nadia for the boundless energy she spends taking care of me and being my friend. I love and miss you, N.

To John for reinstilling my faith in love and family. I look forward to a long and happy life with you. I love you, Mulli.

To Jeff and Susan for their unconditional love and support.

To Cade and Savannah for giving me unconditional love
and hope for the future.

CONTENTS

ACKNOWLEDGMENTS

THE AUTHORS WOULD LIKE TO THANK OUR AGENTS AT IMG, SUSAN Reed and Sue McCarthy-Dorf, for putting it all together. At Contemporary Books, senior editor Matthew Carnicelli envisioned what this book could be from the start and edited the manuscript with enthusiasm and insight, while senior project editor Heidi Bresnahan and managing editor Marisa L'Heureux performed brilliantly under the pressures of time. Dr. Richard Steadman of the Steadman Hawkins Clinic in Vail, Colorado, and Dr. Robert Scheinberg of Texas Orthopedic Associates in Dallas helped us get the medical facts straight. Ann Marie White provided the invaluable gift of research. We would also like to thank Jeff Cordes and Paul Robbins for the clips, Jalbert Productions for the footage, and Rick Kahl, Helen Ollson, and Bill Grout at *Skiing* magazine for the support. Sally Jenkins generously shared her wisdom and advice. Danielle Drake of Team Street worked that cell phone like nobody's business.

We are also indebted to the coaches, teammates, colleagues, and friends who shared their memories, expertise, and the occasional phone number: John Atkins, Pat Bauman, Muffy Davis, Herwig Demschar, Wendy Fisher, Ernst Hager, Brad Hunt, Nadia Guerriero, Matt James, Mike "Cookie" Kairys, Olle Larsson, Sue Levin, Paul Major, Sean

McCann, Tamara McKinney, Lane Monroe, and Andreas "Gnarly" Rickenbach.

Finally, this book could not have been possible without the help, hospitality, and stories of the Street family: Ron, Baba, Lauren, and especially Dee. Once again, you were the glue.

INTRODUCTION

I GREW UP ON STORIES.

My family lived in a tiny community near Sun Valley, Idaho, called Triumph, population thirty-five. Our home was an old mining cabin with plastic taped over the windows and a hardworking woodstove for heat. We didn't have a TV—my parents considered it a corrupting influence—but we did have a stereo. This was the 1970s and early '80s. I could sing along to Fleetwood Mac, but Wilma Flintstone was a stranger to me.

So we had to entertain ourselves. At night, especially if we had company, Mom and Dad would throw a few sticks of kindling on the fire and talk. About everything: stuff that happened when my older brother, Baba, and I were babies, who was doing what in Triumph, how the workday went, and whatnot. My family called it "talking story." I'd be playing in another room and half listening to Dad—he was the main storyteller—holding court in the living room. Dad's stories were dramatic and always seemed to involve some ill-advised adventure or freaky brush with disaster.

For example, there's the story of the time I escaped death at the tender age of one. My parents and their friends loved exploring the mountains, long before that became a trendy thing to do, and they'd hike into the high country for three weeks at a time, packing kids and supplies on a horse or mule. After setting up camp, they'd tie a log to the animals to keep them from wandering. One day Mom and Dad were hanging out at a friend's campsite with Baba and me when the friend's horse went wild—a bear must have spooked him—and he came ripping through camp, dragging that log behind him. Mom threw herself over me, and when she pulled herself up, she spotted a hoofprint pressed into the dirt a mere inch from my head. So you could say I've been living on the edge since I was in diapers.

Dad's stories taught me things. After hearing the tale about the horse and my head, I understood the narrow margin that separates life and death. My story is told within that margin.

Downhill ski racers know there is a fine line between going for it and holding back and surviving—a fine line that, at the world-class level, very few observers can define or even detect. But that tiny, indefinable margin can make a huge difference in how a skier feels, and therefore what his or her results are. A lot of athletes talk themselves out of winning. They come up with excuses as to why they aren't able to win, or don't deserve to, or aren't good enough to. And so they don't.

Before I was introduced to fear, I never talked myself out of winning. At every race I went into the gate with the unwavering belief that I would be the fastest skier in the field. This confidence was my trademark. I lost that confidence high on a mountain in Switzerland in the spring of 1998 after a fall that left me broken and traumatized. I have spent three years trying to get it back.

With its high speeds, hairpin turns, and bone-crushing crashes, downhill skiing has been called the NASCAR of winter sports. A ski racer slams into the rock-hard ground the way a racecar spins into a wall on the final turn. I've had my share of impacts; my body has paid a price. I have more scars than a woman should, and every one of them tells a story. I'm not proud of my scars, particularly the ten-inch Bride of Frankenstein number on the outside of my left thigh. These souvenirs of pain don't make me feel tough or successful as an athlete. They are signs of failure, of a loss of control.

Skiers risk everything for their sport, and sometimes they pay the ultimate price. More often they just get really badly hurt. I've had a few close calls myself and have been injured more times than I can count. This is the risk the ski racer accepts, and if you're demented like me, you push the envelope because that's where joy lies.

I've always been the kind of person who's stretched the limits, tested the boundaries, and challenged the rules. Conformity is not my thing. I grew up a poor kid in a rich kid's sport, a girl among boys, a free spirit among hard-asses, an American in a sport ruled by Europeans. I don't camouflage or censor myself. If I see bullshit, I call bullshit. The biggest lesson I took from my childhood was to keep it real, and maybe I've been a little too real for some people. My inner fire burns hot, and I believe that passion and intensity are two of the reasons I've achieved more success and fame than your average ski racer. Oh, and one more thing: never underestimate the power of a memorable name.

I am an all-or-nothing person, and my life has been marked by extremes—highs and lows, peaks and valleys. I've achieved an athlete's greatest accomplishment—Olympic gold—and experienced an athlete's greatest fear—a crippling injury. The crash of 1998 pulverized my left femur and shredded my right knee. I had to use crutches for months. *Two* crutches. People thought I had polio. I made fun of myself in a Nike commercial where I zoomed around a hospital in a wheelchair, but at the time there was nothing funny about the way I felt: stunted, like an animal caged in my own body. I had to literally rebuild my body and my mind. I had to learn to ski all over again and to face real fear for the first time.

What my story shows is that you can have a signature sneaker, big-time endorsement deals, and a string of TV commercials, but at the end of the day what matters is having a dream. My dream is to ski in one last Winter Olympics, the 2002 Games in Salt Lake City. This is the biggest comeback of my life, and some people don't think I can do it. A lot of people don't understand why I even want to try, why I didn't just give up and walk away three years ago, leaving my career on that mountainside in Switzerland. All I can say is when I have a dream, I'm like a pit bull with a chew toy: I won't drop it.

I can also say I'm just not ready to retire. Speed is in my system. I drive fast, talk fast, ski fast. My doctors say my blood runs through my body faster than most people's. I love to ride full throttle on my snowmobile, skipping across the surface of the earth for fifteen miles. I grew up believing I could do anything, that I was invincible. I have always had confidence in the physical realm, but I also had to learn not to be embarrassed by my strength. This is the central girl problem, but I learned what all girls need to learn: that you can kick ass, and you should never be ashamed to do so. Don't let anyone or anything slow you down.

Which brings me to another story.

A few years ago I had to get home in a hurry. Baba's wife, Lauren, had just given birth to a son named Cade, and I needed to see him. I was living in Portland, Oregon, at the time and couldn't get a flight to Sun Valley. So as I've done many times before, I decided to fly to Boise, rent a car, and drive.

There is a stretch of pavement on Interstate 84 where I really like to open it up. I come around a corner, crest a hill, and drop into the straightaway, and on this particular day, just as I'm getting up to speed, there it is, coming at me in the other lane.

"Damn!"

The police car whips around, and the flashing red lights pop into my rearview mirror.

I get pulled over a lot, but I usually get out of a ticket if the officer is a guy. The cop steps out of the car. A woman.

She leans into my window and says, "Where's the fire?"

I whip out my Idaho driver's license and hand it to her.

"Well, you're obviously familiar with the area," she says. "I'm just wondering why you felt you needed to drive so fast."

"I'm on the way to see my new nephew, ma'am. And, quite frankly, I'm comfortable at eighty miles an hour."

"Well," she says, "and what is it that you do that makes you so comfortable at eighty miles an hour?"

"I'm a ski racer."

She reads the name on my license, looks at me (freckles, red hair, etc.), and a lightbulb switches on. But she does an excellent job of hiding the fact that she's recognized me. Cops have to practice that.

"This isn't a ski hill," she says finally.

"I realize that, ma'am. I'm just really anxious to see my nephew, and I have no excuse whatsoever. I'm driving fast. I'm in a hurry. I'm excited. I can't help it."

"All right, I'm going to let you off. But not for free."

I sign a couple autographs. Then she looks at me and says, "Don't let me see you again."

"Hopefully, I'll see you first, ma'am."

I AM A SKI RACER.

Those words have defined me for twenty years. They gave me the green flag to channel all my energies into my sport. Sometimes that meant I wasn't my best as a person. I swore too much or stepped on people's toes or let my competitiveness build a wall around me. It can be hard to flip a switch and come back to earth. A former coach once told me that he couldn't expect me to act like an ordinary person when I spend my time perfecting the extraordinary.

My story has been told in bits and pieces over the last eight years by a lot of writers and reporters. Sometimes they get the story right, but often they don't. So as the daughter of storytellers, I think it's only right for me to tell my own story, once and for all, and describe the people, events, and especially the place called Triumph that shaped me.

I'm still trying to figure out who I am off skis, and my story is about that evolution. I've been searching for my old, fearless, invincible self for the past three years, but the person I've found is new—changed by adversity into someone more human, more humble, more compassionate.

This is the story of how I grew up.

PICABO

KARMA

WHEN YOU DANCE WITH DEATH EVERY DAY, IT HELPS TO BELIEVE IN A power bigger than yourself, something to help make sense of the risks you take on skis. I believe in karma. What goes around, comes around. It's a question of balance, a cosmic seesaw. If you experience an incredible high point, then an equally dramatic low point must occur for balance to be present. In one month in 1998 I saw both ends of the spectrum. In February, my greatest dream came true in Hakuba, Japan. Thirty days later, in Crans-Montana, Switzerland, my worst nightmare kicked my ass.

I try to live my life in a way that creates good karma. Be a good person, give to others, show respect, mind your manners. Sometimes I fall off the wagon—I snap at a flight attendant, for example. But then I work extra hard to cover the deficit and ward off the bad karma.

But I still don't know what I did to deserve what happened to me in Crans.

I don't like to think about that accident. I don't like to look at video footage or photographs of it. And I will never go back to that mountain. You couldn't pay me to step foot on that Swiss rock pile.

Hakuba, on the other hand—I'd go back there in a heartbeat.

Wednesday, February 11, 1998

The Winter Olympic Games, Women's Super G, Hakuba, Japan

I'm not supposed to be here.

Fourteen months ago I shredded my left knee in a fall during a downhill-training run and had to have the joint completely rebuilt. I rehabbed like a maniac and cut the normal two-year recovery time in half. I started skiing again only two months ago after more than a year off the snow. I've got only a handful of World Cup races under my belt this season, with my best result a fourth in the downhill in Cortina, Italy. Twelve days ago I took a huge digger in Sweden and knocked myself unconscious, ending up in the hospital with whiplash and a concussion. My neck is stiff and my head still aches. So does my right ankle, which I sprained two days ago playing volleyball. The ankle puffed up and turned black-and-blue, and the only reason I can stand on it is the castlike support of my stiff plastic ski boot.

Otherwise, I feel pretty good.

I'll be the second skier out of the gate for the Women's Super G, so the snow should be firm and fast. I wore bib Number 2 the last time I competed in Japan, at the 1993 World Alpine Ski Championships, where I won a silver medal. It's all coming together.

The Super G is a speed event, shorter than the downhill, and with more turns. I've never won an international Super G competition, and everyone expects me to contend for gold in the downhill on Saturday. This race is a warm-up, but it's also a chance to strike.

"If I pull it off," I'd told *Sports Illustrated*, "it will be a miracle."

I show up at the ski room bright and early on race day to pick up my warm-up skis. Expecting to find Super G skis waiting for me, I see a pair of downhill boards hanging up outside instead. They're dense, meaty, and fast, more like two-by-fours than the newer, high-tech Super G skis other racers will be using.

I grab the skis and slide open the glass door. My ski technician, a 6'8" Canadian cowboy named Mike "Cookie" Kairys, is sitting on his toolbox, smoking a cigarette.

"What gives?"

"The course is like a downhill, baby!" he crows. "You don't need those other boards. That thing is set wide open, and it's got your name all over it."

I let out a whoop. *Oh yeah. This is happening.*

Unlike the downhill, there are no training runs in the Super G, only a course inspection before the race. This is supposed to make the competition more exciting and spontaneous. As I sideslip along the course on my warm-up skis, I see that the course fits me like my skintight speed suit. It's a wide-open run, aggressive and long, without a lot of big, hard turns. The course starts above the tree line and flows down the mountain like water.

After inspection I take a couple of warm-up runs elsewhere on the mountain. The weather has been iffy all morning. The men's downhill is supposed to take place first, but a storm has socked in the mountain, and at around 11:00 A.M. it is announced that the men's event is canceled. Almost immediately afterward, the heavens part like the Red Sea, giving the women blue skies and sunshine for the Super G.

I don't like to hang out at the start, so I head up the mountain just thirty minutes before race time. I ride in the gondola with a young teammate, Jonna Mendes, and at one point she turns to me and says, "Peek, there's no reason you can't win this race. I have confidence in you, and I think you should go big today. Go for the gold."

I haven't always had the support of my teammates, and knowing that they're behind me today means everything.

I get off the gondola, skis in hand, and head to a chairlift that will take me to the top of the course. Suddenly I hear my older brother's whistle; I'm sure of it. I turn around and spot Baba and my agents, Brad Hunt and Nadia Guerriero. They'd gone to the top of the mountain to take pictures and are about to get on the gondola to head down to the bottom. Baba asks me what I'm doing with downhill skis. When I tell him, he yells, "Yeah!" and gives me the thumbs-up. "Go get it!"

The start area is almost empty when I get there. Skiing down from the lift, I hear Ken Read, a CBS commentator, talking to a television camera about my prospects today. He says something about how I've had limited starts this year but that a low start number might help my prospects because the course will be in good shape. I'll show him.

Cookie and I have a prerace routine. I step out of my warm-up skis and set my backpack down. Sometimes I look at him; sometimes I don't. I find a spot off by myself, just me and my headphones. Music has always helped me concentrate, lock me into competition mode. This morning I'm listening to Tupac Shakur's "Never Had a Friend Like Me," an aggressive song that drives its take-no-prisoners attitude straight into my brain stem.

Next comes my visualization exercise. I've never skied this course, but I've seen it, and that's enough to imprint the terrain on my brain. I steer my hands like skis through the imaginary course, dipping and gliding and jumping, Tupac merging with every turn and roll into a rhythmic, sinuous, flowing whole.

After a series of stretches, I strip down to my downhill suit and exchange my headphones for my helmet, which has a graphic of a roaring tiger, painted so that you can see my face between its sharp teeth.

After gearing up I walk over to Cookie, who's standing at the start gate holding my race skis. He's nicknamed them my Olys, short for "Olympics"; they're the same skis I wore when I won a silver medal in the 1994 Winter Olympics in Lillehammer, Norway. I jump up and down three times on both legs as high as I can, then pop into my skis. Still standing, I kick each ski on its end, so that the tail lodges in the snow and the tip points straight up, and I stretch my hamstrings while Cookie wipes the bases and the edges down. As soon as I lower the second ski, I hit his hands, a low ten, and he hits mine.

I lower my goggles, and I'm ready.

Helen Marken of Norway is the first racer out of the gate. I watch her attack the first section of the course and think, *Right on, I can get it, because it's smooth and it's nice and it runs well.* I switch into attack mode.

I've only got four gates to gain as much speed as I possibly can to carry me into the flat section that follows. I'm known as a great glider, and if I can hit the flats with enough momentum and fly into a long series of S-turns, I have a good chance. I've got to work every inch of this terrain.

When Marken is halfway down the course, I move into the start house.

Television does not do justice to my sport. To the average viewer watching the race from his or her easy chair, this first pitch looks like a kid's sledding hill, but in reality it's like standing at the top of a roller coaster's steepest drop, poised for free fall. As the ten-second countdown begins, I position my poles over the start wand. Cookie sidles next to me and holds a two-way radio to my helmet. My coaches—Jim, Chip, Gnarly, Herwig, and Marjan—are stationed at crucial points along the course, and as Marken passes them, they bleat advice into the radio on how the course is running.

Suddenly I'm not listening anymore. I'm doing it. The last thing I hear is my teammate Kirsten Clark yelling "Go Peek, go!" and her passion sends me down the hill.

As I drop into my tuck, I work my feet in my boots over the rolling terrain, the way a dolphin surges through water. I smack the first gate and drive my inside hip and milk that first pitch for everything it has to give me. So far the run feels great; the snow is smooth, and my speed feels easy. I fly onto the flats at forty miles per hour, catch some air off a short jump, smack another gate as I whiz by, and I think, *Wow, I'm really having one. I've got to stick with it.*

I cruise through the S-turns, but the most difficult section lies ahead: a big knoll that leads into a ninety-degree blind turn that falls away steeply and ends with another knoll.

This is where I screw up. I don't suck my feet up enough going off the knoll and I catch too much air. My weight falls back and I fly through the air with my legs straight out in front of me and land too low out of the jump, putting me out of position to make the turn around the next gate. Missing the turn means I'll crash into the orange safety fence. Instead I crank the turn hard, my outside leg shaking with the G forces, and power my skis around the gate, trying to hang onto my speed.

Suddenly my motivation switches to anger: *You idiot, you dork. You're going to throw it away. I can't believe you made that mistake!* I come out of the turn so pissed I dive on the next four gates and cut the line off immensely, barely on the edge of control. I pass another gate and scream around a corner and down through a slight compression to hit the first big jump. I'm going at least sixty by now, a little fast, so I check my speed a bit and launch. I think, *Wow! I caught a lot of air*, and then I'm on it again, aggressively working the terrain on the bottom of the course. As I approach the last jump, I know exactly where to launch because I can still hear Marjan's advice: "I know you're going to come in here hauling ass, so make sure you go off that jump left of center. You cannot go center or right or you're going to have a problem."

If I jump to the right, I might panic, change my body position in the air, and blow it. *Get back, get back, get back!* I jump left of center and drift right, landing just before the finish, and sneak just inside the outside finish post.

Yeah! That was a good run! I pump my fist and skid to a stop in the finish corral while looking at the clock. My time is 1:18:02, almost two full seconds ahead of Marken, a canyonwide lead. The crowd roars and I wonder how I could have beaten her by so much. I'm in first place. And with the rest of the field still to come, all I have to do is stay there.

I click out of my bindings and, with my helmet still on and breathing hard, do an interview with Mary Carillo of CBS. Mary says the skiers in the teens may have faster conditions. I tell her I skied well. I had some pretty good jumps, so I'm happy, and we'll see how my time holds up.

I watch as skiers reel down the mountain. *Nobody's catching me; nobody's catching me.* Alexandra "Meisi" Meissnitzer, an Austrian who's one of my best buddies on the World Cup tour, crosses the finish line three one-hundredths of a second behind me and pulls into second.

I wait at the bottom for what seems like an hour. People and television cameras swarm, but I'm too nervous to say much. At one point I say to the camera, "If I win this thing, man, I am a true racehorse."

The best racers in the world give it their best shot, but they can't beat my time. I watch as they cross the finish line, look at their times on the scoreboards, and hang their heads in disappointment: Isolde Kostner of Italy, Heidi Zurbriggen of Switzerland, my good buddy Pernilla Wiberg of Sweden. Even my archrival, Katja Seizinger, a German I call the Executioner for the way she decimates the competition, can't catch me. Sorry, Katja, not today. The biggest scare comes when Number 18, Michaela "Micki" Dorfmeister of Austria, another friend, beats my split time two-thirds of the way down the course. She blazes across the finish line, a mere one one-hundredth of a second behind me. She pops into second, bumping Meisi to third, and collapses on the snow in mock frustration. I run to Micki and give her a hug. She was racing with a broken thumb—a tough cookie, just like me.

After Micki fails to unseat me the magnitude of my victory starts to set in. What seems like ten thousand photographers have their cameras trained on me, and everyone is watching and cheering and offering congratulations. In wonderment, I cover my mouth with my gloved hands. *Wow, I did it. I won.* Meisi, Micki, and I have finished within three one-hundredths of a second of one another, and later I find out it's the closest margin of victory in Olympic Alpine skiing history. But all I know at that moment is a feeling of disbelief and even a little fear. *How do I behave? What do I say?* I want to calm everybody down, to tell everyone, *No, wait! This is the moment I've been waiting for all my life! I'm not ready; hold on; I've got to go powder my nose or something; give me a second!*

Patrick Lang, my translator, says, "Peeky" and motions toward the crowd. I turn around and see Baba; my dad, Ron; and my boyfriend, J.J., standing a few yards away amid a phalanx of cameras. Somehow they've managed to sneak into the finish corral. "How did you get here?" I cry, and I grab my dad and we embrace. His smile is so big, and he is so happy, and he just hugs me tightly and says, "You're so incredible. I'm so proud of you. I'm so honored to be your dad." J.J. gives me a discreet hug, and then I hug Baba, my burly big brother. "Way to go there, little sis," he says, looking misty-eyed.

Dad, Baba, and I embrace harder than we ever have in our whole lives. That hug at the finish line is the culmination of years of sacrifice and effort. We had set out for this when I was ten, and now it has finally happened. They were there for all of it—the sacrifices, the physical and emotional struggles, the injuries, and the arguments. We're living our dream, and it's almost too much to comprehend.

There's only one person missing.

Dad looks at me and says, "There's something over there waiting for you." I turn around and Tom Kelly, media director for the U.S. Ski Team, is handing me a cell phone. "It's your mother."

I grab the phone and find a private spot away from the hysteria to talk.

"What's going on?" Mom asks. It sounds as if she's just woken up.

"Mom, I won!"

"What? The downhill hasn't happened yet."

"I won the Super G, Mom!"

"Oh my god! Oh honey, that's great!" And then she starts crying, and then I start crying. I tell her that I miss her and I wish she were here. Then I tell her I'm going to win the downhill and bring two gold medals to Maui, where the family plans to celebrate after the Games.

I look up and there's a CBS camera right in my face, transmitting my intimate moment with my mom to millions of people around the world. Oh, well. Then I tell Mom that I love her too and ask her if she wants to talk to Dad.

The next few minutes click by like a slide show. Cookie appears and takes my skis and hugs me, on the verge of tears, just like he was in Lille-hammer four years earlier. My cheering coaches hoist me up on their shoulders for a photo op. When I look at that photograph now, I remember how intense and immense the moment was and how numb with joy I felt. Every-thing was happening so quickly when all I wanted to do was grab that moment and slow it down, to let the details sink in.

So I do more interviews and there's more hoopla and then it's time for the flower ceremony. The official medal ceremony will be later tonight, but this gives the crowd of twenty thousand spectators closure. Officials drag a podium out to the middle of the finish corral. The announcer says each of our names, starting with Alexandra Meissnitzer, the bronze medalist. Still in her ski suit, Meisi steps up to the lowest platform and a pretty Japa-nese girl hands her a bouquet of dried flowers. It is destiny that Meisi and I have both finished in the top three. Less than a year earlier, when she was in the States for the World Cup finals, she had hung out with me at home in Portland, Oregon, for two weeks. We'd made a pact to climb the podium together at the Olympics—and here we are.

Next to mount the podium and take her flowers is Michaela Dorfmeis-ter, the silver medalist. When my name reverberates throughout the arena—*Picabo Street!*—and I step up on the podium, the crowd goes wild. This is the moment I've been waiting for all my life. Clutching my bou-quet, I raise my arms triumphantly in the air, and twenty thousand people roar their approval.

Then I kneel on the podium and bow my head, trying to send my energy to Mom, to somehow get her to feel what I've done.

Afterward it's time to pee in a cup. The doping-control station is a secure area set up near the finish, and when I reach it, there's a line of athletes ahead of me. All I want to do is get this over with because there are so many places I'd rather be than here trying to prove I'm not a cheater. But it does give me my first moment to sit and breathe. My skis and my suit are examined to make sure they aren't rigged. I see Meisi and give her a big, long hug. Then I go to a press conference, after which I head back to my Olympic pad, a beautiful log house tucked into the woods not far from the ski lifts.

When I get there everyone is celebrating, even the cooks. They've prepared my favorite lunch: a ham and cheese sandwich, chips, and apple juice. Dad, Baba, J.J., and my agents, Brad and Nadia, are rejoicing, hooting, hollering, and high-fiving, while I perfect the art of eating and grinning simultaneously. Everything is going a million miles a second, and before I know it, it's time to get ready for the medal ceremony in downtown Nagano, an hour and a half away. It's already 5:00 P.M. I don't even have time to shower. I dig around in my bag for my medal-ceremony outfit. What was I supposed to wear again? These pants, this jacket, those gloves.

Two cars arrive, and the Japanese drivers expect us to separate. I'm supposed to ride down in a big bus with a camera on me, but I refuse; I want to stay with my group. I announce we're all riding together, and we pack ourselves into one car. By now it's dark, and the snowy road is twisting and narrow. "Look," someone says, "the moon is full," and I peer through the car window at the sky. Suddenly I'm eight again and back in Idaho, sneaking out of our house in Triumph by moonlight, headed for the chicken coop. A red hen I'd raised from a chick was about to lay eggs, and Mom had told me they might be brown. I couldn't wait to see them, to hold those first warm eggs in my hand, and I kept waking up before dawn to see if she'd laid them yet. I was afraid of the dark and would have waited until daylight had it not been for that big bright spotlight of a moon, illuminating my path to the coop, across the street and behind the garden. Tonight the moon is doing it again, shiny and round as a medal, leading me to a prize at the end of the road—just another perfect moment in a perfect day.

The medal ceremonies are held in Nagano's town square, and when we get there the driver wants to drop me off by myself. "No way, man. I think someone should stay with her," Dad says, and I choose Baba, the family bodyguard because he's big and strong and crowds make me nervous. Then we're told that Baba doesn't have the proper credentials to enter a secure area and will have to watch the ceremony on a closed-circuit TV. I'm adamant that Baba stay with me, and just as it looks like I'm about to pitch a fit, the Japanese officials cave in. They know how mad Americans can get when provoked. So Baba ends up with a ringside seat near the stage. He's the last person I see as I climb the stairs to the medal platform.

As I take the stage, I feel like a rock star strutting her stuff. After taking my position behind the top podium, I hear an announcement in English that Jean-Claude Killy, the legendary French ski racer, will be giving me my medal. I scan the stands for Dad, find him, and mouth the words, *Did you hear that?*

My dad and I have this funny thing we do when we get emotional. We look up at the sky and stretch out our chins and necks like turtles. This tightens the skin and muscles and prevents us from crying. I see him stretch his neck out, and I know that he understands the significance of this moment. I had never met Killy, but Dad had many years earlier, and now our lives had come full circle.

I lower my head so Killy can reach me. "I've been waiting for this moment for a long time," he says as he drapes the medal around my neck.

"I think I've been waiting for it longer."

"I know you have. I'm going to be back here Saturday. What about you?"

"I sure hope so. See you Saturday."

What do you do after someone gives you a gold medal? I want to jump up and down and scream and yell with joy. But I know I have to keep it formal, keep it together.

I am a patriot. My dream as a kid was to fight for my country, but since women aren't allowed on the front lines, I opted to ski for the United States instead. I always knew that the ultimate reward would be to hear "The Star-Spangled Banner" playing just for me and to see the American flag rising into the night sky. Now that it's happening, I cry. The turtle maneuver isn't working this time, and I cry from the moment I step onto that podium to the moment the anthem ends. I can see Dad and the flag at the same time, and as I sing along, I can see everything I care about—my family, my flag, my coaches. I sing for all of us, as loudly and proudly as I can, my heart a balloon about to burst.

I DON'T WIN THE DOWNHILL. I FINISH SIXTH, FOR REASONS I'LL GO INTO later. But it almost doesn't matter. I've got my gold, and we're in Hawaii by the next afternoon. Mom has been waiting for us in a big house we rented for the occasion. She didn't go to the Olympics this time because the Olympics are all about walking, and walking is hard for her. When I finally get to show her my medal, she holds it in trembling hands, and the crying begins all over again.

Maui is perfect. We spend ten days eating, drinking, celebrating, and admiring my jewelry from Nagano. I let everybody wear the beautiful medal, to share in the feeling.

But all the time I know that the World Cup season isn't over. I have two more races, one in France and one in Switzerland. As much as I want to stay here, I have to finish what I started. I have to prove that Nagano was legit, that I deserved to win. I'll make pit stops in Los Angeles, Las Vegas, and Portland before heading to Europe for three weeks. "I'll come home safe," I tell Mom. "I promise."

I fly to Geneva with my agent, Nadia, who has never seen me ski in Europe. After arriving we connect with the rest of the team. There's only one other skier, Kristina Koznick; our coaches and support staff outnumber us two to one. We get to Morzine, a French ski resort that straddles the French and Swiss border, only to find there's not enough snow for a regulation downhill. For five days we hang around Morzine until officials finally decide to cancel the race. Most of the Europeans go home, leaving the Americans, Canadians, Norwegians, and Russians looking for something to do before the next race in Crans-Montana, Switzerland. We end up staying in Morzine a couple days to train, but I feel distracted and restless. I'm half inclined to pull the plug, but I know that all these people—Cookie, Herwig, Gnarly, Jim, and Chip—have traveled here just for me. Not only that, but a good finish in Crans will raise my ranking in the downhill and set me up for next season.

I'm not a superstitious athlete in the conventional sense. I don't believe in jinxes or that wearing the same underwear at every race guarantees success. I don't have a favorite necklace or good luck charm. I just have karma. That's why I should have seen it coming. All the signs were there, telling me to go home.

The cancellation was the first sign. The next one is a fall that comes out of nowhere. I'm in my tuck on a really flat run when I catch an edge and slam into the snow, hitting my head. It's a lame fall, and I can't believe it happened. My head is still back home, and it hurts so much that I call and ask Mom to send me a new helmet because I'm afraid there's something wrong with this one. Finally the team packs up and piles into the team van for the long drive to Crans.

Friday, March 13, 1998

World Cup Downhill Finals, Crans-Montana, Switzerland

I don't particularly want to be here.

The course is mushy, the weather is foggy, and the race is late. I've been sitting in the lodge since 9:30 A.M., waiting for the downhill to start. It's already been postponed once, and if it's going to happen, it's got to happen today. The officials keep changing their minds. The race is off, then on, then off again.

About one hundred of the world's best ski racers, both men and women, mill around the lodge, wasting time. The morning falls into a routine: kick it in the lodge for an hour, take a run, eat something. Lather, rinse, repeat.

Finally, at 11:00 A.M., there's the announcement: the downhill is on, and the men will race first. That takes two hours. Finally, the women are up.

Michaela Dorfmeister is wearing bib Number 1. I'm wearing Number 2, just as I did at the Olympics, only this scenario could not be more different. For one thing, I'm on new, unfamiliar skis, and I miss my old boards immensely. The sun has gone on sabbatical. Fog moves in and out, throwing a damp towel over the atmosphere and softening the spring snow. The visibility is horrible. The course keepers have scattered pine boughs on the snow to aid in depth perception, but I can't see the line I want to run very well. Before the race I ask the start ref if he's going to put more pine boughs on the course.

"There are pine boughs," he answers and walks away.

I go into the start gate mad. *Focus, Peek. Just get this day over with.*

The toughest part of the course is only six turns down: a sharp turn that leads into a big jump. I hated that jump the second I saw it.

I pass the first split-time timer and approach the jump, but as I go into the turn, my skis turn more sharply than I expect them to and I hit the jump too far to the left. *Damn! What the hell was that?* I fly too far and land too low. I go straight into my tuck, but my weight falls back so that my butt almost skims the ground.

Ski racers know when they're about to crash. They can feel it—a leaden *ping* in their gut. In a millisecond they veer from confident to desperate, scrabbling for options that flash through their head and are discarded just as quickly.

I switch into survival mode. *Oh, shit, I've got to pull this off.*

Okay, throw that one out. I'm crashing. How am I going to control this crash?

I have two options: kick my feet out to the right or the left. If I go to the right, I could skim the bottom of my skis along the fence. Then I realize I'd catch the outside gate with my shins and get whiplashed into the fence headfirst. Since I'm going so fast, the impact would probably snap my neck. The other option is to kick my feet out to the left and try to spin out as hard as I can to go into the fence bases first. If I go in tips first, I'm going to get hurt—badly.

Left or right? Live or die?

I have no intention of becoming the second woman to die in a World Cup ski race. I kick my feet out to the left and spin my body. I don't get all the way around and I slam into the fence tips first. My body goes from sixty to zero in a split second, crumpling my left leg like a piece of paper. My skis explode off my feet and my poles go flying.

I lie perfectly still for a moment, chest heaving. I can't feel my legs. *Oh my God, how bad is this? Am I paralyzed?*

I roll over and try to sit up. My legs drop lifelessly away, like marionette legs, and a wave of pain blasts over me, as if someone has switched on a blowtorch inside my leg.

That's when I start to scream.

I look at my left thigh. It looks shorter than it should and cocked to one side. I reach down and feel a knob of bone. Have I dislocated my kneecap? I search farther down and find my kneecap in place. It's not my knee. It's the end of my thighbone. My femur has snapped in two. The searing pain I felt when I tried to sit up was the jagged bone end ripping through my quadriceps muscle.

It's bad this time, really bad. I've blown my left knee apart twice in the past, but this is a whole new level of suffering. It's bone, not tissue, and I can hardly identify this pain. It's so foreign, so unlike anything I've ever experienced. And there's another sensation that's even less familiar: sheer terror. The last time I hurt myself, in December of 1996, I felt furious. I didn't lie there afraid. I pounded the snow in anger, and had I been able to stand, I would have destroyed something. Now I'm lying here, shocked and afraid. This is new territory, and I have no idea what I've done. Have I destroyed myself?

"Herwig!" I am screaming my coach's name. "Herwig!"

The first person to reach me is Gunther Hujara, chief race director for the World Cup tour. In photos of the aftermath Gunther is the guy with the moustache holding me from behind with his legs wrapped around me, trying to get me to lie down and relax. I have two choices: fight the pain or succumb to it. I decide to keep fighting.

Out of the corner of my eye I spot someone zoom by me. A few moments later, Dr. Bob Scheinberg, our team physician, hikes up to me from below. He had run across the course in his ski boots, lost his footing, and started sliding, narrowly avoiding me and sliding into the fence below me.

He approaches and says, a little sheepishly, "Hi."

He inspects my left thigh. "Oh, boy."

The first thing he has to do is stabilize the leg and stop the muscle spasms to ease my agony. He tells me to relax and take breaths and focus on my breathing. Then, without hesitating, he grabs my leg at the crux of my knee and pulls. The bone straightens out and I grunt in pain.

He's leaning on my foot as he does this, and I think that's what's making my leg hurt.

"Stop it! Let go! Quit pushing on my toes!" I scream. He looks at me and says as calmly as he can, "Why don't you lay back then."

I lean forward and push on his chest. "Quit pushing on my leg; you're making it hurt!"

"I'm trying to make it *not* hurt anymore," he says gently.

By now I've stopped screaming and am reduced to grunting long, guttural moans, the sound a wounded animal makes.

Fuck! I can't believe I came here and did this. I'm so tired of this sport. I'm not doing this anymore. I'm done. I'm finished. What did I do to deserve this? All I wanted was one more good race.

Thank you very much for the gold medal. I really appreciate it.

Herwig clicks out of his skis and runs toward me. I look into his face and see sadness and anxiety—and a little guilt. Last night we'd had a huge fight in the hotel bar. He had sensed my ambivalence and refused to let me race unless I was focused. "Make a decision tonight," he'd said. "In or out." I should have said out, but my pride and ego overruled my instincts. I know this is the last place Herwig wants to be, holding another injured ski racer in his arms, hoping for the best. At that moment, I know I will never ski for him again. It is over. And I sense he knows it, too.

"I'm sorry," he tells me with his eyes. And I tell him with mine how sorry I am, too.

Herwig hovers worriedly, holding me, letting me go, asking Bob questions. I rattle off orders in English to the medics and Herwig translates everything I say into German.

"I'm really hurting and I'm getting tired of being up here."

"There's too many people around me; get away."

"Okay, now I'm cold; come back."

A nervous medic tries to insert an IV but keeps missing. He makes a couple desperate attempts, jabbing my hand, until finally I yank it away.

"Look, buddy, you've got one more try. Because whatever you're going to put in there isn't going to make me feel better anyway."

They want to lift me up to scoot a coat under me, but I'm too tough for that. I try to lift my butt off the ground, but when I push down on my good leg, it doesn't feel so hot. I tell Bob I think I might have done something to my right knee. Neither of us knows it at the time, but what I've done is rip the ligaments apart and displace my meniscus cartilage. But the pain from the broken leg overwhelms the other injury.

Time crawls by. Bob keeps holding my legs and overseeing the medics. I can hear the rescue helicopter faintly in the distance, but why isn't it here yet? Is it grounded by fog? Is it ever going to reach me?

Meanwhile, I see a couple of officials walking up and down the fence, testing it to see why it didn't give. Why did I get hurt so badly?

When I hear the comforting *thwok thwok thwok* of the chopper approaching, my spirits lift. By this time Bob and the medics have splinted my legs, sandwiched a board between them, and strapped them together. The helicopter lands on the other side of the course, its rotors kicking up a small blizzard. I am strapped to a stretcher, carried to the helicopter, and slid inside. Bob climbs in next to me and we lift off for the short flight to a hospital in Sion, Switzerland.

I feel claustrophobic in the small, dark space, and I struggle not to panic. The noise of the helicopter is soothing, but at the same time I want to hear myself make noise as if to affirm my sanity. Every time I breathe out, I make some kind of grunting, whining, or groaning noise, bearing down like a woman giving birth, pushing the pain out. My leg feels like it's about to explode. My thigh has ballooned to three times its normal size, an overwhelming mass of pressure from my knee to my hip. All I want is someone to relieve the pressure, to take a needle and pop it.

The helicopter lands outside the hospital, and I'm rushed into the emergency room, cursing like a sailor. Nurses come up to me in an endless stream, asking me questions in English: Am I allergic to any medications? Would I like some water? Is there anything they can do to make me feel more comfortable?

"Yeah," I answer, "make the pain in my leg go away." Finally I've had enough. Whatever was in that IV didn't have much of an effect. I'm a buck fifteen into this ordeal, and I want some relief.

"All right, listen," I say to a nurse. "I'm not answering any more fucking questions. I'm not talking to anybody else until somebody makes this pain stop."

A chubby anesthesiologist enters the room and tries to quiet me down. I look at him and say, "I'm fucking hurting and I have been for over an hour now, and you're doing nothing about it. So if you have something to make the pain go away, wonderful, bring it on. Otherwise, fuck off and get out of my room."

Before I have a chance to tell him to fuck off again he turns on his heel and is gone. A few minutes later he returns and inserts an IV into my groin. A glow of well-being travels down my femur to my kneecap, and a sound escapes me that could be banned in thirty countries, a long, sustained *ahhhhh* of pure, unadulterated, indescribable relief.

The medication takes the edge off and calms me down. I drift in and out of consciousness, and every time I come to, I'm wearing fewer clothes. I wake up and my ski boots are gone. I wake up and my downhill suit has been cut off and replaced with a hospital gown. I demand to know who undressed me. My thigh is huge and the skin looks shiny and gross, an overstuffed sausage.

I pass out. I wake up and my coaches are standing around me, sadness in their faces. My first thought is to apologize. I'm going to get knocked out and have surgery and wake up in the middle of the night hungry. I know this scenario. They have to fly home without me and think about my accident the whole way home.

"I'm sorry, guys," I tell them.

"What? We're sorry. You're the one laying here hurt."

I'm not mad at Herwig. I have no right to blame him. We've traveled to this place together. He gave me the choice to race the night before, and I took it. The decision was mine. My fate was in my hands.

Besides, we don't have time to discuss our feelings. We have business to attend to, a press release to write, people to contact and to reassure.

I pass out. I wake up to the phone. Bob has called my orthopedist, Dr. Richard Steadman, who practices in Vail, Colorado. There is talk of flying Richard here to do the surgery or of transferring me to a hospital in Geneva an hour and a half away. Finally, Richard, Bob, and the Swiss doctors agree that we can't delay the surgery. The fracture is hideous. It consists of two main femur fragments with dozens of pulverized bone fragments in between. One potential danger is a fat embolism, where marrow leaks out of the bone, travels to my lungs, and kills me. The leg must be repaired immediately.

The ligaments in my right knee are totaled and will need extensive surgery, too. But Bob plays it down because he doesn't want to hit me with too much bad news all at once. "We'll determine how bad it is once we get to Vail," he says.

Nadia calls my parents and breaks the news to them. For fifteen years I have risked my neck on the world's high, white places, and for fifteen years my parents have sat by the phone waiting for me to call them after each race and tell them I'm okay. This is the call they dread, the call that tells them I am not okay.

By the time I talk to them, they sound upset and afraid. They are so far away, and I feel terrible for causing them pain. A sense of responsibility overtakes me, and I hear myself saying, "Look, I'm okay, I'm not in pain anymore. They're going to take care of me; this is a great place to be for bones. I'm really, really sorry I did this. I'm sorry, Mom, that I didn't keep my promise to come home. But I need you guys to be strong for me now because I've got a big surgery to go through."

A doctor and two nurses come in to give me an arteriogram. They'll pump a dye through my lower extremities and take an X ray to make sure the arteries and veins are intact before they do surgery. The nurses post themselves at my arms and chest while the doctor inserts the IV. I ask the nurses why they're standing so close when suddenly a burning sensation like liquid fire courses through my broken thigh. The nurses restrain me as I lunge and try to sit up. Then I let out a groan and a nurse slides a little pan in front of me and I turn my head and vomit.

That is the icing on the cake. It's bad enough that I sustain a potentially career-ending injury in the last race of the World Cup season. We've got to add vomiting to the experience.

Three hours after arriving in the ER I'm ready for surgery. The doctors will bolt my femur together with an eight-inch steel plate. Bob will assist, and as I'm being wheeled into the operating room, he looks down at me and says, "Don't worry. Just relax. I got you."

I look at him and say, "You'd better, damn it."

The last thing I remember is the sound of Bob pulling on his latex surgical gloves. *Snap*.

TRIUMPH

I'VE ALWAYS BEEN THE UNDERDOG, A TOMBOY WITH A FUNNY NAME WHO was born in a scruffy old mining camp. Kids from Sun Valley and Ketchum, the wealthy resort communities up the road, called Triumph "Weirdsville," and they called me worse. When I defended myself with my fists, I was standing up for my hometown, too. With this many strikes against you, winning becomes an uphill battle. But I learned to like it that way. The underdog can only surprise you.

You can't find Triumph on some Idaho state maps, but that tiny town was my whole world as a kid. I loved growing up there. I'm not saying living there was all sweetness and light, but the rough times shaped me, too. That place and its people taught me to be resilient and adventurous. They taught me to be tough.

"Why did you choose Triumph?" That's the question people always ask my parents, Ron and Dee. They usually laugh and answer, "Because it was cheap." But the reasons go much deeper than that.

My parents arrived in Triumph in 1967 with the same high hopes of the miners who settled the town in 1882. The prospectors had looked for silver; my parents were looking for freedom. Like a lot of young people in the late '60s, they decided to "turn on, tune in, and drop out." In 1966, Dad was twenty-eight, managing Bundocks, the nicest restaurant in Reno, and was unhappily married to the boss's daughter. Mom was nineteen and a coed at the University of Nevada, studying foreign languages and singing protest songs at antiwar rallies. They met when a date took Mom to dinner at Bundocks. Six months later, after Dad's marriage ended, they hit the road in a Dodge van with Dad's motorcycle in the back and an old trailer hitched to the bumper. Dad wanted to escape the "craziness." Mom wanted Dad; she didn't care where they ended up. "He swept me off my feet," she says, "and grew me up the way he wanted."

They ended up in Grass Valley, California, doing odd jobs on a horse ranch for the summer. Then they headed to Mexico City and put thirty-nine thousand miles on that old van, eventually wandering back up north to look for winter work. Someone told them that Sun Valley ski resort in the Wood River Valley was hiring and that anyone who worked there got a free ski pass. This sounded good to Dad, who was an avid skier. They landed jobs in Sun Valley's Trail Creek Cabin, a restaurant in the woods where tourists arrived by a horse-drawn sleigh for a prime rib dinner and a little entertainment. Mom prepped and Dad cooked. Idaho is a common-law state; after living together for forty-eight hours they considered themselves married, and Mom took Dad's last name.

They rented a furnished house in Triumph for fifty-five dollars a month from the Reverend Ernie Harr. In the late 1950s, after the mine had shut down, Ernie and his brother, Milton, had bought the entire town from the Triumph Mineral Co. and installed a sewage system and water lines. The Harrs were deeply religious people who also happened to believe in UFOs. Triumph itself was rumored to be a rest stop for flying saucers on their way to wherever flying saucers went. I was too young to comprehend the Harrs' eccentric brand of spirituality, but some of it soaked in. Mom and Vernette, Milton Harr's wife, would sit and talk about spiritual matters, particularly karma. Vernette believed you created positive and negative karma, that every choice you made affected your life for better or worse. Nothing happened by accident; you held your fate in your own two hands.

It bothers me when people portray my childhood as some kind of dirt bag, hippie lifestyle where my parents weren't making any money. That's not the way it was. My parents were civic leaders in Triumph. They helped establish a community board and tried to start a food co-op. And they busted their butts to own their own home just like anybody else. When I was two, the only decoration on our Christmas tree was the title to the house. Ernie sold it to my parents for four thousand dollars. When my parents first moved to Triumph, Dad would go on unemployment when the resort closed down for the summer, but after I was born, he always had a full-time job, first as a chef and then as a stonemason. Mom worked alongside Dad on his restaurant and masonry jobs, kept books on the side, and did housekeeping for several wealthy residents of Sun Valley, including Clint Eastwood. On top of that she held down the home front and still found time to perform folk songs in local bars and at private parties. She sang more for fun than for money. That describes my parents' life philosophy in a nutshell: having a lot of material possessions didn't matter; having a good time did.

My parents were living a hybrid version of the American Dream. They made a living off the Establishment but went home at the end of the day to a place where they answered to no one. My parents' lifestyle was a little eccentric, but then everyone in Triumph was eccentric. It's easier to label them "hippies" than to try to understand them. Sure, Dad had a ponytail and smoked weed and thought the war was wrong, but those things didn't make him a hippie. They made him his own man.

The second winter Dad started running the resort's employee cafeteria, which was housed in a Quonset hut not far from the famous Sun Valley Lodge. He scheduled his day with a ski bum's inventiveness. He'd arrive at work at dawn and get the kitchen ready for the day. Then he'd head to the lifts at nine, ski until noon or one, and go back to work until seven or eight. Mom helped him in the kitchen. They lived paycheck to paycheck, commuting from Triumph to Sun Valley in a series of beat-up old cars and vans. Baba was born on March 19, 1969, delivered at the Sun Valley hospital. Baba describes his birth like this: "Doc Saviers walked in, busted out his catcher's mitt, caught me before I hit the floor, handed me to a nurse, and said, 'I'm going skiing.' "

In the spring of 1970 Dad butted heads with resort management—they wanted him to cut his hair, among other things—and he walked. He found work as a chef in Ketchum, a sleepy railroad town that had become a resort area when the first ski lifts for Sun Valley went up in 1936. That summer, he and Mom took Baba on a twenty-two-day backpacking trip in the Sawtooth. I was conceived on that trip, at an altitude of eighty-five hundred feet, which may help explain why I've felt an energy from the mountains for as long as I can remember.

I was born at home on April 3, 1971, with Dad playing midwife. Mom says that when he handed me to her, she smacked my butt. Instead of crying I laughed at her and went to sleep, and she says that's how she knew I was going to be a handful.

That year Dad started training as a stonemason because he liked the outdoors and the work wasn't as seasonal. He'd drive to construction sites in Sun Valley and Ketchum on his motorcycle and come home covered in rock dust and sweat. Dad had a gift for building with stone, and over the years he worked for some of the area's most famous residents, including Bruce Willis and Arnold Schwarzenegger, a.k.a. "Arnie." Drive around the valley's most exclusive neighborhoods and you'll see Dad's handiwork everywhere: chimneys, walls, security gates.

Only fifteen miles separate Sun Valley and Triumph, but they're worlds apart. Sun Valley is a world-famous ski destination that reels in tens of thousands of tourists each year. Triumph's population fluctuates between thirty-five and fifty people, depending on who is coming or going. Sun Valley rivals Hollywood in materialism and conspicuous consumption and is a vacation-home magnet for industrial tycoons and show-business celebrities. No one goes to Triumph without a good reason. When they first moved there, my parents had to bribe the county snowplow driver with a bottle of whisky to get him to clear the road from Triumph to the highway.

Triumph is still there, if you want to find it. Drive north out of Hailey on Highway 75, hang a right after the iron railroad bridge, and go six miles on East Fork Road. The town is at the end of the pavement: seventeen buildings—some more shacks than houses—tucked into a narrow canyon. The town's mining history is everywhere. Triumph Mineral Co. used to send its ore carts to Ketchum, where the metal was smelted and shipped out along a miles-long cable system. The timber lift towers that supported the cable still stand in the hills behind town; hike into those hills and you'll find boarded-up shafts among the sagebrush. Drive a little farther into town, pass a ruined mill and an abandoned boardinghouse, and look to your left. You'll see three small houses all in a row. The white one in the middle with the tin roof was ours.

Triumph rubs up against wilderness, so maybe that's one reason I turned out so wild. Where the houses stop, the landscape begins, stretching as far as the eye can see. Off the right side of East Fork Road, which divides the town in two, is a marshy, aspen-clotted meadow where I picked morels after the spring rains. Black bears are known to prowl the area. Way in the distance, through a V in the horizon, the snow-capped Pioneer Mountains loom. Baba climbed the tallest, the 11,800-foot Hyndman Peak, with Dad when he was six. I never managed that, but I did like to scramble up the steep green mountain that rose right out of town. We called it Mindbender because hiking it was such a mind-bending experience. The mountainside is gouged with avalanche chutes where the snow crashes down in winter, wiping out everything in its path and sometimes blocking East Fork Road for days. When Dad took Baba and me up Mindbender to chop down a Christmas tree, he always chose one growing in an avalanche chute because it was doomed anyway.

As my parents saw it, there was integrity in simplicity, and this philosophy extended to the way they raised Baba and me. We ate mostly grains and vegetables grown in Mom's huge garden and eggs from our own chickens. We had rabbits that my parents slaughtered for food, and for a while we had a pig named London, though it eventually ended up as pork chops and bacon. Once a week we'd drive three miles up the road to trade eggs for milk from Rupert and Bonnie House, an older couple who owned a cow. Rupert and Bonnie had moved here in the 1930s when Rupert got a job at the mine. They raised five kids followed by a series of foster kids. Rupert ended up owning a lot of the land in the area, and my parents respected the Houses because they embodied the original pioneer spirit.

Our parents' goal was to give Baba and me the basic essentials we needed to survive, but where we put any extra money was different than most people. We went clothes shopping once a year for school in Twin Falls; I wore Baba's hand-me-downs, thrift-store finds, and handmade dresses (when Mom could get me into them). Our house had no doors inside: a slab of sheet rock separated the bathroom from the kitchen, and the curtain to our large, communal shower was a sheet of plastic held in place by a rock. Dad fastened plastic over our bedroom windows with duct tape because we couldn't afford glass. On stormy nights the wind made that plastic membrane thump like a heartbeat—*shoop, shoop, shoop*—and I'd lie in bed and pray that Dad's tape job would hold.

Any extra money went, not into new cars or TVs or windows, but to hiking and backpacking gear (and later, my ski racing career). At night my parents huddled near the woodstove thumbing through the REI catalog, dreaming about which new hiking boots and tents to save for. They headed for the mountains every chance they got. They'd spend weeks in the White Clouds, living on grains and nuts and cutthroat trout caught in the high-altitude lakes. Baba spent his diaper years wedged between sawbucks, along with Mom's guitar, on the back of Tom, our pack mule. After I came along I rode, too.

That mule had something Baba and I didn't: a name. Mom and Dad wanted to wait until we were old enough to choose our own identities, so our birth certificates read only "Baby Boy Street" and "Baby Girl Street." We did have nicknames, however—lots of them. My brother was dubbed Baba because that's what he called his bottle, but he also went by Baba Jomo and Jimmy Jomo. I loved the game of peekaboo, so Mom called me that from my diaper days. She also called me Squeak because when I yelled my voice sounded like a squeaky hinge, and eventually that nickname spawned such variations as Squeakers and the dreaded Squeakerbuns.

The story of how I got to be officially called Picabo has been told a million times, so I'll get it out of the way early. As you'll see, I have a love/hate relationship with my name, just as I do with my dad, but I've come to accept both of them as key to my success.

Though we lived in the middle of nowhere, my parents were determined to mold Baba and me into world citizens. Dad had moved around a lot as a kid and spent six months in the marines after high school, and he didn't want his kids growing up without knowing what a brown or a black person looked like. So when I was three, he took out a loan to finance a trip south of the border where it was warm, culturally interesting, and cheap.

Baba and I obviously couldn't go anywhere without a passport, and we weren't getting a passport with names like Baby Boy and Baby Girl. The Establishment had spoken.

Mom remembered seeing a sign for a town called Picabo on the day she and Dad were driving to Sun Valley for the first time. The name had stuck in her head because it was pretty. The town was named for a nearby river that the Shoban tribe called Picabo, or "shining waters," after the way it gleams when the sun hits it. (The white man called the river Silver Creek, and today it's a world-famous trout-fishing destination.) Dad pointed out that the name happened to sound the same as peekaboo, my favorite game.

So they asked me what I thought of the name Picabo. I said I liked it. I was three—what did I know? Soon enough Picabo was shortened to Peeky, Peek, and Boo. Dad flirted with naming my brother "Juan Way Street" but fortunately was talked out of it. He got a more conventional name: Roland Wayne Street III, after his father and grandfather, but everyone still calls him Baba. (If a phone call comes in for "Roland," we know it's someone he doesn't want to talk to.) Mom got duplicate copies of our birth certificates made with our new names and then asked a friend, Kenny Dickens, to take a black-and-white photo of the three of us. She took the photo and the birth certificates to the Blaine County courthouse in Hailey, where she wrote Roland Wayne Street III and Picabo Street on the passport application.

In the summer of 1974, we drove to Arizona, parked our Toyota pickup in Tucson, caught the train to Nogales, and traveled through Mexico and Guatemala. I remember the trip in bits and pieces: bouncing along dirt roads in hot, crowded buses; the women who sold clothes and supplies out of big bags at the bus stops; the old woman with the baskets who showed me how to make corn tortillas from scratch. (To this day the smell of fresh corn tortillas takes me back.) I learned who to befriend and who to avoid, which peddlers were a bargain and which a rip-off. By the time I was ten, I'd been to Mexico four times and New Orleans twice. Dad had friends in New Orleans, and we made sure to visit when Jazz Fest was happening. New Orleans blew me away. The racial diversity, the food, the way people talked—I loved it all. I ate it up. I'd wander among the crowds at Jazz Fest, dazed by the kaleidoscope of sounds and tastes and skin colors, all mixed up in one big, beautiful, happy, dancing whirl. I was so overstimulated that Mom thought I was going to pop.

In a way, those early travels prepared me for my future as a globe-trotting ski racer, when I'd be going places and meeting new people on my own. Back then, though, Dad took us everywhere and was almost fanatical about keeping us together. "If my family's not invited, I won't be there either," he would say. He didn't even believe in baby-sitters.

So it made a huge impression on me at age four when my parents left us for the first time, though it was only for a few hours. We drove to Marysville, California, where Dad had lived as a teenager, and stayed with our grandparents while he and Mom attended his high school reunion. Five years later Mom's grandfather died and my parents left Baba and me with our neighbors, the Bells, while they drove to Wichita for the funeral. In 1983, Dad took me to his father's funeral in Marysville, and that's when I met my half sister, Sunny Mayne Street, for the first time. I'd known that Dad had a daughter by his first marriage, but he never talked about her. I was twelve; she was ten years older than I. What I remember the most about our meeting is that her jaw was wired shut. She'd had surgery to realign her jawline, and she couldn't open her mouth. There we were, long-lost sisters, and she couldn't say a word to me. She just sat there sucking on pieces of bread.

I never saw Sunny again, though I did get a letter from her after I won the Olympic silver medal in Lillehammer, Norway, in 1994. She explained who she was and included a photo of herself and her three kids. But we aren't in touch. Maybe one of the reasons Dad wanted to keep Baba and me so close was because he didn't want to lose any more kids.

THE STORY OF HOW I GREW UP THE ONLY GIRL AMONG SEVEN BOYS HAS been told many times. Billy and Jamie and Baba and Sam and Pat and Andy and Josh were my gang, friends through thick and thin, no matter what. For the fourteen years I lived in Triumph we spent as much time together as we could. We ate dinner at each other's houses. We hated each other one minute and loved each other the next. Those boys were my best friends, so I'd like to introduce them.

Billy and Jamie Collins were the oldest. When I was eight, Billy was thirteen and Jamie was eleven. They lived at the far end of town in a house with a lawn where we played football. My brother was a year younger than Jamie. Baba was a burly redhead whose role alternated between bodyguard and bully.

Sam Urbany and I were two years younger, so we were always very competitive. And we were both rebels. Sam didn't have much fear of consequences. He was like the dude in boot camp who smirks at the drill sergeant.

Then came Pat Hastings. Pat was into macho games, like cops and robbers and army commandos. Once Pat and I stole cigarettes out of his mom's purse because we thought smoking was cool. We coughed for twenty minutes and decided it wasn't.

Andy Boender lived a mile up East Fork Road. His family was well-off—his dad owned a construction company—so he had the most stuff. When Andy got a new basketball, we all got a new basketball.

Josh Martin was the youngest. He and his mom had a really tight bond because it was only the two of them. Josh was a sweet kid who loved toy soldiers. His room was one big battlefield sectioned into battle scenes, from cowboys and Indians to Vietnam. He and Pat would spend all day in his room reenacting history's great conflicts.

We spent most of our time outside. There was so much diversity in our little world. Living in Triumph was like getting to eat what you wanted at every meal. In the summers we'd get up in the morning, do our chores, and ask ourselves, "All right. Should we play cops and robbers in the old hotel or army in the mining ruins? Go swimming in the lake or catch tadpoles at the river? Ride horses at Rupert and Bonnie's or go to Carl Massaro's place and talk him into letting us play with all the weird junk in his yard? What will it be: Dungeons and Dragons at Andy's or football or Butts Up or 500?"

If it was hot, we'd hit "the beach." The "beach" was a crescent of black sand that bordered our "lake," a low-lying tailing pond with green water. The black sand was all over town, a product of mining tailings mixed with the town's soil. My friends and I had some vague idea that arsenic had been used to separate the ore from the rock, but our parents' warnings to stay out of the sand only intensified our desire to roll around in it. God, we were dirty little buggers! Pat's mom wouldn't let him in the house until he cleaned up; she'd hand him his dinner out the window. I'd come home with dirt in my ears, my nose, and the creases of my eyes. Dad would say, "Look at you, you little grimy dirt bag," and send me to the shower. People outside Triumph called us "black sand babies."

In the early 1990s, Triumph was declared a public health hazard. The Environmental Protection Agency considered making the old mine a Superfund Site, and many of Triumph's residents have had their blood tested for lead. By the early '90s, I was one of the country's most promising young ski racers, and in 1993 some local environmental activists, eager to make me a toxic-hazard poster girl, urged me to say that playing in the black sand had given me lead poisoning. I refused. It's not in my nature to worry about something that I can't control. As kids, all we thought was, *Cool, we've got a beach and a lake. We've got swimming in the summer.* We swam in that water. We swallowed it. How could a blood test change the past?

When I won the Olympic silver medal in 1994, the issue was dropped. My blood, whatever was in it, seemed to be just fine. I'm still not worried about it. I've been in and out of so many hospitals in the past five years and had so many blood tests that if lead were a problem, I'd know.

Besides, a little lead wouldn't have scared us away. We were the Triumph gang, and we were hardcore. We were athletic and strong and had an attitude. I was one of the guys. Other girls had dolls; I had a BB gun.

The old hotel was a favorite haunt. Our houses were small and the hotel was huge, so we liked to play there: cops and robbers, army, games that required an element of surprise. It was a decrepit, two-story building with a collapsing floor and dozens of tiny-paned windows—perfect for target practice. We'd lie on our bellies on this grassy spot across the main street, pick a pane, aim our BB guns, and see who could get closest to hitting it. We tried not to take too many windowpanes out at once because we wanted to make them last. Also, our parents used the hotel for town meetings, and Mom played the old piano in there in the afternoons before we got home from school. We wanted to minimize the number of holes so the grown-ups wouldn't catch on.

Of course they did. One day we were summoned to the hotel, and when we got there, the entire population of Triumph was waiting for us. Actually, it was only our parents, but in a community that small it might as well have been the whole town. They were steamed. Shit, it felt like a dam of anger was about to break on top of us. When one of the adults asked us why the windows were shattered, we fidgeted nervously, casting panicky, sidelong glances at one another.

Suddenly, Pat or Sam, I can't remember which (probably Sam, knowing him), came to the rescue.

"It was an extreme accident," he piped up.

The rest of us grabbed that excuse like a lifeline: "Yeah, that's right, an extreme accident, yeah, yeah."

This act of desperation broke the tension, and our parents could hardly suppress their laughter. Then one of the big, bad dads, either mine or Sam's (probably mine, knowing him), told all the kids to leave so they could come up with a punishment. "But I'll tell you right now—and I know I speak on behalf of everybody else—the guns are gone."

We went outside to await our fate. Once in a while one of us would get up and go eavesdrop at a window, but finally we gave up and sat in a silent huddle. Ten minutes later we were called back in and told that our penance was to go from house to house on weekends, cleaning our yards. We also had to sweep the glass off the top floor of the hotel. Our parents locked our guns away for a while and told us to find something else to vandalize.

Unfortunately, everything else in town was pretty thrashed, so we turned our destructive impulses on each other. Our games became more intense and physical, and I got no slack whatsoever for being a girl, even if the game was tackle football.

"You can play with us," Baba told me, "but we're not going to do anything to protect you or anything like that. If you're going to play with us, you're going to play all the way. You'd better show up and be ready."

And I was. When I got the ball, they tackled me just like everyone else, and I tackled back. I rushed straight-armed, head down, ball tucked under my arm. Baba went on to set school records as a linebacker at Wood River High School, so he was the undisputed football god, but for my size and ability, I held my own. And I liked that. It worked for me. It defined me. I would prove myself physically not just to them but also to myself.

One day, I can't remember what year it was, we were playing pickle in the street. I was the runner, and the guys were throwing long bombs with a hardball. I wheeled around to run to the other end and that ball hit me smack in the forehead. I dropped to the ground and was out for at least thirty seconds. I came to under a ring of concerned faces and a chorus of "C'mon, Peeky, get up! You're okay!" I pulled myself off the road and groggily kept right on playing.

Fall down. Get up. I excelled at it.

I HEARD A FACTOID SOMEWHERE THAT IDAHO HAS PRODUCED MORE Olympians per capita than any other state in the United States. That makes sense to me. Idaho is a hard land with high standards. Work is a source of pride. If you grow the biggest potato in town, no one can say you didn't hoe that spud.

I am a third-generation Idahoan. Dad was born in Orofino, my grandmother in Helmer. Her father, my great-granddad, was a lumberjack and the biggest guy in town. He was the guy the townspeople would pit against the prizefighters who came through town. My mother was born in Wichita, Kansas, but raised in Salt Lake City, Utah. Her father was an FBI agent and a journalist. He was also an alcoholic, and Mom says one thing that attracted her to Dad was that, other than a glass of good wine now and then, he didn't drink.

My parents are very different people, and they've played very different roles in my life. My mom is the family peacemaker and my best friend. Our relationship has always been noncompetitive and nurturing. We sing and compose music together. Mom is a great whistler. I remember how, when darkness was falling, she would step outside and send two perfect, high-pitched notes drifting over town, calling me and Baba home.

I was a tomboy, and while Mom accepted that, she also tried to cultivate my feminine side. She encouraged my domestic skills, such as sewing, and made me pretty dresses that I wore only for birthdays and special events. Eventually I did discover my girly side, and I have the big-hair photos to prove it.

Behind Mom's low-key personality lies an iron will. Just consider what she faced when she came to Triumph. Here was a city girl who grew up with central heating and big cars, who had never felt sweat on her belly until she was nineteen, plopped down into primitive circumstances with no alternative but to make them home. The soil in southern Idaho is rocky and arid, and the growing season is about an hour long, but after reading a few books, Mom carved out a masterpiece of a garden across the road from our house. It was twenty-three rows wide and one hundred feet deep and boasted every vegetable from acorn squash to zucchini. Its greenness stood out against the brown hills, and it was so impressive that people would drive by just to admire it.

Mom says athleticism skipped her generation. She preferred cross-country to downhill skiing, which scared her. I must get my physical gifts from Dad's side of the family. His mom was a champion basketball player and hurdler in school, and Dad went to the Junior National Championships for pairs roller-skating in the early '50s. His nickname is Stubby because he was under five feet tall until he was a high school junior. They thought he had a birth defect until he grew eleven inches in one year and was big enough to play football. He joined the marines right out of high school, and in 1960, after he got out, he went to live with his parents in Lake Tahoe, California. The Winter Olympics were in Squaw Valley that year, and watching the ski racers tear down the mountain inspired Dad to learn to ski. His first wife was a ski instructor at Mount Rose, a ski area near Reno, and he became a good skier by trying to keep up with her.

Dad liked to go fast. At Sun Valley he'd rocket from top to bottom in a tuck, his ski poles wedged under his armpits and sticking out behind him like airfoils. The story goes that the ski patrollers finally gave up trying to slow him down; they just didn't want to get into it with him. Instead they'd walk up to him at the bottom and say, "You know, you could turn once in a while."

It's funny that Dad had a problem with authority figures since he was such a disciplinarian himself. In a way, he was only emulating his father's behavior. His dad had been a nurse in the navy, and even after Granddad went into banking, he ran his family like a military platoon.

A certain moral standard prevailed in our household. Dad set strict rules in our house: say please; say thank you; don't reach across the table. I didn't care much for school—the lessons I learned from Dad were more important. He warned me against lying because one lie led to another and pretty soon you couldn't remember what the truth was anymore. I never forgot that advice, even if I didn't always follow it.

Baba and I had to get permission to do just about anything. We had a long list of chores to do every day after school, from chopping wood to weeding the garden, and we couldn't go out and play until our chores were done and done right. Dad had very exacting standards. There should be no soap left on the dishes after they were rinsed, and they should be toweled dry and put back in the cupboard spotless, not stacked by the sink. The floor should be vacuumed, not swept. Trying to meet his standards is probably what made me a perfectionist at a very young age, though sometimes I deviated. I'd use the broom instead of vacuuming, even though I knew that when Dad got home he'd inspect the floor for telltale pieces of straw. If he found them, I got a tongue-lashing: "Why are you doing it wrong? Should I show you how to do it again? Do you have a problem with vacuuming the house?"

I was supposed to do as I was told. It was the principle of the thing. *Be a good person!* To this day I don't know why I didn't always vacuum. Maybe it was my way of saying, "Screw you. I'm not going to do everything you say."

Dad's rules ran head-on into my own obstinacy. If he told me to do something, my first response was, "Why?" For instance, an order to gather the eggs would elicit a string of questions. "Why should I do it? What am I gonna get out of it if I get 'em? What could I be doing instead? Is it really my turn?" And on and on. I worked every angle. I wanted all the information there was to know, and if there wasn't enough, then I had to make a decision to play along or not.

Ironically, our standoffs were a bonding experience. I think Dad enjoyed the back-and-forth, the give-and-take. I reflected his intensity like a mirror. He loved seeing himself in me. I wasn't afraid to challenge Dad because I knew he saved his considerable temper for more serious infractions. He never got mad at me just for the sake of getting mad. There was always a good reason, and it usually involved some near-death experience on my part. Mom likes to say her main job was "keeping Baba fed and me alive" because I seem to have been born with a homing device for risk.

Here is a partial inventory of the nonskiing injuries I suffered in my formative years: I got the first of my five concussions at age ten when I jumped from the monkey bars to the uneven bars at school, lost my grip, and landed on my head. I received a second-degree burn on one arm when I got up to answer the phone and answered to the red-hot woodstove instead. In fifth grade, I lost a front tooth when I was chasing some girl who'd teased me, slipped on some ice, and fell down mouth-first on the curb. I still have a scar on my chest where I shimmied too quickly under some barbed wire and another scar on my ankle where I ran into a sharp metal rod that was sticking out of the ground. It ripped my skin open and bled like crazy. I looked down at the wound, said "Oh wow," and kept right on running.

Whenever I'd drag myself home with some new wound, Mom would just shake her head and reach for the soap and water to scrub it clean. Her archenemies were Jack Frost and infection.

If I did something really stupid, like ride my bike across the busy main road and crash into a fence, Dad would have to get my attention. He knew I hated the dark, so one punishment was to stand in a corner with the lights out for what felt like forever. Sometimes he made me touch my nose to the wall so I couldn't cheat and look around. Sometimes the punishment was harsher.

One of my main chores was chopping the kindling. Baba and I alternated, so every other week it was my job to make sure the kindling box stayed full, even if it meant I had to go out to the chopping block four times on a Saturday in the dead of winter. Wood heated our stove, and that stove fed us and kept us warm. Not only was it mandatory to have a full box, but the wood had to be cut a certain way. There were three sizes. The thin pieces were the "starters" because they combusted quickly. The medium-sized ones were "fillers" and got the fire going good and hot. The big chunks, the "overnighters," kept the fire burning until dawn.

I was really good when it was my week to cut the kindling because I knew how painful the product of my efforts could be. When I got into trouble, I had to pick my own piece of wood and hand it to Dad. Then I'd stand with my toes on this line in the kitchen, bend over, touch my toes, and get whacked. I'd always put my hand back there and get smacked on my hand, then get another spanking for having covered my butt. So I'd have a hurt hand and a hurt butt, but not for long, given my toughness and tolerance for pain. Disappointing my parents was worse than the actual spanking. I couldn't give a shit about that.

In fact, the harshest punishment Dad could mete out was to make me sit in my room by myself, especially if there was a house full of fun stuff going on. Being alone was the worst. Fortunately, I rarely was.

TRIUMPH HAD TWO GENERAL TYPES OF INHABITANTS. THERE WERE FAMI-lies like ours, with kids who went to school and parents who went to work. Our dads were in construction and our moms waited tables and cleaned houses in Sun Valley. They helped make the tourist economy run. We ate together on holidays, showed slide shows to each other, played cards, and talked story.

On the other end of the spectrum were the drifters, the hippies, and the hermits. Some of them just wanted to be left alone; others dealt and did serious drugs. We did our best to coexist; in a town that size, we didn't have a choice.

The trailer court saw a lot of action. Milton Harr parked four trailers at the end of our little street before the turnoff for the main road and rented them out to an ever-changing cast of characters, including a Vietnam vet with a hair-trigger temper named Mike. Sophie lived in one of the trailers. She was the other girl in town, the one nobody has written about. She couldn't even ride a bike, so she didn't count. She lived with her mom in Triumph for a couple of years before they moved to Hailey. Sophie's dad was the first dead body I ever saw. He died of an asthma attack, and there was an open casket at the funeral home. I'll never forget looking down at his face, Willie Nelson's "Blue Skies" playing in the background.

Winter arrived in October and left in May and presented my gang with a whole new set of recreational options. We'd make snowmen and dig igloos and forts. We'd go hooky-bobbing, hanging onto the fenders of cars and letting the drivers haul us down the street while we tried to stand upright. There was a big tailing pond down by the East Fork Wood River that froze over in the winter, and we'd shovel it off for bone-rattling, fully padded games of ice hockey.

Blizzards had a purifying effect. They buried the abandoned cars and the black sand and restored Triumph to its former self, a bleak little outpost in an all-white world. The dark houses would be banked in snow to the rooflines. There was so much snow that we wore boots, jackets, hats, mittens, and snow pants everywhere we went. There was so much snow that I could ride my Flying Saucer to the bus stop and stash it at Josh's house, where it would be waiting for me when I returned. There was so much snow that some mornings we couldn't open the front door. Fortunately, shoveling was Baba's job.

I skied for the first time the winter I was five, on a small hill behind our house. I'd grown tired of watching Dad and Baba head off to Sun Valley without me, so one afternoon, when the snow was deep enough to bury the sagebrush, I borrowed Baba's boots and skis. The memory is sketchy because I was so young, and while I do remember falling a couple times, I'm positive I reached the bottom standing up, feeling triumphant. This was the way I mastered everything: through trial and error, until I got it right.

Sun Valley's beginner hill was called Dollar Mountain, but Dad didn't want to spend the money on a lift ticket until I could snowplow—a novice maneuver in which you point your ski tips together and splay the tails out, like a pizza wedge—and stop. I spent the next winter skiing on the road behind our house. The road pitched slightly toward the trailer court and then made a sharp right down to the main road, and the county snowplow driver kept it packed and smooth, just like a groomed ski trail. Mom skied with me, until one day she hooked a ski tip under a power line that we had snaked across the road, fell, and dislocated her collarbone. She skied occasionally for the next five years before giving it up completely. She was scared of getting hurt again, a concern I did not share.

I got my first skis in 1978, when I was seven. They were eighty-centimeter K2s with red and white graphics—very patriotic. Dad bought them cheap at the annual ski swap in Ketchum, where people sold and traded their used gear. That December my parents took me to Dollar Mountain for the first time. All four of us piled into our truck for the fifty-minute drive to Sun Valley. If there was any doubt that I was my father's daughter, that day erased it.

Baba and I clamped our boots into our skis and shuffled into the lift line. I watched as the chairs, which seated two people, descended on the cable, scooped up the skiers, and transported them high above the ground to the top of Dollar. The next skiers in line had to push themselves quickly into position or risk being knocked on their asses when the next chair swung around. The only thing that kept us from falling off that chair was a thin metal bar that Baba pulled down in front of us. I was terrified that he would push me off or that I'd slip under that bar like a letter under a door. And since I hated being afraid, by the time we got to the top I was completely pissed off.

At the bottom, Mom and Dad were waiting with other proud parents to watch their kids come down the mountain. Other kids began making slow, methodical turns, but I was nowhere in sight. My parents scanned the slopes, and just about the time they were getting worried, somebody pointed out a tiny figure rocketing downhill. No question who that was. I was so furious I'd abandoned all thought of turning, pointed my ski tips downward, and thrown myself on the mercy of gravity. At the bottom everyone gave me shit and told me I should turn more—Dad included. But I think he was secretly proud.

Before long I was jumping off the chairlift before it reached the top.

The philosophy behind Dollar Mountain was that the novice skier could progress slowly in order to be ready for the steeper, more challenging slopes of Bald Mountain across town. I was skiing Baldy after two days.

In fact, the next thing I remember I'm skiing balls-out down Baldy, following Dad. He wasn't very patient, and neither was I, so we were completely compatible. All I saw that first winter was his back. I kept my eyes glued to him, shadowing his every move. He was so big and I was so small that I had to fly to keep up with him, on the verge of losing control, my skis practically flapping with velocity. I didn't have time to be afraid; I was too busy trying to keep up. If I didn't, the next time I'd see him was in the parking lot at 4:00 P.M. I skied so I wouldn't be left behind. Sunny days were the best. We would start on the east side of the mountain and head west as the day progressed, following the sun across Baldy's face. Baba was usually with us, which gave me someone else to chase. It was all about speed. G forces.

At the end of that season, Sun Valley hosted a kiddy race on Dollar called the Kindercup (Sun Valley was designed by a homesick Austrian). Just for the heck of it, my parents signed me up. And just for the heck of it, I won.

After I started skiing, Mom gave me a whole new set of nicknames. "Ski" and "Peek" became Skeek. Skeek became Skeeker and, worst of all, Skeekerbuns. Mom called me that nickname everywhere: at the ski hill, the grocery store, the parking lot, school. "Skeekerbuns!" she'd yell. And I'd throw her a withering look that said, "Mom, will you please shut up? I can't believe you're calling me that."

"Oh. Sorry, Peeky."

IN THE SUMMER OF 1978, DAD WENT INTO THE ROCK BUSINESS. IF YOU stand outside our house and look to the north, you'll see Porfrey Peak, elevation ninety-five hundred feet. The peak was a volcanic plug that had thrust out of the earth millions of years ago, shedding a mantle of talus as it cooled. Dad and Kenny Dickens used to hike up Porfrey and ski down, and one day they realized that all the loose rock could be quarried. Dad and Kenny brought in a third partner, a geologist from Reno, and they started lining up the necessary permits. They negotiated rights with the Forest Service, the Bureau of Land Management, and Triumph Mineral Co. and put in a new road. They opened the quarry with a 50 percent down payment from their first customer, a wealthy Dow Chemical executive who was building a house in Sun Valley. Soon Dad was supplying stone not only to the jobs he was working on, but also to construction sites throughout the valley.

On most summer weekends Baba and I would throw our bikes into the back of Dad's truck, jump in next to them, and hang on for the three-mile ride up Porfrey Peak. Dad drove, with Mom or Kenny in the passenger seat. The road had three big switchbacks, hairpin turns so severe that Dad couldn't make them in one shot. A two-point turn meant Dad had to back up twice to get around them, a four-pointer, four times. Back up and go a little bit, back up and go, the gears grinding and the rear tires flirting with thin air. The road was so steep and the drop-offs so terrifying that women had been known to cry the first time they were driven up.

All day Baba and I worked in the quarry. But rock hauling was one chore I didn't mind because of the reward that awaited us when we were done.

The quarry was a vast, lunar-looking field of loose basalt, all sizes and shapes, hot to the touch in the summer heat. There were two or three color patterns in the quarry: dark tones to light, from a pink with lime green tones, flecked with black quartz, to a deep rust color we called orange. Dad would look for particular shapes, sizes, and colors, depending on the project. He'd point out the ones he wanted and Baba and I would pick them up and haul them to the truck. Or, if the rocks were far away, we'd slide them down a plank. One misstep could result in a twisted ankle, so I had to step precisely and carefully. Each rock, depending on its weight, would shift my center of balance, so I was constantly readjusting my balance. Working that quarry made me coordinated, dexterous, and strong. It was challenging and fun. We got dirty, drank a lot of water, and broke our nails. Meanwhile, the whole time we'd be eyeing that road.

By five o'clock the truck would be full, and Baba and I would be astride our bikes, ready to rip. Sometimes the gang would ride up to meet us.

While the truck lumbered along behind us, we'd take off in a pack across the flat ridgeline, zigzag down the ridge, and haul ass toward the first switchback. We usually approached it together, and before we hit the turn, we'd drop our bikes sideways, hit the brakes, and slide around that switchback, then pedal fast and furious down the next stretch. At that point, someone usually broke out into the lead and it became a race to catch the leader by the next turn. Hit it right and you could slide inside and get an edge, then pedal, pedal, pedal, pedal down the straightaway. Missing the turn was not an option. God, it was a long way down. You just didn't want to think about it.

Baba held the quarry-road record of eleven minutes from top to bottom. But some days we'd take it slow, absorbing the experience. We'd catch air off the side and splash through mud puddles, just screwing around, enjoying the ride.

There was one ride I didn't enjoy. Every weekday from September to June Baba and I rode the school bus for forty-five minutes to Ernest Hemingway Elementary School (Hemingway lived and died in Ketchum, and there is a memorial for him in Sun Valley). We were the first ones on and the last ones off. No one wanted our route, and our drivers had bad attitudes. When a new driver showed up, we'd gauge his or her attitude and then calibrate ours to match. The driver would say something snippy, we'd respond in kind, and the relationship usually went downhill from there.

With a name like Picabo, it was only a matter of time before I got teased for it. As the bus filled up, the taunts began. "Hey, can we sneak a Peek? Pick a booger, any booger, just don't pick a Peek a booger."

Baba always defended me, and at one point the principal wanted to expel him for being a bully. My parents informed the principal that Baba was instructed to kick the ass of any kid who gave me a hard time.

One day I got off the school bus and stormed into the house. "That's it! I'm over it," I fumed. "I want to change my name."

"Okay," Mom said in her usual calm fashion. "Let's come up with a new one."

I lay on my bed and pondered the alternatives. Jennifer, Michelle, Krista. Everybody had those names. So boring, so normal. As hard as I tried, I couldn't think of anything better. Ultimately, I did choose my own name, just as my parents wanted: for better or worse, I was Picabo.

Believe me, there are times I've reconsidered my decision. In a 1997 article in *Newsweek*, the famous sportswriter Frank Deford wrote that I have "a name out of Disney that sounds like a red-light district." I could go on for pages with such analogies. My name has been a running joke most of my life, and while I've come to accept it as a mixed blessing, it wasn't funny when I was a kid. One time, after I confronted another ski racer who was making fun of me, she asked me why I didn't get a "real" name. The irony is that she is now married to one of my major sponsors, a corporate executive who pays me good money to have my name attached to his product. But at the time it hurt.

I didn't take the taunts lying down. There was one girl who never let up, some funny-looking chick whose name escapes me. One day on the bus I hauled off and punched her in the face. I got in big trouble when Dad found out. I'd never shrink from a fight—I'd hit first, ask questions later. Baba and I went at it so often that our parents finally bought us boxing gloves.

Life in Triumph had one set of rules, life outside Triumph another. Outsiders considered Triumph a sort of third-world moment amidst affluence, but at first I was oblivious to such social distinctions. Then I started noticing who got picked on at school and who didn't, who was cool and who wasn't. Eventually I put it all together. The rich kids were the popular clique. There was a pecking order, and by the second grade I was very familiar with it. But I knew that dwelling on it would only make me feel bad. Nice clothes and new cars were important to some people, but since I felt as if I didn't need them, none of the criteria for being popular made sense to me.

What did make sense were sports. I wasn't overly big in grade school, but I was strong for my size and very coordinated. Sports were easy for me, and when I channeled all my energy into something, I did it well, whether it was shooting an arrow or throwing a ball. So the more alienated I felt, the more I turned to my athleticism to bail me out and win me respect.

The summer I was nine, my family went to New Orleans for two months and lived with friends, Frank and Peggy Shipman. While Dad helped Frank build a chimney, I hung out with their kids, Otis and Nadine. I got to be friends with two African-American girls who lived next door. Their sport was double Dutch, and I picked it up right away. It was aggressive and feminine and challenging all at the same time. I brought double Dutch back to Ketchum and taught it to the other girls. They had to be tough and play hard. Double Dutch was a hit, and after that whatever I did ruled on the playground. There were a couple other girls who were competitive and coordinated, and we set a new standard for what it meant to play like a girl at Hemingway Elementary.

I set extremely high standards for myself, even as a third-grader. I ski raced in the winter and competed in bicycle motocross from June through October. The BMX track was shaved out of a field in Croy Canyon west of Hailey, and it was essentially a mud hole with jumps and whoop-de-dos. Hay bales lined the outside of the course. Each Saturday evening about one hundred kids showed up, and we'd race in packs by age group in a frenzy of dust and wildly churning limbs. Girls my age weren't much competition, and by the end of my first season, I had cleaned up. They decided to run boys and girls in the final race, and all I had to do was finish to claim the girls' overall title. But I didn't care about the girls. I wanted to beat the boys.

I went out fast and hard. Too hard: on the first turn I packed it in. Somebody behind me literally ran over me, leaving a tire track down the back of my T-shirt. "Get up, Picabooooo!" Mom yelled, mercifully using my given name. "All you have to do is finish!" I got back on my bike and pedaled limply across the finish line. Despite being the top girl, it took all my willpower to keep a lid on my emotions. I didn't want people to see me cry because they might misunderstand my tears. I wasn't crying because I got hurt. That was nothing. What really hurt was not doing my best.

MY FIRST SKI TEAM WAS THE SUN VALLEY SKI EDUCATION FOUNDATION. It was a breeding ground for nationally ranked ski racers, the place to be if you had aspirations. I started on the Farm Team with the other little kids, and the older I got the better I skied.

But I wasn't overly serious at first. Skiing was a part of the fabric of everyday life in the Wood River Valley, just something almost everyone did. Businesses opened late on the morning after a big dump. Not much got done on powder days except skiing. Students got discounts on season passes and were let out of school early twice a week to go skiing. Olympians and national champions ate breakfast at the same diners and shopped at the same markets as everyone else. Gretchen Fraser, the first American to win an Olympic gold medal in Alpine skiing, in 1948, was from Sun Valley, and she had a run on Baldy named after her: Gretchen's Gold.

I didn't start out wanting to join that tradition, or hoping that one day I, too, would have a run that bore my name. But I do remember the day the dream hit me. I was ten, and Mom and Dad had come to watch me race. Afterward we trooped through the parking lot to the car. I was carrying my first-place trophy, Dad was carrying my skis, and we were all huddled together against the cold. Suddenly the rightness of that moment, of us being a family combined with the heft of that trophy in my hands, caused some greater notion to click into place.

I tugged on the sleeve of Dad's coat and made him stop walking.

"Dad, I want to go to the Olympics," I said. "I want a gold medal."

He kind of blew it off as a ten-year-old moment and kept walking.

"Dad, I mean it. I want to ski race." I grabbed him again and said once more, "*Dad*, I want to go to the Olympics."

He stopped and looked down at me for a few seconds. "Well, that's a pretty big bite," he finally said. "But if you really want it, I'll be with you all the way."

Later he said that he could see the fire and passion in my eyes, and from that moment on, winning was all he wanted for me.

3

ALMOST FEARLESS

I'm standing outside the entrance to Sawtooth Title in downtown Ketchum, gathering my courage. It's the middle of February in Idaho, but my palms are sweaty. I've been going from business to business for a week knocking on doors, but that doesn't make pushing them open any easier.

Don't be a weenie. Who cares if they feel sorry for you? You're on a mission.

I'm standing here because I've qualified for the 1985 Western Regional Junior III Olympics at Mount Alyeska, Alaska. The Junior Olympics are the biggest event of the year, my chance to see how I stack up against the best girls in the West, other thirteen-year-olds I've seen in the points standings but never raced against.

I'm standing here because doing well at the J.O.s will improve my national ranking, which will improve my chances of making the U.S. Ski Team, getting me one step closer to my dream.

The trip costs eighteen hundred dollars. I have two weeks to raise the money. If I don't, another skier will go in my place.

"Jesus Christ, we don't have that kind of dough," Dad had grumbled.

We have four hundred dollars from Mom's mother and another five hundred dollars from family friends. I'm standing here because if I want the rest, I'll have to ask total strangers for it.

I wipe my palms on my jeans and push open the door. A bell jingles. I see a big brass nameplate, and then a desk, and then a guy in glasses sitting behind the desk. He looks up at me curiously. I don't know him, and he doesn't know me. I'm just some kid who's walked in off the street.

I begin by introducing myself. "My name is Picabo Street."

My pitch goes something like this: "Here's my deal. I'm going to Alaska for these ski races. It's really far away and I have to fly up. We need plane tickets and the whole thing is kind of expensive and my family can't afford it. I'm gathering donations, and if you'd like to be a part of this, please give me a check. Cash works, too."

I hand the man a piece of paper with some numbers written on it. "This is how much I have, and this is how much I need."

He takes the paper and looks at it, looks at me, and smiles. Then he reaches in a drawer and takes out his checkbook. After I've pocketed the donation, he wants to engage in a little small talk, and since he wrote me a check, I decide to hang out and chat for a few minutes.

"I'm thirteen, sir. I've been ski racing seriously for three years. My goal is to go to the Olympics someday." He shakes my hand, and I'm on to the next door.

My mission is a success. I go to Alaska, where I win two out of three races as well as the overall title. I get three medals and one of those shallow pans prospectors used to find gold in streams.

WHEN I THINK ABOUT MY EARLY YEARS AS A SKI RACER, I THINK ABOUT sacrifice. I think about swallowing my pride and doing whatever it took to make my dream happen. And my parents did the same, though it was rarely easy.

Skiing is called a rich kid's sport for a reason. In the early '80s, the parents of a junior ski racer had to shell out between fifteen and twenty grand a year. You needed money to ski on the team, to pay the coaches' salaries, to enter the races, to travel to the races, to buy the lift tickets at the races. Getting outfitted in skis, boots, poles, and ski clothes could run you another thousand bucks, minimum. My coaches said I had "talent" and "promise," and every spare dime my parents made was channeled into cultivating that promise. After almost fifteen years in Triumph, my parents decided a few creature comforts couldn't hurt, but there wasn't enough money to go around. Mom, Dad, and Baba gave up so much so that I could ski race: new cars, new clothes, a new stereo, a new stove.

Having a kid who's a ski racer is like playing Vegas. My parents took their hard-earned money and put it all on the line, gambling that it would pay off. And from the very start, it did. For three years, from age ten to thirteen, I was almost unbeatable. Idaho was part of the U.S. Ski Association's Intermountain Division (IMD), along with Montana, Utah, and Wyoming. The ski season started around Thanksgiving and lasted until April of the following year, and I spent most weekends traveling to IMD races with the Sun Valley team in crowded vans with ski bags lashed to the roofs. During the 1982–83 season, when I was eleven, I won every IMD age-group race I entered except one. I placed second in that race. I also began to get sponsored by equipment companies that sent me new gear every season, so my parents were spared that expense at least.

The financial demands put a strain on the household. I'd lie in bed at night and hear my parents arguing in the kitchen about money and about me. How much spending money should I get for the next trip? Where would the money for the plane fare come from? And on and on.

I hated it when they fought over me. I felt guilty that my family gave up so much, and I wanted to ski well so their sacrifices meant something. Baba and I had what we needed; we just didn't always have what we wanted. I'd lie in bed, trying to ignore those raised voices in the other room, and dream of a richer future. *Boy,* I'd think, *we sure are going to have a lot when I make it. We'll have everything we want.*

ALPINE SKIING COMPETITION IS DIVIDED INTO FOUR TYPES OF RACES: slalom, giant slalom (GS), super giant slalom (Super G), and downhill. Up until age twenty-one, I skied all of them. A brief explanation of each one will help the rest of my story make a lot more sense.

Slalom and GS are called "technical" disciplines, meaning the priority is turning. Slalom skiers make short, snappy, nonstop turns through several dozen pairs of flexible plastic poles stuck at regular intervals in the snow, usually on the steepest, iciest trail the course setter can find. Each set of poles is called a gate; miss a gate and you're out of the race. A GS course is longer and the gates are spaced farther apart. A GS gate consists of two sets of double poles connected with a nylon banner. In both slalom and GS your finish is based on a combined time from two runs. The slalom and GS have an added incentive: if your first run isn't among the thirty fastest, you don't make the cut for the second run.

The downhill is a speed event, and it's by far the most dangerous. The course can be up to a mile and a half long and strewn with one terrain landmine after another: clifflike drop-offs; huge jumps; treacherous knolls; banana-shaped turns; side hills so round and steep that skiing them is like trying to turn on the side of a basketball; ruts and bumps and dips so hairball you practically need an all-terrain vehicle to get through them, and all you've got is a pair of legs. Oh, and you're going up to eighty miles an hour in the process. More serious injuries occur and more careers are ended in the downhill.

The Super G is about 15 percent shorter than the downhill and combines the turns of a GS with the speeds of a downhill. Both disciplines are the ultimate test of strength, balance, reflexes, and nerve. The downhill ski racer is a speed-seeking missile, a gravity groupie, a momentum monger. Everything—body position, the slippery one-piece suit, even the way the poles are bent to hug the body in a tuck—is designed to trim milliseconds off your time. The fastest way down the mountain is called the fall line—it's the path a snowball would take if you rolled it downhill—and the more time you can rack up with your skis in the fall line, the faster you'll go. Throwing your skis sideways is slow. Getting too much air is slow. Standing up or opening your body is slow. You have to keep your upper body curved and then on the flats and straightaways drop into a deep, aerodynamic tuck, the upper body parallel to the thighs and the head tucked between the arms, which are extended straight ahead, fists together, clasping the pole grips. I've always had a hell of a tuck. My hips are extremely flexible, and I can drop so low into my tuck that my torso is lower than my thighs. I am a bullet, an arrow always pointing down, down, down, going faster, faster, faster.

Until I was introduced to fear, I rarely felt as if I got up to full speed. And when I did, it was only briefly, and it was the greatest feeling imaginable.

I was eleven when I got the fast thing going. The Sun Valley downhill coaches would have us do "nonstops"—run after run without a break—on downhill skis to get the feel of those big boards under our feet. Sometimes they'd set up a few gates on Saturday morning and we'd practice big, fat high-speed turns while the slopes were empty of people. It was always an adjustment to go back to those narrower, more constraining technical courses. The only reason I ever made turns was to slow down.

I took to the downhill immediately. It was simply a wintertime version of ripping down the quarry road on my bike. I lived to push the edge of the envelope and accepted crashing as an inevitable by-product of finding where that edge lay.

My first big downhill was a revelation. It was an IMD race in Park City, Utah, on a run called Payday. I was twelve, and I was wearing a blue ski suit handmade by a woman in Hailey; Mom hired her because it was cheaper than buying a suit in a store. The run was relatively flat, a starter course, but to my young eyes it seemed huge and wide open, the possibilities for speed endless. The snow was smooth, the visibility was perfect, and there was nobody in my way. It was almost too good to be true. My parents had driven the five hours south from Triumph to watch me, and Mom remembers watching my run through her fingers. Crazy, fast, and fun—that's how I remember that race. I loved the wind and the rush, the control of that intensity wrapped up so tight, the run unwinding like a ball of string, and I was the kite.

Ski racing seems simple in theory—whoever gets to the bottom the fastest wins—but it's the variables that complicate things. Any number of factors, natural and manmade, can affect the outcome of a race. Snow conditions can vary from soft as a Slurpee to hard as an ice rink and can change from one extreme to another in the course of an hour. The weather might be warm enough for sun block and shades or cold enough to turn your toes black with frostbite. The way the gates are set on a course (tight or loose), the type of wax on your ski bases, even the tint of your goggle lenses can make or break a race.

Then there's the fear factor. Skiing is 90 percent mental. One of the ironic things about high-speed sports like skiing or car racing is that caution can equal danger. It can be safer to ski aggressively. This is where confidence comes in, a commodity I possessed in abundance. A lot of skiers fixate on falling. They ski *not* to fall. When you're scared and skiing defensively, you are an accident waiting to happen. As a kid, my fear threshold was just as high as my pain threshold. Playing with the boys had taught me to think like a boy.

I may have been brave, but I wasn't an idiot. A big jump might make my heart thump the first time I saw it; the key is that I never let fear stop me. If something made me hesitate—usually it had to do with going airborne— I talked myself through it: *keep breathing; lift your heels; pull back your toes; breathe at the takeoff.* I kept everything flowing and visualized myself doing it successfully. I crowded my brain with so much information that fear got elbowed to the back of the room.

People seem to think I'm utterly fearless. I'm not. I'm afraid of the dark. My friends don't understand how I can fly one hundred feet through the air on skis and land on a surface with all the traction of a steeply pitched mirror yet refuse to leave the drapes open at night. I'm afraid of what I can't see.

But if you define fearlessness as possessing a daredevil, thrill-loving, adventure-seeking spirit, then yes, I am fearless. Always have been.

Dad had a friend named Bud, who was a bush pilot. One morning he flew into Hailey to pick somebody up and found himself with an hour to kill. So he called Dad at 6:30 A.M. and offered us a ride. Baba was spending the night at a friend's house, so Mom, Dad, and I jumped in our car and headed to the airport. Well, this was no sightseeing tour; Bud did some crazy shit. He did barrel rolls and loop de loops and flips. He corkscrewed through a narrow canyon and put the plane into a steep dive, pulling up right before we kissed an alfalfa field. He buzzed Baldy and he buzzed our house in Triumph and he buzzed downtown Hailey. He flew so close to one rooftop that Dad could inspect the mortar work in a chimney he'd built for the house's owners.

Dad and I were loving the ride, but Mom got sick. I felt guilty because I was sitting next to her, completely in heaven, while she ralphed into a plastic bag. Dad and Bud offered to set the plane down right away, but Mom steadied on. "No, no," she insisted. "We don't have that much time and I don't want to ruin it. Let's keep going." That was Mom: willing to feel crummy so we could get our kicks. She puked again on the way home, right in the middle of downtown Hailey.

Dad and I shared an intrepid spirit, but to be honest I wasn't allowed to be afraid. There was no place in Dad's worldview for cowardice or failure. " 'Can't' is not in our vocabulary," he'd often say. If my job was to collect the eggs, then I'd damn well better collect the eggs, regardless of the personal peril it entailed.

Our hen house behind the garden was ruled by a macho, chick-producing stud rooster with talons a ninja warrior would envy. Every encounter was a showdown. I'd enter the dark hen house, basket in hand, and he'd attack me, white wings flapping and evil talons extended. Half the time I had to fight him off with a pitchfork. He was probably as afraid of me as I was of him, but that didn't make egg collecting any less terrifying. Coming home with an empty basket was not an option, so I was forced to dream up a way to outwit the enemy. First I'd make sure the rooster was outside. Then I'd sneak into the hen house, bar the door with a pitchfork to keep him out, grab the eggs, and get the hell out of there. I hated that little bastard. I hope he ended up as someone's main course.

NOT LONG AFTER I DECLARED MY OLYMPIC INTENTIONS, A FRIEND OF Dad, a fellow mason named Billy Baybutt who'd been in the air force, gave him a large American flag with the provision that if I ever went to the Olympics, Dad would bring that flag along when he came to cheer me on. Dad agreed. He nailed the Stars and Stripes to the living room wall, right by the front door. It's funny, but even though I looked at that flag every day for several years, I didn't understand its significance until years later. But Dad did. He understood very well, and he did his best to keep his promise to Billy Baybutt.

I had a lot of coaches, but Dad was my guru. On race days he'd get up early and work on my skis, smoothing the metal edges with a big file and waxing and repairing the bases. I can still smell the fumes, like melting candles, as he heated the ski wax on the stove and then smoothed it on with an iron. After the wax had cooled, he'd scrape off any excess with a straightedge until the bases were silky and fast. Then he'd fix me breakfast and drive me to the hill in his truck. On the way we'd discuss my strategy for the race, who my biggest competition was, how I was feeling. He'd pick me up at the end of the day and drive me home, my knees packed in ice.

Dad's expectations were as high as always, and nothing pleased me more than meeting them. I lived for calling home after a race to tell Dad I'd done something spectacular, to hear him exclaim, "Wow!" or "Yeah, Boo!" I wanted to blow his mind, to prove my toughness. But if I didn't ski well, his reaction could swing the other way. He'd grill me about the race, going over every mistake, every miscalculation. Or worse, he'd call the coach and grill *him*. Our conversations often ended with me slamming down the phone in frustration.

Getting praise out of Dad was always a challenge, and as time went on, I gravitated to coaches who were similarly stingy. If a coach was generous with his approval or was always blowing sunshine up my ass, I didn't take him seriously. The more a coach withheld praise, the harder I worked because I assumed I was doing it wrong. My favorite coach growing up was a wry Frenchman named Michele Rodigoz. Michele coached me on and off for a long time, from my preteens to early twenties. I had to wait seven years to hear him tell me I'd had a good run.

Maybe that's one reason why I always felt capable of going faster and skiing better, no matter how many races I'd won. There was a feeling I was looking for, a perfection on my skis, a feeling that kept me going and going, and still does even today.

No matter how well I did, I was still a Triumph kid, always having to prove myself. My teammates' parents pulled up to the mountain in Rolls Royces and cheered on their kids in furs and nugget-sized diamond earrings. Dad pulled up in an old pickup wearing muddy clothes from a day mixing mortar and laying rock. Mom cleaned their houses, and sometimes I helped her after school, dusting and vacuuming the "McMansions" that were springing up all over. The local mandate that material wealth equaled success didn't hold up on the ski hill, and a few parents began to resent my success. Where did I—a girl from Triumph who skied in her brother's hand-me-downs—get off beating their kids, who had the best of everything? Mom remembers how one parent used to clap whenever I fell or straddled a gate.

I believe that in their hearts most of the Sun Valley parents admired the fact that a kid with so little was working so hard to make it happen. But they weren't letting themselves thrive in those feelings. They wanted to resent me as a way to ease their disappointment about me beating their kids.

Dad loved the idea of a Triumph kid spanking the rich kids. Mom, on the other hand, didn't relish our underdog status. I don't think she completely bought into the no-frills lifestyle she ended up with. She accepted her life and made it work because she loved Dad and she loved us, but it also embarrassed her a little. That's why she took such pride in seeing me atop the middle step of the podium at the end of the day, why she loved getting kudos and congratulations while some woman in a fur coat and dark glasses was ignored. My victories were her small slice of the pie.

Winning went to my head. I was brave and fast and I knew it. I was faster than girls two years older than I, faster even than many boys. Boys and girls in different age groups would race on the same day, and our times would be posted on one big scoreboard at the bottom of the course. One day my time was better than one eighteen-year-old guy's, and his friends teased him so mercilessly that he cried.

The entire family's status rose on the tide of my success. Mom felt my behavior reflected on all of us, and nothing made her madder than seeing me brag or pitch a fit. I had to watch myself when she was around, but oftentimes my race-day demeanor was less than exemplary. I was brash, overconfident, and intensely competitive. My moods were as unpredictable as the mountain weather: hugs and smiles one minute, sound and fury the next. There was no saying how I was going to act when I got to the finish, especially if I felt I hadn't skied well. I'd throw tantrums or whack the snow or a lift tower with my pole. I could be pissed off for an hour—marching around, shooing people out of my way, throwing and kicking things, and being generally obnoxious. I loved to take my aggression out on my skis. I'd put them together, get a firm grip, and kick them hard with my heavy plastic boots so that they would flip over each other a couple times before hitting the ground. That was fun for me but bad for my skis. One time I swore so vociferously that someone's mom asked me to leave the scoreboard area.

As I see it now, I was getting to know my temper. Anger made me feel passionate and alive. It stoked my competitive fires. I have more of my father in me than I wish I did. But the feistiness and the perfectionism I inherited from him are what helped to make me a champion.

BY THE SEVENTH GRADE, I WAS A JOCK FOR ALL SEASONS. I PLAYED VOLleyball in the fall, ski raced in the winter, ran track in the spring, and rode BMX in the summer. I moved among several cliques that rarely overlapped. It was like juggling different worlds. I had my Triumph homies, who were tight all the time no matter what. There was the ski team, with whom I spent most of my after-school hours in the winter; the other athletes at Wood River Junior High; and the popular girls, who usually happened to be the rich girls as well. My best friends among the rich girls were Terri Chavez and Julie Grant. They lived in my general vicinity, so I spent time at their houses. Terri was my Triumph-friend Andy's cousin, so we had an automatic bond. She and Julie would bring magazines like *Vogue* and *Teen Beat* to school. I'd sit outside at recess with them, looking over their shoulders while they breezily flipped through the pages, pointing out the models and the pop stars by name.

I tended not to have close friends on the ski team. I was so competitive with my teammates and didn't care if they liked me or not. The closest I got to having a friend on the team was a tall, slender blond girl named Muffy Davis. She was the other hot young racer in town. We started competing against each other when I was eight and she was seven. We were more rivals than buddies, but in a healthy way, always pushing each other to be our best, whether we were skiing, mountain biking in the off-season, or playing ice hockey to build stamina.

Muffy and I often roomed together on road trips, but outside of sports our lives didn't mesh at all. Her father was a wealthy doctor in Sun Valley, and her mother sold real estate. Muffy's younger brother, Christopher, had a severe disability and was confined to a wheelchair. He lived an hour away at the Colorado School for the Deaf and Blind, and Muffy visited him on weekends. Every December she'd miss an afternoon of training to attend the school's annual Christmas party with Chris. She possessed an inner strength you couldn't help but respect.

Because Muffy was a year younger than I, we didn't race against each other that much, and when we did I usually won and she was usually second. It happened so often that we started calling ourselves "the Muffy and Picabo Show." When she won, it infuriated me, and I did whatever I could to prevent it. I remember a race at Rotarun, a dinky ski hill out by the BMX track three miles from Hailey. It was nothing special, just a little hometown race, and everybody was competing in her ratty old ski clothes and sweats—except Muffy, who showed up for a GS event in her slick one-piece downhill suit. This was like going to a square dance in a ball gown. Everybody snickered at Muffy, until she proceeded to dust us on the first run. At lunch all the other girls drove home and got their downhill suits—including me. I won the second run, but Muffy was nice about it. As usual, she went up to all the coaches, shook their hands, and thanked them. Then she came over to me. "Great race, Peek," she said, patting my back and smiling, her braces glinting in the sun.

Muffy may have had better people skills than I had, but otherwise we were similar in many ways. We both got teased for our names (at least nobody called me "McMuffin"), we both were fiercely competitive, and we both wanted to ski in the Olympics. That was every young skier's dream, the highest goal you could aspire to. Saying "I want to go to the Olympics" was automatic, like saying you wanted to get married or have kids. I remember how the team would be hanging out in the locker room or riding in the van to a race, hollering out our big-time aspirations. "Me and Muffy are gonna win Olympic gold medals," I'd brag, and Muffy would nod her head, grinning. When our teammates scoffed, we'd drape our arms around each other's shoulders and say, "Laugh it up now. When we've got those medals around our necks, we'll see who's laughing. It'll be the Muffy and Picabo Show. You guys just wait."

I LEFT THE SUN VALLEY TEAM AFTER THE 1982–83 SEASON, WHEN I WAS twelve. There were a lot of reasons, but a big one was what my parents considered a general lack of supervision. The team could get pretty rowdy on road trips, throwing chairs, punching holes in walls, falling off balconies, that sort of thing. Demolition wasn't something I engaged in; I had enough of beating up on old stuff in Triumph. Besides, I knew my family didn't have the money to pay for any property damage. I also left the team because I wasn't getting along with a few coaches who liked to boss me around for no reason. (If you're going to boss me around, you damn well better have a good reason.) Dad also felt I could use more one-on-one attention. The town of Hailey had started its own ski club, so we jumped there, and Dad arranged for me to travel to races separately with my own coach.

The Hailey Ski Club had more pluck than money. We trained mostly at Rotarun, though we'd go to Sun Valley for downhill training because Rotarun was so small. Back in the '80s, Hailey was a working-class community. The parents of the other skiers were beauticians and cops and hardworking entrepreneurs. (This was ten years before Bruce Willis and Demi Moore bought up half the town and everybody became a real estate agent.) Not only was I still beating the rich kids, I was doing it as a member of the lowly Hailey Ski Club.

The 1984 Winter Olympic Games were held in Sarajevo, Yugoslavia. The Olympics, always a big deal in Sun Valley, were particularly exciting that year because Christin Cooper, a hometown girl, was competing. Billy and Jamie's parents had bought a satellite dish, so we went to watch the ski racing at their house. Boy, did I like what I saw.

Americans have always struggled in the shadow of Alpine powerhouses like Austria and Switzerland, but in Sarajevo, the U.S. Ski Team exceeded all expectations. It started when Bill Johnson, a brash, one-time car thief from California, declared he was the one to beat in the men's downhill, and then went out and won, shocking the world. Phil Mahre took the gold in the men's slalom, and his twin brother, Steve, won the silver. The American women bagged three of the top four places in the GS, with Debbie Armstrong taking the gold and Christin Cooper the silver. Tamara McKinney, probably the best woman skier the United States has ever produced, was fourth, just out of the medals. For the first time in Olympic Alpine skiing history, the United States finished on top in the medal count.

When I was growing up, Tamara and Christin were my idols. I'd see them in person when they blew through town with their coaches for races or training. They awed me. They were strong, pretty, and friendly, wore cool uniforms, and skied so well. I wanted to be one of them. I wanted that uniform so badly.

That May, I took one step closer to getting it. I came home from school to find Mom waiting for me, holding a letter. The envelope was addressed to me and bore the logo of the U.S. Ski Team. I could tell the flap had already been opened and resealed. If I remember correctly, Dad was fiddling with the stereo, acting all nonchalant.

"What's this?" I asked, but I knew what it was before I even opened it.

"Dear Picabo," it began, "on behalf of the coaching staff of the United States Ski Team, I would like to invite you to attend an on-snow training camp at Mt. Bachelor, Oregon, from July 9 to July 21, 1984.

"This training camp will be an excellent opportunity for you to receive some high-quality training in slalom and giant slalom, to get acquainted with your peers from around the country, and to be exposed to the coaching staff of the U.S. Ski Team. We feel this is a very important step in your development and that it should take precedence over other summer training opportunities."

Yeah, like hauling rocks in the quarry.

The letter went on to say that I was responsible for paying for my own transportation to and from Portland, Oregon, and that I should come in good physical shape and be prepared to work hard. It was signed Bob Harkins, assistant alpine director.

Oh, how I celebrated. I got in Dad's face, crowing, "I've arrived!" while prancing around the room, waving the letter like a tiny flag on the Fourth of July. Dad just sat there looking smug, trying not to smile. We'd both known it was only a matter of time.

The camp location ended up being changed to Mount Hood's Palmer Glacier an hour east of Portland. At 11,237 feet, Mount Hood is Oregon's tallest mountain, a gothic-looking peak jutting out of fruit orchards. In the summer the snowfield is crowded with ski racers bagging some hot-weather turns, trying to keep their edge. To save money I begged a ride with one of my Sun Valley coaches, a former Olympian named Abbi Fisher who was going to coach another training camp at Hood. We talked and ate doughnuts as we drove. Abbi told me that when she was on the U.S. Ski Team, she didn't eat junk food for ten years, not even a candy bar. *Oh my god,* I thought with a mouthful of doughnut, *will I have to do that?*

There were two dozen girls at Hood, up-and-coming skiers like me from all around the United States. At thirteen, I was the youngest. We ran gates in T-shirts and got sunburns. We stayed in the Cascade Lodge, and one of the girls snored so badly we threw shoes at her face to shut her up. I still have a group photo of all of us. Several of those girls went on to make the U.S. Ski Team with me. But of all the girls in the picture, I'm the only one who's hung with it.

I skied with the Hailey Ski Club again in 1984–85 and had another good year, cleaning up at the Junior Olympics in Alaska. I ended the season with high rankings in the 1985 Intermountain Cup final standings: fifth in the downhill and tenth overall, among girls two and three years older than I was.

That spring I got a call from a coach named Paul Major, who was in charge of recruiting new talent for the U.S. Ski Team. He told me that they had some open slots to fill on their development squad, and I had made the cut. He explained that the team would fly me to summer and fall conditioning camps at its headquarters in Park City, Utah, and to on-snow camps as far away as South America. I'd travel with the squad to a few races, but for the most part ski and train with my local ski club, competing on the junior circuit.

I was going places. But that meant leaving one particular place behind.

THE MINERS HAD THEIR HEYDAY IN TRIUMPH, AND THE STREET FAMILY had theirs. The house next door to us changed hands several times, and when I was eleven John and Jane Majors moved in. This began what I call "the drama years." It was the beginning of the end.

From the start, John and Jane didn't get along with anyone. Jane had a little boy by a previous marriage, but they weren't interested in joining Triumph's family scene. They yelled at the gang when we ran through their yard, and as time went on, Jane's behavior became increasingly unpredictable. She'd scream at Mom: "You don't have to sing all the time, and your garden's ugly anyway!" Jane conjured some absurd conspiracy where Mom was throwing weeds from her garden into Jane's. She and her husband didn't like Dad at all, and they seemed to resent my success. They didn't miss a chance to make our lives miserable.

Neither did their dog, a German shepherd determined to set a world record for nonstop barking. That dog infuriated everybody in town, particularly Mike, the Vietnam vet who lived in the trailer court. Mike drank too much, and Baba liked to sneak around his trailer and eavesdrop on him and his buddies bullshitting about their exploits in 'Nam. Mom called Mike "a ticking time bomb," and he'd been spoiling for a fight for a while.

He got it one summer evening around dinnertime. Mom was out in the garden. I was doing homework. Dad had just gotten home from work and was taking a shower. John and Jane's dog was yapping as usual.

Mike, who was drunk, walked out of his trailer and starting shooting off rounds at the dog. (He missed.) Undeterred that Mike had a loaded pistol and seemed willing to use it, John ran out of his house and down the hill toward Mike, determined to kick his ass. But before he could get one off Mike popped John in the mouth, knocking out his front bridge.

Dad was just drying off when he heard the shots. He threw on some clothes and charged outside, and I ran after him. By the time Dad reached the trailer court, John had dragged himself to his feet and was ready to go again with Mike. Dad got between them, and John decided he'd throw down with Dad, too. I arrived just in time to watch Dad kick John's ass a bit. He and Mom had both taken up karate years ago after a close call with four would-be banditos in a train station in Mexico, so Dad knew how to defend himself. He settled into a karate stance, cocked back his arm and, *boom*, punched John smack in the middle of his chest. John flew backward through the air about six feet and landed on a hay bale.

Figuring he'd taken care of him, Dad turned and yelled at Mike to get back in his goddamn trailer, then started up for the house. Meanwhile, John had gotten up and dusted himself off, breathing heavily and seeing red. As Dad was walking away John lunged at him from behind.

"He's coming, Daddy!" I screamed. Dad whirled around to take care of John some more. Fortunately, somebody grabbed Dad and somebody grabbed John. The fracas broke up with everybody shuffling away and mumbling about what a pussy John was for attacking Dad from behind.

Life in Triumph was never the same after that. The good vibes had gone sour. But then I was changing, too. I was a teenager, for one thing, and while I was still one of the boys, it was also becoming clear that I was a girl. I obviously had more complicated emotions than they did. I had also discovered the telephone. Out-of-town races had become social as much as competitive events, a chance to find out what clothes other kids were wearing, what music they were listening to, and what movies they were seeing. It was about who was the fastest at the end of the day and who was partying with whom at the end of the night.

One of the last races of the 1984–85 ski season was held at Nordic Valley, Utah, near Ogden. There, a former French ski team member named Scott Sanchez approached me and said he'd been hired to coach at a new ski academy called Rowmark Ski Academy. The program had about twenty skiers, who took classes at Rowland Hall-St. Marks School, a prestigious prep school in Salt Lake City. While they studied alongside the nonskiing student body, Rowmark students had no afternoon classes in the winter. Instead, they trained at one of the many ski areas outside the city and traveled to races around the West. Scott asked me if I was interested in checking the place out.

It was a tempting offer. A lot of top young racers go to ski academies as a way to work with international coaches and rise faster through the ranks. Olle Larsson, the director of skiing, was one of the country's top experts on ski technique.

That spring we drove to Salt Lake City. We toured the Rowland Hall-St. Marks School, an imposing brick building big enough to hold every house in Triumph. And we met Olle, a hilarious, bighearted Swede with a laugh you could hear two rooms away.

Enrolling me at Rowmark would mean even more sacrifices. Baba would have to leave Wood River High, where he was excelling in football and dating, to spend his junior year in Salt Lake City. Dad would have to put his stonemason work on hold, leaving his partner Kenny Dickens to run the quarry. Mom would have to leave her garden. Olle told us that Rowmark could help a little with the tuition, but because the school was so new it could offer only a modest scholarship. We'd have to make up the rest.

Olle had a highly developed moral conscience, and it bothered him that my coming to Rowmark could deplete our already meager resources. At one point during our tour, he pulled Baba aside and asked if he could speak with him in private.

"Baba," he said, "if Picabo's going to come here, all your parents' savings will have to be directed exclusively to her. How do you feel about that?"

Baba thought a minute and said, "Personally, it's fine with me."

It was fine with all of us. John and Jane ended up pressing battery charges against Dad, and the case would drag out for three years. Starting fresh seemed like a good idea. Besides, I was tired of being the only chick in town. I liked TV and magazines and telephones. I was ready for the world.

In August 1985, we closed down the house, packed our stuff in a U-Haul, and drove out of Triumph.

From the start, city life was not our bag. Everything about Salt Lake City seemed dirty: the air, the water, the buildings. And there were so many temptations. I was curious about everything except skiing.

We rented a place on Sherman Avenue about a half-mile from the Rowland Hall-St. Marks School. It was our first real house, a cute bungalow-style place with doors on the rooms, a gas stove in the kitchen, and a bathroom with tile walls and shower doors made of glass. There was a bedroom for my brother and one for me. Mom and Dad got jobs managing the equipment-rental department at a ski shop in Park City, an hour away. Baba enrolled at East High, just down the street, and made the football team. East High had two thousand kids as compared to five hundred at Wood River High, and it was an easy place to get lost.

Attending Rowmark Ski Academy was like stepping into that old Molly Ringwald movie, *Pretty in Pink*. Many of the students at Rowland Hall-St. Marks were troubled rich kids whose parents sent them there to clean up their acts. They drove expensive cars and wore trendy clothes. In Idaho I had dressed for durability and warmth; here, all the girls cared about was whether the guys thought they looked cute. Like the twenty or so other students in the skiing program, I played other sports, particularly volleyball and soccer. This made me a jock, which gave the other kids one more reason—along with my name—to give me a hard time.

I retaliated in small yet significant ways. One guy at school used to leave his Maserati idling in front of the school (we all assumed he was dealing drugs). One day at lunch, when no one was looking, I hopped in and took it for a ride. That car was all horsepower and hunger, and when I gunned the engine it surged like a thoroughbred out of the gate. We had a lot in common, that car and I. I drove my new toy around for about thirty minutes, got a little lunch, and returned it to the same parking spot before its owner even knew it was gone.

I also "borrowed" my brother's car, the same beat-up old Beemer we'd driven to New Orleans when I was ten. When Baba wasn't home, I'd steal his keys and take his car for a joyride. I didn't have a license, but that didn't stop me. Driving was just another way to go fast.

Around Thanksgiving, the team started its on-snow training. I spent the mornings in the classroom and the afternoons on the ski hill. Every day a van would pick up the team for the forty-five-minute drive into Big Cottonwood Canyon, where we trained at a ski area called Solitude. It was strange to drive through a city to get to the mountains. It didn't seem right.

But the thing that bothered me most was that Mom and Dad weren't healthy. I knew it. I could feel it. They were out of their element. All their money was going into my expenses, which only added to my guilt. They seemed to do nothing but drive to work and drive home. They weren't eating or sleeping well. On weekends, they just sat around, doing nothing. When they bought a TV, I took it as a sign.

By Christmas, we'd made a decision: at the end of the school year, we were out of there.

My year at Rowmark wasn't a total loss, thanks to Olle. We got along well. I saw in him someone with a genuine passion for the sport. He saw in me a raw talent he could cultivate, a skier who, he felt, was equally gifted in the technical and speed events. His ideas about ski racing technique, especially how to generate speed out of a turn, were so far ahead of their time that what I learned from him fifteen years ago is still helping me today.

And it was Olle who discovered I possessed a unique mental skill that would become a secret to my future success.

The Rowmark ski team competed every weekend. One weekend we had a three-day downhill competition in Grand Targhee, a beautiful, remote ski area in Wyoming, not far from Jackson Hole. The mental side of skiing fascinated Olle, and in the evenings back at the hotel, he'd gather the team together for imaging exercises. He'd put on some classical music, and after we were good and relaxed, he would have us visualize running the course we'd trained on that day. With Olle prompting us through the course and a parent manning the stopwatch, we'd imagine the entire race, from the countdown in the start gate to every gate, every jump, every roll and dip. When we crossed the "finish line," each of us would pop up our index finger to signal the timekeeper.

Other kids would be off by seconds, but I'd come within three or four tenths of a second to the time I'd skied on the actual course. Each day, as my real times got faster, so did my mental times. To this day, Olle says he's seen nothing like it.

My grades weren't quite as remarkable. Not only was the curriculum at Rowland Hall-St. Marks extremely challenging, but all the traveling to ski races made it hard to keep up with my schoolwork. My status was "borderline" the entire time. My mom recently dug up my academic evaluations from that school year. Here's a sample:

"Picabo could be an A student if she only wanted to be. She has excellent pronunciation and participates actively in class. She, however, has not been doing her assignments and has not been studying for tests." (Spanish)

"Picabo began the quarter in good fashion, but her effort gradually dropped. She had particular problems at the end in making up work she missed due to skiing. Several of her early tests were Bs, so she can do better if she applies herself." (World History)

"Picabo has handed in only one of six homework assignments, even though she is often reminded. She needs to take responsibility and exert the effort. She will be reminded no more!" (Earth Science)

"Picabo is a very good math student. She tends to make careless errors when she rushes. If she stays calm, she can do very well." (Algebra)

"Picabo has learned a great deal about herself and what she needs to do to prepare for races. Her skiing at the J.O.s was excellent, especially her slalom, where she was by far the most aggressive. Picabo needs to work on actually racing, not on victories, attention, trophies, etc., before the race. These things will come *after* good racing." (Olle)

Olle always accentuated the positive, but I wasn't happy with my skiing that season because I didn't win many races. Nevertheless, in February 1986 I was one of six skiers chosen to represent the United States at the Topolino World Juvenile Championships, a prestigious international event for eleven-to fourteen-year-olds. It was my first trip abroad. We flew into Munich and drove to Austria, where we trained for a few days before the two-day event in northern Italy. Europe was a trip. For one thing, the mountains were huge, unfolding endlessly as far as the eye could see. We ate in restaurants every night, ordering whatever we wanted off the menu. If we didn't like it, we ordered something else. One of our team members got scarlet fever and had to be rushed to the hospital. I finished sixteenth in the downhill there, but I was more disappointed by my performance at the Western J-II Junior Olympics in Park City. I got only one top-three finish, a second in the GS.

I also sustained my first skiing injury while at Rowmark—ironically, at a downhill in Sun Valley. I remember exactly where it happened: at the intersection of River Run and Olympic Lane. I was hauling ass through a big gully when I came around a corner, lost control, and started heading straight for a lift tower. I tried to redirect the trajectory of my fall in the direction of a safety fence, and in the process of tumbling ass over teakettle I whacked my chin on my knee. I peeled myself off the ground with a bit tongue, a bloody lip, and four broken teeth. My parents weren't there, so a coach drove me to a local dentist, Dr. Chris Mazzola. He bonded my broken teeth and X-rayed my jaw, shaking his head the whole time. The X rays revealed numerous hairline fractures in my lower jawbone. Dr. Mazzola wanted to wire it shut, but I refused. No way was I going to end up sucking on pieces of bread like my half sister Sunny.

I considered an injury serious only if it put me out of commission. Getting hurt was no big deal. It was like the time Josh got shot in the eye with a BB gun and had to go to the hospital and have the bullet removed from his eyelid with tweezers. Josh didn't need a stitch, and the next day you couldn't even tell he'd been shot in the eye. My broken jaw was the same thing—a war wound. You couldn't tell it was broken. In fact, I thought it was kind of cool.

I became one of Dr. Mazzola's best patients over the next few years, and he did the work at a discount. Finally, in early 1994, he promised to give me free dental work for life if I won an Olympic gold medal.

Dr. Mazzola is just one of the people in Sun Valley who helped me out when I was a young ski racer. So let me amend the statement I made at the beginning of this chapter. When I think of those years, I think not just of sacrifice, but of generosity, too. A few people may have doubted me, but at least as many supported me financially in those early years, some anonymously. To this day I don't know who they are. I owe them a debt of gratitude.

I also owe the people who, when I asked them for help, opened their wallets purely on faith. Whether they said yes or no, the bottom line was that they treated me with respect. And disrespect was the thing I feared most.

4

THE GREAT WALL

ALMOST EVERY YOUNG ATHLETE REACHES A POINT WHEN LIFE THREATENS to blow him or her off course. The forces that tug on any teenager pulled at me, too, only I had to choose between toeing the line and giving in to temptation. It was touch and go for a while. Adversity roared around me like an avalanche off Mindbender Mountain, blocking the road to my dream.

After returning to Idaho from Salt Lake City in May 1986, my parents decided to settle in Hailey. Mom wasn't particularly eager to live next door to John and Jane again, and she wanted Baba and me to have a shorter drive to Wood River High, where he'd be a senior and I'd be a sophomore. My parents found a house in a subdivision on Carbonate Street, seven blocks off Main. Dad and Baba spent the summer with Kenny Dickens, quarrying rock for local construction projects and selling it by the ton. They'd get half the money up front, quarry the rock, and then receive the second installment upon delivery. Dad was picking up the occasional masonry job as well, a fireplace here, a stone wall there. Mom got a job as a customer service representative for Cablevision in Ketchum. She handled the complaints.

My year in Salt Lake City had taken me out of the social loop, so when I wasn't at conditioning camp with the ski team, I was reestablishing old friendships and making new ones. It was great to see Terri Chavez and Julie

Grant again, and we had a lot of adventures. Julie's mom was a saleswoman for Mary Kay, and she had a pink Volkswagen Cabriolet she used to drive around town on sales calls. Julie and I would put the top down on that pink car and take off. We'd rip down the unpaved back roads of Hailey, catching air off bumps and plowing through mud puddles. By the time we were done that car looked like a pig after a mud bath.

That was the summer I met Tiffany Timmons. I was introduced to her by friends at a Fourth of July party, and after they disappeared, Tiff and I ended up spending the evening together. We really hit it off. She was fun, open, and ready for anything. She had a nice family and a nice car. She was outdoorsy like me, and while she didn't ski race, she was a great skier, so we had that in common, too. We spent a lot of time together that summer, hiking, swimming, and tubing on the Wood River. My friends and I engaged in a local pastime called river boarding. We'd attach a wooden plank to a bridge with a long rope and then stand on the plank, riding it like a surfboard in the strong current.

In August, I took my biggest adventure: a two-week ski camp in Las Leñas, Argentina, a ski resort high in the Andes. Because our summer is winter below the equator, South American ski resorts are deep in snow from June through September, and ski teams from all over the world make a beeline to train there. I felt comfortable in South America, maybe because I'd spent so much time in Mexico and Guatemala as a kid. I practiced my Spanish—Mom was fluent—and I liked being able to order from a menu and say hello to the locals. Actually, the first thing I did in Argentina was flush the toilet. *Wow,* I thought, *the water really does go down the other way.*

I was still finding my place on the U.S. Ski Team. It had a definite hierarchy. At the bottom were the rookies like me, members of the development, or D, team. The A team was the most seasoned competitors. They spent the winter on the World Cup, the highest level of international ski racing. We called them the "big girls." The idea was to ski well enough to climb through the ranks, from D to C to B and finally to the A team. Only about 1 percent of D team members actually get that far. It is so easy for a young athlete to get sidetracked by injury, puberty, family problems, or just plain burnout.

I was determined to make it, to be a big girl. But I had to play the little girl games—eat with the other little girls, let the big girls ski first, and so on. There is always a sense of resentment among the veterans when new blood arrives; no one wants to get beaten by a young upstart. And being a rookie with a certain attitude, all I wanted to do was to beat the big girls.

All the big girls were in Las Leñas. Among the speed specialists were Pam Fletcher, Adele Allender, Chantal Knapp, Hilary Lindh, Kristin Krone, and Tori Pillinger. The technical team included Eva Twardokens, Diann Roffe, and the ultimate big girl, my idol, Tamara McKinney. Tamara was a small-boned twenty-four-year-old with shoulder-length brown hair and huge green eyes with mile-long lashes. Like mine, her upbringing had been unconventional. She had seven brothers and sisters, and her mom home-schooled them all. She spent her summers on her father's horse farm in Kentucky and her winters near Reno, skiing the Sierras. She finished third in a World Cup slalom when she was sixteen. She'd had an incredible run of success in the early '80s, winning the World Cup GS title in 1981. In 1983, she won the World Cup GS title again, finished second in the slalom, and, most impressively, won the overall title—the first and last time an American has done that. Tamara was awesome, the best on the team. All I wanted to do was beat her in competition. I never got that chance—her career was ebbing as mine was beginning—but I accomplished something even better: we became friends.

We'd met in Sun Valley, but in Las Leñas I got to know her as a person rather than a hero. During camp, I looked at her with eyes that said, "Teach me; teach me." Tamara must have received the message because one day at lunch she approached me and said, "A bunch of us are heading out to do an afternoon hike and ski. You're welcome to come if you like."

I couldn't believe it. An invitation from Tamara McKinney to go skiing with the big girls. "Oh, yeah," I answered.

A group of us set out at around one o'clock, under a sky the color of a new denim shirt. We shouldered our skis and hiked in a long line up a narrow ridge through thigh-deep snow, making our way above the tree line toward the jagged peaks. As we hiked, Tamara talked to me about how the team worked, what to expect from different people, how to behave. After two hours, we reached the top of a series of bowls filled with pristine powder snow that was almost blinding in its whiteness. I watched Tamara float down through the snow, making one effortless turn after another, and thought to myself that she looked as graceful and beautiful in the powder as she did on the racecourse. It was a perfect day: rock, snow, sky, sun, and skiing with Tamara.

The next time I saw Tamara was a month later, on a glacier in Saas-Fe, Switzerland. By now I felt comfortable enough with her to give her a little grief. One morning the team was lined up, waiting our turns to take a GS run. Tamara was ahead of me, taking forever in the start gate. While she tried to get her focus, I was getting increasingly restless, until finally I was practically pawing the ground and snorting with impatience.

"Hey, old lady," I said, "you'd better hurry up and get out of the start or I'm gonna beat you down."

Tamara turned, looked at me, and responded, "Not yet you're not." Later she admitted to me that she'd turned back around and thought, *Oh shit*. But that exchange really bonded us. She saw that I could dish it out, and I saw that she could take it.

BACK AT WOOD RIVER HIGH, I STARTED DATING MY FIRST SERIOUS BOYfriend. His name was Brad Jakes, and he was a star athlete like me: the point guard on the basketball team, the center forward on the soccer team, and the quarterback on the football team. Everybody called us the "all-American couple." I was only fifteen, and our relationship was pretty wholesome; we'd hold hands and kiss once in a while. Baba was the star linebacker on the same team, and I'd stand on the sidelines with a pad and pencil, keeping stats for John Blackman, the football coach, and watching Brad get pummeled, play after play. Between his football and basketball and my skiing, Brad and I spent more time apart than together, and eventually we broke up. We realized we were more like buddies than boyfriend and girlfriend, so we called it off before our friendship suffered.

All that time on the road was making my grades suffer. It was Rowland Hall-St. Marks all over again. Some of my teachers at Wood River High felt I was putting the U.S. Ski Team ahead of school, and frankly they were right. I felt my studies had no impact on me whatsoever in the short term.

I wanted that ski team uniform a lot more than I wanted a high school diploma.

I got the uniform that November, at our final preseason on-snow camp in Copper Mountain, Colorado. It was very ritualistic. The ceremony took place in a hotel meeting room. First the A team entered the room, followed by the B and C teams. The rookies entered last. When Paul Major handed me my uniform, it was one of the greatest moments of my life. I had been admitted to an exclusive sisterhood of speed. The color scheme was light blue and maroon. There was an article of clothing for each discipline—technical and speed—along with warm-ups and a hooded parka, not to mention a ton of accessories: hand warmers, shin guards, goggles, glasses, and helmets. It was like Christmas. I'd never gotten so much new stuff at one time in my life. I tried everything on in my hotel room later and checked myself out in the mirror, imagining how I'd look standing on the podium wearing it.

My dream was burning brighter than ever. At home in Hailey, I drew the Olympic rings on a piece of paper, cut them out, and taped them to my bathroom mirror. I saw them when I brushed my hair and washed my face. They were the first thing I looked at in the morning and the last thing I saw at night.

I spent the rest of 1986 trying to juggle my ski team obligations with my schoolwork and my social life. Ultimately, I didn't want to try anymore, and halfway through my sophomore year, I dropped out of Wood River High. Paul Major did the right thing. He hired a private tutor named Jimmy Woods to travel with the team and signed me up for the same Alaska-based correspondence school that Tommy Moe, another promising junior skier, was enrolled in. Now I could study on my own time.

Let me say right here and now that leaving high school is not something I'm proud of. I don't want kids to adopt the same attitude toward school that I had. Over the past few years I've tried hard to convince young people that you can succeed in both school and sports. Five years ago I established the Picabo Street Award at Wood River High, with which I give a one-thousand-dollar college scholarship to a senior boy and a senior girl who excel in the classroom and on the playing field. It's my way of making amends.

I spent the winter of '87 competing in the North American Ski Trophy Series, an elite race circuit in the United States and Canada. The Nor-Ams, as everyone calls them, were my chance to prove I could hold my own against the best amateur ski racers on the continent, as well as a few European skiers. I finished the season tied for eighty-fourth overall and thirty-fourth in the Super G—not bad for a fifteen-year-old competing against skiers sometimes twice her age. I came on strong in the spring, garnering five top-ten finishes in slalom and GS. I'd rejoined the Sun Valley ski team after returning from Rowmark, and I'd train with them whenever I was back in the area. I'd always gotten along with the director, Lane Monroe; he respected my talent and made sure I had a ski club to come home to.

Dad spent the winter behind the wheel of a big yellow bus. He'd broken his arm blocking a kick in karate class, and it hadn't healed correctly because he didn't have medical insurance and couldn't afford a good doctor. That bad arm made it hard to lay rock, so he went on the Sun Valley payroll. The ski resort has three separate base areas—Dollar/Elkhorn, Warm Springs, and River Run—and Dad's job was driving a shuttle bus to each one, picking up skiers in the morning and ferrying them to the mountain. At the end of the day, he'd pick them up at the base areas and drive them home. He followed a prescribed route, and varying from it could get him fired. One morning he pulled up in front of a lodge and saw a famous face waiting to board the bus.

Understand, Dad was not easily impressed by celebrity. Almost thirty years earlier, he'd met the world's most famous actress and hadn't even known who she was. The cast and crew of *The Misfits* were staying in Reno during filming, and they used to eat at Bundocks a lot. Dad was working as the desk clerk one night when a petite blond in a leopard-skin pillbox hat stopped to buy postcards. She and Dad talked about life for a few minutes, and then she left and entered the dining room, taking a seat between Clark Gable and Montgomery Clift.

"Hey, you know who that was?" the bartender said excitedly. "That was Marilyn Monroe."

To this day Dad just shrugs when he remembers her: "She was about this tall and real plain."

But he did recognize the person waiting for the bus on that winter day in 1987. He was Jean-Claude Killy, the most famous ski racer of all time, winner of three Olympic gold medals in Grenoble in 1968 and the first two World Cup overall titles, in 1967 and 1968. Now *here* was a celebrity. Killy lived in France, but he skied in Sun Valley regularly. Dad figured a man of Killy's stature shouldn't have to wait for the bus, so every day for a week Dad took a shortcut to drop Killy off at his lodging. Dad risked his job so Killy wouldn't have to wait. Still, Dad was too bashful to speak to him. Then one day, as they approached Killy's stop, Dad got up the nerve.

The Great Man was standing by the driver's seat as the bus came to a stop. Dad made his move.

"You know, my daughter is a young ski racer," he told Killy. "You're an inspiration and an idol to her. Her dream is to go to the Olympics and win a gold medal for America."

"Really?" Killy responded. "That's spectacular. What's her name?"

"Picabo Street," Dad answered.

"I'll watch out for her," Killy replied as he stepped off the bus.

Eleven years later, Killy put the gold medal around my neck in Nagano. Sometimes I'm amazed that moment ever happened.

BY THE FALL OF 1987, OUR TIGHT FAMILY UNIT HAD STARTED TO UNRAVEL. I was gone half the time, and Baba had started attending Boise State University. Dad wanted to drive the shuttle bus for a second winter, but he had to pass a physical in order to get certified. He went to the hospital for tests, but the blood work turned up some scary numbers. The average blood-sugar level is 80 to 120; his was 917.

Dad hadn't been feeling well for more than a year. He'd gained weight, his vision was blurry, and he was drinking gallons of water because he was thirsty all the time. He also had to urinate constantly, and sometimes he was incoherent, as if drunk; only he didn't drink. Now we knew why. Dad had severe adult-onset diabetes. The doctors wanted to admit him immediately, but Dad refused because he had to pick up Mom from her job. They said he wasn't going anywhere except to a hospital bed.

"Look, man," Dad argued, "I've been living with this for a year. What's fifteen more minutes to go get my wife?"

The diagnosis was incomprehensible. Dad was the tough, no-excuses guy with the constitution of an ox. The idea that he had a life-threatening illness was surreal. Mom was overcome with worry. She stood at the foot of his hospital bed, crying and asking if her husband was going to die.

For the rest of his life, Dad would have to inject himself with insulin twice a day and monitor his blood sugar and diet obsessively. My parents faced a mountain of medical bills. One bright spot was that they no longer had to pay for my ski racing expenses.

Dad's diagnosis was a huge distraction, but my parents explained that there was nothing I could do about it, so I needed to stick to my plan and concentrate on what I could control: my skiing.

I spent the winter of 1988 racing Nor-Am events and in the last week of January traveled to Italy for the World Junior Alpine Championships in Madonna di Campiglio. I got sixth in the downhill—my highest international finish to date—and in the Super G, I learned a lesson I never forgot. Halfway down the course I had a time that would have put me in the top five. But I got too far ahead of myself, missed the third to the last gate, and was disqualified. "Stay focused and in the moment," Paul told me afterward. "Don't cross the finish line until you're finished." This lesson applied to my attitude as well. I was more concerned with the end result—podiums and trophies and accolades—than the effort it took to get there.

The junior team did extremely well at the World Junior Alpine Championships, winning four medals and finishing ahead of Austria in the medal count. The big girls, on the other hand, had a dismal showing at the 1988 Winter Olympic Games in Calgary, Alberta. I was competing at the time and didn't watch it on TV, but I heard secondhand accounts over the course of those two weeks in February. The Games got off to a nightmarish start when Pam Fletcher, America's best hope for a medal in the downhill, broke her leg colliding with a course worker during a training run. Tamara McKinney skied as well as she could considering she'd broken her ankle three months earlier. The U.S. Ski Team failed to win a single medal; its highest finish was Edith Thys's ninth in the Super G. It was a shocking reversal of fortune after the team's triumphant showing in Sarajevo four years earlier. Several coaches quit or were fired, and Paul Major was tapped as the new head coach of the women's squad.

Paul was about thirty, a mild-mannered, smooth-talking, redheaded guy nicknamed Stick Man because he was so skinny. He'd been a ski racer himself before getting a degree in civil engineering. In 1982, he coached the women's ski team at the University of Colorado, Boulder, to a national title before coming to the U.S. Ski Team. Now he was The Man, and his priority was to cultivate his group of gifted junior skiers.

I won both the downhill and Super G at the 1988 J-I Olympic Championships at Mt. Bachelor, Oregon. I was now arguably the nation's top young skier in the speed events. I got third in the slalom as well, which underscored my versatility. That March Paul put me in my first World Cup event, the Aspen-Subaru Winternational.

The weeklong event was more for the experience than anything. I skied all four disciplines and finished in the top thirty in the overall. My parents called me every day, which was a little strange, since I usually called them. As it turned out, there was something they weren't telling me.

When I got home, they sat me down and gave me the bad news. While I'd been in Aspen, Dad had been hospitalized in Twin Falls for diabetes-related complications. He had called me from his bed but never told me where he was. They worried that upsetting me would affect my performance. My needs took priority, but below the surface, other concerns were beginning to swirl. Dad had spent a decade catering to my goals, and I think his brush with death got him wondering where his own life was headed.

That April, Dad had recovered enough to go to Hawaii. He and Mom were flown over there by a wealthy businessman from Long Beach, California, named Gary Cecil. He owned property in Sun Valley, and Dad had done some masonry work for him. Gary had a house in Maui as well, and had decided the house would not be complete without a stone privacy wall surrounding it. Gary wanted Dad to design and build the wall, so he flew my parents to Maui to check out the site and to see if they were interested in living there. Dad was still trying to adjust to having to manage his diabetes, but they went anyway.

This was not your garden-variety wall. It would have four sides, 250 feet on each side and 50 feet on each end. Dad estimated it would take four years to build. After he and Mom got back, we spent all summer debating whether they should take the job or not. Their first concern was whether Baba and I could get along without them. Baba was nineteen and a college sophomore; I was seventeen and on the road half the year with the ski team. You could tell Dad wanted to go. He loved Maui. Mom seemed on board with the idea, too, but now I know that deep down she had misgivings. She knew she was leaving her kids at a crucial time and wasn't sure how she would support us from four thousand miles away. But she also felt she had to stand behind her man. He needed someone to make sure he ate well and followed his insulin regimen. Besides, this was his dream, his plan, and she didn't want to be apart from him, even though the move was contrary to everything they'd ever stood for.

My theory is that Dad was building a wall between us on purpose. He had lived vicariously through me for years. This was his way of taking his life back.

By August the decision was made. My parents would move to Maui, Baba would live in Boise, and I would live in Sun Valley in a condo owned by Gary Cecil.

My reaction was two-sided. On the one hand, I couldn't believe that my parents, who had always been there for me, were bailing. On the other hand, I was secretly thrilled. I could do anything I wanted. I had to answer to no one. I didn't realize what a blow their departure was until later, when that attitude came back to bite me in the ass. It would be easy to blame what happened on their absence, but I've come to believe my rebellion was inevitable.

My parents packed up the Hailey house and left for Hawaii in September 1988. One of the last things I did before leaving was to scrape the Olympic rings off my mirror with a razor blade.

WHEN ONE-HUNDREDTH OF A SECOND CAN LOSE A RACE, I GO FOR EVERY possible advantage. The strategy begins in the start gate. The clock begins when your legs pop open the start wand. I place my poles over the start wand and press my legs against it so it bends and torques before opening. It's just me and the wand. If I can get that wand to flex an inch and a half or two inches before it pops open, I've gained a tiny margin that can make all the difference.

In a sense, that's what I was doing for the next two years: seeing how far I could push the wand, bend the rules, and still stay on the U.S. Ski

Team. Paul Major was my biggest advocate, but I didn't make it easy for him.

One big bone of contention between us was my fitness level. Physical conditioning had been an issue from the start. I loved to mountain bike and in-line skate, but those activities were as much fun as they were cardiovascular. Hitting the gym was not my idea of a good time. Every summer the U.S. Ski Team would mail me a workout to do on my own time so that I'd be in shape for the dry-land conditioning camps. I resisted the idea from the beginning. I was naturally big and strong, and I felt I could succeed purely on my natural physical talent. Yet Paul and his staff of trainers wanted me to change everything. For two years I'd gone through the motions, but let's just say that I was no star in the gym.

My parents were in Maui. Baba was in Boise. When I wasn't skiing, I was on my own in Sun Valley, still struggling to find my place in the world. I had begun to resent the responsibility that came with being a member of the U.S. Ski Team. All my friends had to do was go to school. I had to do my correspondence courses and go to the gym and watch training videos. Finally I stopped doing all those things. My workout would arrive in the mail and I'd leave it unopened. I hit the refrigerator, not the books. I'd spend the day roaming around town or hanging out in the park, wasting time until my friends got out of school. It was only a matter of time before they drifted over to the condo. "Picabo's pad" was freedom central, an adult-free hangout where we could watch TV and avoid homework. Sometimes Baba drove down from Boise with friends to check up on me, but that only added to the distractions.

My buddy Tiffany Timmons went to school in Sun Valley, so she was usually the first person to reach me. Sometimes she'd pick me up after school and we'd go to her house, or I'd ride my bike to her house and be there when she got home.

I'd constantly ask Tiffany's opinion about what I should do. "Do you think I'm crazy for wanting to be normal?" I'd ask her. "If I quit skiing, will it come back to haunt me later?"

"Peek," she'd answer, "you're happiest when you're skiing; you think about it all the time. All you want to do is go to school and be normal. You know what? You can go to school and be normal any day. Not everybody can be an Olympian. You need to go do that. That's your dream."

When I was seventeen, Paul promoted me to the C team for the 1988–89 season, and I began competing on the Europa Cup, the European counterpart to the Nor-Ams. Since the Europeans were the world's best skiers, my Europa Cup results would be crucial in my climb up the ski team ladder. I finished seventh in the downhill in Eben-in-Pongau, Austria, a terrific start.

The 1989 World Alpine Ski Championships took place in Vail, Colorado, that January. The Winter Olympics get all the attention, but the Worlds, which are held every two years, are almost more prestigious to the skiers themselves. There's no figure skating or ice hockey to steal the limelight; ski racing takes center stage. Having the Worlds in the United States was a rare event, and it was great to have the Europeans come to us for once. Almost four hundred competitors, men and women, showed up. I was selected to forerun the downhill course, a huge honor. My job as a forerunner was to ski the course before the racers to make sure it ran well, that the gates were well placed, and the timer worked. This was my first exposure to Olympic-caliber skiing, and I loved every minute: the festive opening ceremonies, the TV cameras, the media mob. Tamara McKinney, who had been flirting with retirement, bounced back from her disappointing showing in Calgary in fine style. She and Vreni Schneider, the great Swiss champion, waged a dramatic battle for the combined title. This two-part event is the ultimate test of a skier's versatility. Competitors run a special downhill and a slalom—disciplines requiring completely different skills—and whoever has the lowest combined time wins. Tamara won the combined, as well as a bronze in the slalom, giving the U.S. Ski Team a huge morale boost. Tamara was my idol and my friend, and here I'd forerun for her and then watched her kick butt. I was on cloud nine.

After the Worlds, I raced in several Nor-Am races in Colorado. My best finish was a sixth in the downhill in Steamboat Springs, but that's not the reason I remember that race. I remember it because that's when I heard about what happened to Muffy Davis.

Muffy made the development team a couple years after I did, and in the winter of 1989, when she was sixteen, she started competing on the Nor-Am circuit. She had been scheduled to race in Steamboat, but changed her mind at the last minute. She felt as if she was coming down with something, so she decided to stay in Sun Valley and save herself for some upcoming Nor-Ams.

The next day, February 4, Muffy decided to join the Sun Valley ski team for some downhill training. The weather was foggy, the visibility almost zero, the snow soft and grabby. Muffy was taking a sharp turn at about fifty miles per hour when she caught an edge and slammed into a tree, hitting her shoulder and back. She bounced off that tree and struck a second tree with her head, cracking her helmet. There was a top back surgeon in town who operated on Muffy immediately and probably saved her life. But he couldn't fix everything. Muffy's spine was severed just below the rib cage, paralyzing her from the waist down.

When I heard about Muffy's accident, I reacted with shock, then guilt. Anytime another skier is hurt you know it could have been you. Why had I avoided tragedy and she hadn't? Our lives had diverged so suddenly—I was in a position to see how far I could take my dream, but Muffy would never walk again. Her dream had been stolen.

In late February, I returned to Steamboat for a World Cup speed event. I finished twenty-fourth in the downhill. The Super G was the next day.

The top of the course was tricky: a straight shot past four gates toward a giant jump that suckered you to just haul ass and launch. The coaches advised me to take it slow, but I didn't know the meaning of the word. Besides, the other girls were tucking the top, and despite the fact that several big girls had blown out of the course, I decided to bomb it, too. I went straight at the jump like everyone else, but somewhere in midair the plan went wrong. My weight tipped back and the wind lifted my ski tips. I extended my legs, trying to touch down prematurely, and came down on the tail of my left ski. I landed so far on the back of my skis that my butt hit my bindings, and I heard something snap in my left knee. Paul was standing right there, and he watched as I spun around and tumbled off course, plowing through a few race staff, the safety fence, a crowd of bystanders, and then into a stand of trees. By the time I came to a stop, I knew my season was over.

When I called Dad that night and told him I'd ruptured my anterior cruciate ligament (ACL), he didn't get angry. He cried. It was the first time I'd ever heard him cry for me. Then Mom got on the phone and we all cried together.

The knees are a skier's Achilles' heel. Most ski racers tear at least one knee ligament during their career. Every World and Olympic champion since 1976, with one exception, has suffered an injury to the ACL, which connects the femur to the tibia. A skier can have multiple knee surgeries in the course of a career. Blowing out your ACL is practically a ski racing rite of passage.

This definitely fit my definition of an injury: I would be out of commission for at least six months. At the time, it was a huge disappointment, but looking back, it seems relatively minor in light of what would come later. And in a way, tearing my ACL at seventeen was a good thing. I got it out of the way early.

My parents couldn't afford to fly to the mainland for the surgery, so I had to go through it alone. The U.S. Ski Team sent me to their team physician, Dr. Richard Steadman. His offices at the Tahoe Fracture Orthopedic Clinic in South Lake Tahoe, California, were ground zero for state-of-the-art knee repair. Not only would I become one of his best patients over the years, we'd become good friends. I owe him my legs.

I flew to Reno, where I was met at the airport by a big man named John Atkins. Atkins had been the head conditioning coach for the women's team from 1980 to 1984, when it was the best in the world, and was now working as Steadman's head physical therapist. "Call me J.A.," he said.

Richard Steadman's nickname is Steadie and for good reason. His gentle, comforting manner was just what I needed. He let me stay at his home the night before the surgery. Using arthroscopic techniques and two small incisions, he stitched my ACL back to the base of my femur. He made three portals in my knee. Through one he inserted a telescope with a camera so he could see what he was doing. He pumped fluid through the second portal to keep the knee joint open, and the third was for his surgical instruments. The surgery lasted less than an hour, and I slept through it.

I spent two days in the hospital. My only company was another kid who'd had surgery. His mom was taking care of him, and she ended up caring for both of us. Mom racked up huge phone bills staying in touch with me. The phone was our lifeline. My parents scraped together enough money for a round-trip flight to Maui, and three days after surgery I checked out of the clinic, my knee in a brace, and flew from Reno to Maui.

Maui was paradise. My parents lived on a hill in Kihei with 360-degree views of the island, from Lahaina to Paia. The sunsets were gorgeous. I could watch the weather patterns shift and merge and see whales migrating from my bedroom window. *Why would you not want to live here?* I thought.

This was a working vacation. Coming back from ACL surgery is a long, grueling process, and the surgery itself is only the first step. It's followed by months of often rigorous physical therapy designed to strengthen the ligaments and muscles around the wounded knee. Steadman referred me to a state-of-the-art rehab facility on Maui. But it was expensive and took a big bite out of my parents' paychecks. Every day for four months they'd drive me to rehab in this big old Cadillac they'd bought and then drive to the other side of the island to work on the wall. While Dad cut and placed rock and Mom mixed mud and pushed a wheelbarrow five miles a day, I was strengthening my knee. I rode a stationary bike, jumped rope on one leg, and did push-ups and sit-ups. On my own time I swam in the ocean and walked on the beach, letting the resistance from the sand work my knee.

I allowed myself one indulgence—a summer romance with a local kid named Steven Kahae. Steven was a native Hawaiian, my surfer boy. When my knee felt stronger, he taught me to skateboard, and we spent hours at the beach, hydroplaning along the water's edge on skimboards. We had a great time together, but our relationship couldn't override my mission: to ski again.

I returned from Hawaii in July hungry to ski. My first stop was to see Steadman to make sure my ACL had healed. "The ligament looks good and tight," he said. "If J.A. passes you, you can ski." It was J.A.'s job to see how the ligament held up under stress. He tethered my waist to a thick black rubber cord that was bolted to the wall of his rehab room. The cord provided resistance as he put me through three-minute sets of deep knee bends, side lunges, and running forward and backward. I did the exercises back-to-back, with hardly any rest. I passed twenty-one out of twenty-one exercises and was pronounced fit to ski.

My parents decided I needed more domestic guidance, so back in Sun Valley I moved in with Tiffany and her family. A few weeks later, I left for a training camp in Chile. It felt great to be back on snow, and I skied aggressively, without a second thought about reinjuring my knee.

Right after I got home, Tiffany left for college in Arizona. We cried and hugged and I told her I wished she could stay. Tiffany's departure hit me hard. My friends were graduating from high school and going to college, and I felt alone and left out. I'd tried to stay in touch with my high school world. I'd gone to the junior prom with a friend of Baba's, a foreign exchange student from Brazil. Terri and Julie were there, and the three of us had scrunched together tightly for a group photo, laughing. I wanted us to stay that way forever, the three amigas, inseparable.

Several times a week, Mom would call and ask how I was, and I'd lie and say I was fine. At one time ski racing had made me feel special; now it made me feel like an oddball at a time when all I wanted to do was fit in. Paul would remind me to "think about the big picture, not the little picture," but the little picture—a normal teenage life—looked so much more appealing. I had lost sight of what I wanted. I knew the Olympics were out there, a fuzzy dot on the horizon that kept fading in and out. I wanted to reach it, but I could no longer see the steps to get there.

After returning from Chile, I had six weeks to kill before the team's first conditioning camp in Park City. You can get pretty out of shape in six weeks; my idea of physical exertion was getting off the couch to get a beer. I ran up a huge phone bill calling my ski racing buddies who lived out of state. The whole idea of going to training camp annoyed me. The team is thrown together and forced to live like high school kids on a field trip. You're given a stipend for the week. You're told, "Here's your hotel room; this is going to be our meeting time; this is our objective for the camp; this is our highlight times and events; the rest of the time we'll go about getting fit."

The workouts took place on the athletic field at Park City High School. It was my field of nightmares. I hadn't done any of the drills on my own, and my lack of preparation showed. I couldn't keep up. It was a vicious cycle: I was pissed that I hadn't done the drills and pissed that I was forced to do them now. Then I'd get pissed that I was there to prove whether I had or hadn't done them. Being pushed through the workouts only made me want to push back.

The ski team has something called the "fitness medal test." It consists of eight drills: the 40 yard dash, 440 yard dash, one mile run, vertical jump, bench jump, push-ups, sit-ups, and shuttle run. Skiers had to meet the minimum performance criteria to be considered physically fit, and failing any of them jeopardized your place on the team. It struck me as ridiculous that my fitness for skiing depended on a bunch of numbers. I was kicking everybody's ass as it was. What made their way so much better?

The team's sports science director, Steve Johnson, thought it would motivate me if I saw other ski team members' medal test results. I compared Tamara McKinney's results to those of a less-successful skier.

"Your results don't prove anything on paper," I said, throwing the physical tests down on the table. "That woman [Tamara] just beat everyone in the world and has been beating everyone in the world for the last ten years. She is one of the greatest skiers this sport has ever seen, but she can't run away from a turtle on the track. This woman here [I pointed to the other set of results] can do everything perfectly on your test, but she gets her ass kicked all day every day on the ski hill. So you're going to try to tell me that she's what I'm shooting for? No. I'm going tell you that Tamara is what I'm shooting for."

I wasn't done yet. "If I'm going to come on board and join your program, then you guys are going to explain to me what the hell it is so I buy into it."

Paul tried to convince me that I'd only reach my potential if I stopped going through the motions and committed myself to getting fit. He lived in Park City, and after the camp he drove five hours to Sun Valley for a talk. He found me at the Timmons' and made me go for a run with him. We ran for about three miles, and by the end I was breathless and red-faced.

"Picabo," Paul said, "you're in no better shape than a bowler."

I just stood there, silent except for the sound of my panting.

"Look, it's your choice," Paul went on. "You can go ski race for some college. Or you can pull yourself up by the seat of the pants and ask for help. You can be the best in the world, but there's a path you have to take to get there. And if you don't want to follow that path, you'd better reconsider your dream."

A month later, I was in Vail for one of the first races of the season when a friend called to give me some terrible news. Terri and Julie had been killed in a car accident while driving home from college for Thanksgiving. A horse trailer had jackknifed on an icy hill and slammed into their car. The three of us had posed for a picture together at the junior prom. Now they were gone.

I would lose a lot of friends over the new few years. They crashed small planes into mountainsides and fell asleep behind the wheel on the way home from concerts. They got crushed under trucks in off-road accidents, drove their Jet Skis into cliffs, jumped into frigid rivers and never emerged. They became drug addicts and blew themselves away in despair. It got to the point where Mom would call and, after hearing the tone in my voice, would ask, "Who is it now?" Skiing headlong down a mountain didn't seem so perilous. Merely living was dangerous enough. What was the point of making a decision about my future when fate seemed to be calling the shots?

I had a lackluster winter. My Nor-Am ranking improved to twenty-eighth, and I won a couple minor races. My best result was a fifth in the slalom at the World Junior Alpine Championships in Zinal, Switzerland. That's where I met my next boyfriend, a young ski racer who was half Swiss, half Chilean and came from a wealthy family. His name was Paolo Oppliger. It's amazing how expensive calling Chile and Switzerland can be, and Mom really resented having to send a check to Tiffany's mom to cover the four-hundred-dollar phone bills. Looking back, I can't say I blame her.

By now I was in full rebellion mode. I questioned and challenged everything. I built a wall around myself. I was eighteen years old, and I didn't want to be told what to do. I took my frustrations out on the team. I was either late for team meetings or skipped them altogether. Paul set a 10:30 curfew; I broke it, again and again. In trying to get through to me, Paul resorted to desperate measures: taking away my precious uniform. The first time was at a training camp in Colorado. He made me pack the whole thing up in a box and carry it out to the team van. He opened the van doors, and I put the box inside.

"You'll get it back when you deserve it," he said and shut the doors. I walked back to my hotel room, sat on my bed, and said, "Shit." For the rest of the camp I had to endure the humiliation of skiing in my grungy old ski clothes, with my teammates asking me where my uniform was.

I would get it back, only to lose it again. This went on for a year. Other coaches wanted me gone. The board of directors wanted me gone. Paul asked them to be patient, to give me a chance.

The season ended in early April 1990, and we had a month off before reporting to a one-week training camp in Park City. I didn't want to go, and I tried my best to weasel my way out of it. I showed up at Park City High School with an attitude and ran into a brick wall: John Atkins. The ski team had coaxed him into leaving Steadman's practice to head the conditioning program again. He had his hat and his whistle, and he was not in the mood to deal with me.

J.A. ran his workouts like NFL boot camps, with lots of wind sprints, push-ups, and strength drills—a real dry-land fandango. I refused to do the workouts, or I did them in a half-assed fashion. I dropped out of the wind sprints complaining of a sore shoulder. J.A. was disappointed at how far I'd regressed, especially after seeing how well I'd done with my knee rehab the previous fall. He thought I was lazy, obstinate, and not worth the trouble.

One afternoon, about three days into the camp, Paul summoned me to his hotel room. I got there to find he wasn't alone. J.A. was also there, along with Brian Williams, the head women's trainer.

It was quick and dirty.

"Look," Paul said, "I've stuck my neck out as many times as I can for you. It's out of my hands."

"We're at the end of our rope with you," J.A. said. "We're going to send you home."

"For good?" I asked, trying to keep a straight face.

"We'll have to see," J.A. answered. "You need to go home and get into shape. And you have to decide if this is what you want to do. If it is, you'll do it our way. If it isn't, then good luck; we wish you the best."

He handed me some training guidelines. I took them, turned on my heel, and left the room. I wasn't upset at being suspended. If anything, I was thrilled. No more listening to J.A. yell at me and tell me what to do. No more curfews and team meetings and wind sprints. I was free. On the way out I passed another delinquent skier who was about to go into the hotel room and receive her sentence. The next day we were high-fiving each other at the airport and yelling, "Wahoo, we're outta there!"

There was only one problem: I knew Dad would freak. So I did what I thought best—I didn't tell him. For three weeks, I hung out in Sun Valley, partied a lot, studied a little, and generally lay low.

One day the phone rang. It was Dad. *Okay, stay cool.*

"Hey, Dad, what's up?"

"What's up with you?"

"I was just out training."

"Look, I know what happened, so cut it out. Paul called me."

Shit.

"I hear you fucked up. I hope you haven't ruined it. They say you haven't."

I held my breath and waited for him to start screaming at me. I was shocked when he started apologizing instead.

"I don't know what's gone wrong, and I'm really sorry that we're away, and our absence may be part of it," he said, using the calm, measured tones of a hostage negotiator. "It's obvious you can't do this on your own, so we've borrowed the money to buy you a plane ticket. You're coming to see me right away. You've got a chance here, and we've got to get you on the right path. It might not be fun, but we need to get it right. You're either coming and doing it my way, or you're on your own."

I found out later that Dad wasn't so calm at first. He'd cried and thrown things and sworn he'd kick my ass when he got hold of me. Thank God Mom was there. She worried that if he tore into me, I'd run in the other direction. She told him she'd hate him forever if he chased me away.

Before we hung up, Dad suggested I make a list of the pros and cons about being a ski racer. So I sat down with a pad and pencil and started to write:

"Reasons to stop ski racing: Go to college. Hang out with my friends. Not to be told what to do."

"Reasons to keep ski racing: Travel the world. Meet all kinds of cool people. Support my family. Make my lifelong dream come true."

Before I was done, I crumpled up the paper and lobbed it across the room. My decision was obvious. Two days later Baba came and got me and put me on a plane. I flew for six hours over the Pacific Ocean, landing squarely in the jaws of Ron Street's boot camp.

THERE'S A STORY DAD LIKES TO TELL ABOUT MY BIRTH. THE BIG EVENT occurred in my parents' bed in Triumph. I took my time coming out, and when I finally made my appearance, I was the color of an eggplant. I didn't move or make a sound. Dad smacked my bottom and I started screaming. Then I became quiet again. They threw cold water on me and I screamed and turned pink. Then I went quiet again. Dad ascertained that a wad of mucus was lodged in my lungs. He looked for the aspirator they had on hand but couldn't find it. (It turned out Baba was using it as a pacifier.) So Dad put his mouth to mine and suctioned the mucus from my throat himself. Then he blew air into my lungs until my chest heaved and I turned rosy. He breathed life into me.

Nineteen years later, Dad breathed life into my career. Yet at the time, all I knew was how much I hated him.

From the minute I stepped off the plane in Maui, I was under Dad's thumb. I was not allowed to talk on the phone, go to the movies, or go on dates. No boys, no phone, no fun. I was nineteen and grounded in paradise.

"If you want our support, you'll have to earn it," Dad said. Every morning I'd wake at 6:00 A.M., don my running clothes, and run around the neighborhood for forty-five minutes. I did sit-ups and push-ups before every meal. Dad called it "earning my food." After breakfast I'd shower and change into my work clothes. Then the three of us would climb into that big old Caddy and drive to the other side of the island, where the wall was waiting.

That summer the project was almost half done. Locals called it the "Great Wall of Kuau." I called it a lot of things, none of them printable.

From ten o'clock until noon, I'd do whatever Dad wanted me to. It was as if we were back in the quarry ten years earlier, with me picking up rocks and putting them where Dad said to. Dad would say, "Move that pile of rock over there," and I wasn't allowed to ask why. If I did, his answer would be, "Because I said so." If I questioned him, he'd make me do fifty sit-ups and *then* move the pile of rock. I sweated an ocean that summer. At noon, I'd have lunch and study until two. The ski team required that its athletes have a GED by age nineteen, so I was under the gun on that score, too.

In the afternoon, Dad would run me through a light workout—push-ups and deep knee bends. We'd have a snack at three followed by more studying. Or I'd help him with odd jobs, such as stockpiling materials or moving still more rocks. We'd knock off around five in the afternoon, and then the fun would really begin.

Dad took the fitness program I'd need to pass to get back on the team and beefed it up. I trained six days a week, with Sundays off. I'd go to a local Gold's Gym and push metal for two hours. I'd head to the beach on my in-line skates to do agility drills and footwork, and bicycle along a narrow, two-lane highway with traffic whizzing by. I'm lucky I didn't end up as roadkill.

Oftentimes we'd head to the track at a nearby school for circuit training. We followed the program to a tee. I'd run two or three 440s—three times around the track—and Mom would average my times and write it down. I'd run a 440, an 880, and a 1,600. I'd run my butt off while Dad clicked away with the stopwatch and shouted out numbers to Mom. Every time I'd round the track and pass Dad, we'd exchange a few words:

"Fuck you."

"Fuck you, too."

I ran till I puked. I ran until I hobbled with shin splints. I ran until I dropped.

"Keep running."

"I've run as fast as I can. I can't run anymore."

"Keep running."

"I've done the suggested workout for the day. Why are you having me do more?"

"Hate me now; thank me later." That was his motto. So I did as I was told. I hated him.

At some point it stopped being about exercise and started being about control. It became a battle of wills, of who was going to push harder and be more stubborn. Dad and I rarely spoke, even in our downtime. On Friday evenings, we'd head to the beach, where Dad would whip up a dinner of grilled opakapaka—my favorite fish—mango salsa, and fruit salad. We'd hang out and watch the sunset and talk story. Creative writing was my favorite course, so I'd go off and sit by myself and write poetry, venting my emotions in free-form verse about life and the beautiful hell I found myself in.

Sometimes my frustration, anger, and exhaustion bubbled over, and I lashed back.

One time in particular stands out. It was Sunday, my day off, and we were hanging out on the beach. Dad said something that ticked me off and before long we were embroiled in an ugly, four-letter screaming match.

"Screw you! I'm out of here!" I yelled and took off down the beach. Mom followed me and found me sitting on some boulders, crying. She sat down next to me.

"I hate him!" I sobbed. "I'm so tired of him dominating me. I don't want to do this anymore."

Mom listened and let me vent, waiting for my anger to dissipate. I didn't know at the time how hard it was for her to watch Dad push me to the breaking point. All I knew was that she seemed to be a neutral partner in this torturous enterprise, mutely writing down my times as I circled the track again and again. Finally she broke her silence.

"I support what Dad's doing. I truly do," she said. "If I didn't, I wouldn't let it go on. I want you to stick with it because it's what you need, and it's going to get you where you want to go. I promise you, I'll always be right behind you, no matter what."

Then she started to cry, too. It was a pivotal moment. I knew she was on my side and that I could get through it.

After that, the routine became easier. I could see my body changing, becoming lean and dense with muscle. By the end of my prison term I was doing 150 sit-ups before every meal.

In early September, my parents drove me to the airport. Dad and I were still at a standoff. I refused to believe that his boot camp had made a difference, and I was too stubborn to say to him, "You just put me through hell for three months, but I forgive you. You were right."

As we said good-bye, I embraced Mom with all my new strength and cried. I gave Dad a quick, awkward hug; he gave me a letter. After the plane was aloft, I opened it. "Dear Peeky," he began, "I know we're not getting along well enough for me to tell you this in person. I just want you to remember that even though we may not mesh at this point in our lives, your best interests are my only concern. I'm your father and I always will be. I'm right behind you. I love you, Dad." And he included a fifty-dollar bill.

I cried when I read that letter. I cried so hard I had to stick my face in a magazine so the other passengers wouldn't see me.

I showed up at the team's fall conditioning camp in Park City, ready to prove to Paul and J.A. how hard I'd worked and how much I wanted to get back on the team. I'll never forget how nervous I was. This was it.

While Paul observed and J.A. circled, whistle at the ready, I went through the drills. I did more sit-ups than anyone else. I did push-ups on my knuckles. My vertical jump was a new personal record. I was flexible and focused. My shin splints made running painful, but J.A. could see that

I'd put in my time. And when it came time for the team activities, I fell right in and was a part of the group. Paul and J.A. were looking for an attitude adjustment, and they got it. When Paul announced they were reinstating me, I was overjoyed, and so were my teammates.

At that moment, I realized Ron Street's boot camp had been just what I needed. My body had changed, and so had my attitude. Those three months convinced me that I could stick with a strict regime, accept being told what to do, and see results. While Dad and I were building the wall, we were literally building the foundation for my future success. I don't think I ever thanked Dad in person, but I thanked him the best way I knew how: by winning.

That winter, I went out and won the Nor-Am overall championships. The next winter I went out and did it again.

And best of all, I got my GED.

I never did spend the fifty dollars Dad included in his letter. I still have it to this day as a reminder of our shared sacrifice and commitment. After I got back on the team, Dad and I reached a new understanding. We were in this as a family. If I needed to make a strategic decision, I consulted with them. If something didn't feel right, I needed to talk to them. Because we had started it together. We had put all our eggs in one basket: me.

5

THE STRAIGHT, LATE LINE

SKIING A DOWNHILL COURSE IS LIKE PLAYING A PAR FIVE ON A GOLF course. There's a perfect way to get from the start house to the finish line, just as there's a perfect way to get from the tee to the pin. Let's say you have three drives to get yourself within range of the green. You look at the course and pick your spots. You think, *That's exactly where I want to hit all three of my balls.* That's basically what skiing a downhill is like. You look at the course and figure out the fastest way to get from point A to point B. You pick your spots: where to start a turn, where to land a jump, where to finesse the terrain, and where to go full throttle. Sometimes it takes days of studying and skiing a course to find the perfect line. Other times, the line simply presents itself to you and says, "Here I am."

I love the straight, late line. Many ski racers will make a nice, big, round turn around a gate. I think big, round turns are slow. I tend to start my turns at least two feet lower and cut a straighter path past the gate. I know I'm strong enough to power myself through the turn, to skirt the fine edge of control.

Of course, the straight, late line can get you in trouble. It narrows the margin for error. As they say in skiing, "The person who falls the least wins the most."

I liked to play with fire, on the hill and off. In the Hollywood version of my story, I returned from Ron Street's boot camp in Maui contrite and humbled, ready to play by the rules. That's not exactly what happened. Despite the grueling hours of hard labor moving rocks and the brutal training schedule, I remained the same irrepressible, push-the-envelope extrovert I had always been. I accepted that skiing was my job, but that didn't mean I was going to start sucking up to the boss. I was still allergic to curfews, and at bed check you were more likely to find me dancing the night away in the hotel disco than getting my Zs. (I love to dance almost as much as I love to ski.)

I spent the 1991 and 1992 seasons shuttling between the Nor-Am circuit in the United States and the Europa Cup abroad. The Europa Cup is the level just below the World Cup, but the competition can be even more intense because the skiers are young, scrappy, and hungry. A World Cup racer might ski in a Europa Cup if he or she had time to kill or wanted to stay sharp between events. I was skiing all four disciplines, but my best results came in the speed events, and I started finishing in the top five against some of the best Russian racers. Now that I was getting results, the ski team was willing to put up with my antics. The coaches and I had reached an uneasy compromise: I'd live in their cage, as long as they left the door open.

Ski racing is funny. Athletes travel as a team yet compete as individuals. Your roommate could be the same person who kicks your ass on the hill. There's no law that says teammates have to be friends (it would be unenforceable), but open hostility can be distracting and even destructive. When I think of my teammates from those early days, I'm amazed at how different our backgrounds were. Not surprisingly, we had a tough time getting along. Tanis Hunt was a classy brunette from Scarsdale, New York, who always wore nice clothes and kept herself done up. Gibson LaFountaine and Gillian Frost were both from wealthy families and argued constantly. Julie Parisien was a very smart, extremely talented skier from Maine who got addicted to Coca-Cola one winter. I helped her kick the habit by hiding the key to the hotel minibars. I was criticized for being too aggressive, and some of the girls got jealous because I preferred to hang out with the guys, playing cards and shooting the shit. My old Triumph habits died hard.

The veteran of our group was Heidi Dahlgren. At twenty-six, she was considered old, but that didn't mean she got much respect, especially from me. Our team van was full of tension, a powder keg on wheels; one time we were traveling in the van to a race when Heidi tried to break up an argument. I turned around and snapped, "Shut up and sit down, Grandma. Your days are numbered."

Finally the fighting came to a head. We rolled into some resort and Chris Poletis, one of the assistant coaches, came around to the side door of the van, slid it open, looked in, and said, "You guys are a bunch of bitches to each other, and the coaches are tired of it. We're going to go get the training ready, and you guys are going to sit here and work out your differences. If it takes you all day, it takes you all day. But when you leave this van, things are going to be different. Good luck." And he shut the door, locked it, and walked away.

We sat there, dumbfounded. After a few minutes, a couple girls yelled at each other. Then a couple girls insulted each other. Then somebody apologized. An hour later everybody was sorry. "Look," I said, "it's bullshit to fight with one another. We need to get along. We have enemies, but they're not sitting in this van." We all tried harder to get along after that, though sometimes it was more an act than anything.

Like actors, skiers tend to date other skiers because those are the people who they spend most of their time with. My boyfriend at the time was a promising downhiller from Alaska named Mike Makar. We first met at the 1985 Junior Olympics in Alaska when I was thirteen, but we didn't start dating until the fall of 1990, after we'd both made the team. I was nineteen; he was seventeen—a younger man. Mike was my first love. He worked as a part-time guide in the Brooks Range, and I spent several summers with him and his family in Anchorage. Alaska reminded me of Sun Valley, but magnified about thirty times. Mike and I could drive thirty minutes and find ourselves in the middle of nowhere. We'd lie on our bellies and watch for caribou and bear and go fishing by the light of the midnight sun. One of my favorite pastimes was sea kayaking in a bay near Girdwood. Killer whales would come right up next to my boat, so close I could touch them. There were vast glacier fields across the bay, and at night we'd lie awake in our tent, listening to the ice crack and break and crash into the water.

Mike and I spent a lot of time apart in the winter because the men's and women's teams traveled on separate circuits, but I did my best to stay true.

I curtailed my flirting, and I called him as often as I could. Unfortunately, that street didn't run both ways, and in the winter of 1992, while at a Europa Cup in Switzerland, I heard that he'd been seeing someone else.

The news tore me apart. I spent hours crying and swearing and throwing things. Julie, who was highly rational, urged me not to do anything rash until I had all the details, but several other teammates urged me to retaliate. I remembered that a French ski racer I'd met in Maui lived only a couple hours away, so I decided to take Michele up on his standing offer to visit him if I ever found myself in the area. I bummed a ride across the border.

Later that night Paul was awakened by the phone.

"Hi Paul, it's Peek."

"Where are you?"

"France."

I explained to him where I was and that I'd missed my ride and couldn't get back to Switzerland.

"That's your problem, not mine. Just get your ass back here; there's training tomorrow."

The next morning I showed up at the hill, ready to ski. The other girls came up to me, eager for details, but all Paul said was, "I see you made it." He never asked me how I got home, and I never told him. (Michele gave me a ride.)

Life was so full of distractions. Chris Poletis used to jokingly threaten to put blinders on me, like the kind the Budweiser Clydesdales wear in the commercials, to help me focus. Paul was frustrated that I wasn't skiing to my potential. After all, there were several Europeans two and three years younger than I who were tearing up the World Cup. He knew I could be the best; the problem was convincing me.

My old friend Tamara McKinney helped do just that. Tamara had retired from the U.S. Ski Team in November 1990 and the following season came to Switzerland as a guest coach. One day we were riding the lift when she told me something I've never forgotten. "Picabo," she said, "you've got this incredible fire. And as soon as you learn how to channel it, you'll be unbeatable."

It blew my mind that someone like Tamara, who had kicked as much ass as she had across the globe, could believe in me that much. She con-

firmed what I knew about myself deep down but hadn't fully acknowl-
edged: that I had what it took to win. I grew up a little at that moment. I
became more serious, more focused on realizing my potential. My self-confidence soared. *I can beat the world; Tamara said so. And if anybody
knows, she does.*

It would take a couple years to convince the world of my potential. The
1992 Winter Olympic team was named in January, and I wasn't on it.
Wendy Fisher, a quiet redhead from northern California who I'd raced
against in the Junior Olympics, had been doing better in the combined, in
which racers ski a slalom and a downhill. Wendy got to go to Albertville,
France, instead. I knew I needed more experience, but I was bitterly disappointed. I wasn't the only one. Mom and Dad were back living in Hailey at that point, in a gray house on First Avenue North. Mom had had
enough of mixing mud and pushing a wheelbarrow, so Dad would fly back
to Maui for weeks at a time to finish the wall. When I called him from
Europe to tell him I wasn't going to Albertville, he was furious.

"Dad," I said over his rant, "I'm not ready yet."

I found out later that after we hung up he put a hole through the wall
with the telephone.

The women's speed events were held in Méribel. The downhill was probably the most challenging course ever run. It was dubbed "the women's
Hahnenkamm," after an infamous men's course in Kitzbühel, Austria. I
was skiing Europa Cups and didn't get to watch much of the Games on
TV. Dad taped the races, and after I got back from Europe we watched
them together. We saw Wendy Fisher, the skier who had gone instead of
me, catch monster air off a huge jump, crash on the icy course, and sprain
both her knees. Dad apologized for getting so mad and told me he was
relieved I hadn't gone.

The United States got two medals that year. Diann Roffe, a pixyish
brunette from upstate New York, won a silver in the GS, and Hilary Lindh
took second in the downhill. I'd known Hilary for years. She was from
Alaska and a couple years older than I. We'd raced against each other occasionally as juniors and attended Rowmark Ski Academy together. Hilary
and I had never hit it off, but I knew she had worked hard for that silver
in Albertville, and she deserved it. At the same time, her success made me
only want my own medal more.

Fortunately, I had only two years to wait until I got my next shot at the Olympics. The Winter and Summer Games had always taken place in the same year, but after 1992 the International Olympic Committee decided to separate them by two years. To adjust the schedule, the next Winter Games would be in Lillehammer, Norway, in 1994. After that, the Summer Games would be in 1996, the Winter Games in 1998, and so on.

I won my second straight Nor-Am title in 1992, and that, combined with my Europa Cup results, earned me big girl status. Every spring the U.S. Ski Team coaches get together and decide who to put on the A team. In the spring of 1992, I got the nod. I was twenty-one and had been skiing competitively for thirteen years. I was also informed that I was now a speed specialist under the tutelage of Ernst Hager, the downhill and Super G coach. Ernst had been my coach at the 1990 World Junior Alpine Championships and had been watching my progress for years. He saw my fiery temperament as an advantage, not a handicap. The dangers of downhill require a different breed, a free-spirited type. I fit the profile. My future was in the fast lane.

"Give her to me," Ernst had said to Paul. "I can make her go."

THE LIFE OF A WORLD CUP SKIER IS MORE GRIND THAN GLAMOUR. YOU ski on mountains most people see only in James Bond movies and stay in four-star resort hotels straight out of travel magazines, but the World Cup circuit isn't about sightseeing. Most of the time, it isn't even about ski racing. It's about waiting.

The American team spends up to ten weeks a winter in Europe. An average week might go like this: Land in Frankfurt or Geneva at the crack of dawn after a ten-hour plane ride from the United States. Pack into a crowded van with a half dozen teammates and drive several hours on twisting, snow-packed mountain roads to the ski resort. Unpack the van, check into the hotel, which might be a five-star palace or a cramped Alpine lodge with a communal bathroom. Unpack. Go to dinner. Go to disco. Get to bed about two o'clock in the morning. Wake up at seven the next morning and drag your jet-lagged ass to the hill by eight for training. Get off the hill by eleven, when the tourists are just finishing their second café au lait. Head back to the hotel for a lunch of greasy potatoes and some form of red meat. Find something to fill the afternoon—get a massage, read a book, watch a movie, go shopping. Repeat this routine for three or four days. On race day there's more waiting in the lodge, more waiting at the start gate, more waiting at the bottom of the course to see how you did. If a race is postponed due to bad weather, wait some more. If the race is canceled altogether, you've done all that waiting for nothing. Pack up and head to the next resort.

The competition makes the grind worthwhile. I call downhill ski racing a lot of hanging out for ninety seconds of joy. And the hardest part is that as soon as you've had your ninety seconds, all you want, more than anything, is to go back up there and do it again.

I was excited to be skiing in the big leagues, but all the downtime drove me crazy. I felt like I was wasting my life away. I liked to stay busy. In every single country I was the first one to figure out how to use the TVs and the telephones. I'd have the stereo and the TV on in my room while talking on the phone and playing cards, all at the same time. My energy could be overwhelming, especially for teammates who preferred to turn their brains off between races. Eventually I was assigned a room to myself.

The European skiers didn't know quite what to make of me at first. The Austrians and Germans, in particular, are a stern, unemotional bunch. Part of their behavior is due to the pressure. There are three main sports in Europe—cycling, soccer, and skiing—so skiers fill the winter sports–idol slot occupied by NBA players in the United States. In the United States, ski racers are lucky to get a column inch on the inside sports pages in a non-Olympic year. In Europe, ski racers are national heroes, front-page news every day. If they blow a big race, the whole country comes down on them.

Like a fast line that can't be ignored, I presented myself to the World Cup and said, "Here I am." The Americans and the Euros weren't exactly chummy, but I refused to play that game. I'd just walk up to an Austrian or a German or a Norwegian and start talking: "Hey, how are you doing? Who are you? Where are you from? You've got a cool name; what does it mean?" I'd yell "Good morning!" to a couple Austrians on another chairlift, and eventually they started yelling "Good morning!" back. I liked to make people smile.

My first close friend among the Euros was Pernilla Wiberg. Pilla looked like Grace Kelly and was a pop singer in her native Sweden. She was sweet, demure, and spoke perfect English. We had skied the Europa Cup together. At the time, I was what we called a "scrub filler," a racer who was filling out the result sheet in the back of the pack, a nobody just getting experience. Pilla, on the other hand, was cleaning everyone's clocks. I'd look at her and ask myself, *Are you going to be a filler or a winner?* One day I approached Pilla and said, "You are an incredible skier. You ski so powerfully, and it's fun to watch and to compete against you." I could tell she wasn't sure who I was. I told her my name—"I'm Picabo Street from America"— and a bell went off. We got to know each other better when we ended up on the World Cup and she started running speed events. Pilla wanted to contend for the overall title, so she had to run downhill. I saw fear in her eyes, and I wanted to help her. I gave her the lowdown on the downhill, and she gave me pointers on skiing slalom.

Ernst was my speed guru. He taught me all the little things you do in downhill that make you fast. He taught me to wring every millisecond out of the terrain, to drive my hands forward and to reach for the next gate, to reach down the hill, to reach for speed. When I did that, everything fell into place: I had my weight on the balls of my feet and was generating speed out of a turn. I learned that the essence of downhill is precision. Without it, you're reacting to the course rather than controlling it. The ultimate goal is to control the course, to be in the driver's seat the whole way down.

I respected Ernst. An Austrian who lived in Lake Tahoe, he had coached the U.S. women's team in the early '80s, when it was the best in the world, and had turned Tamara into a downhiller. He had a thatch of silver hair and three daughters, all ski racers, who earned him the nickname Poppy. Ernst never talked smack or played head games. He was direct, a man of few words. Even his laugh was short and to the point, a monosyllabic burst of sound: "Ha!" And then a pause. And then another "Ha!" Ernst was anything but effusive in his praise, so I worked hard to please him.

When I was a kid at Hemingway Elementary, I had a ritual. I'd get to class and ask the teacher if I could go to the bathroom. Then I'd take my hall pass and walk from classroom to classroom, looking in the windows to see who was there and what they were wearing. When I came back, I'd be ready for class. This was one more way to test the limits, and I learned from the teachers who let me go. I didn't learn a thing from the teachers who resisted me and made me stay in class. It became a competition: *You're going to try to teach me and I'm not going to pay attention to you because you wouldn't let me go to the bathroom. If you have the nerve to control me, then I'm going to control you by refusing to learn.* That was my mentality. I don't know where it came from; that's just the way it's always been.

I could be the same way with coaches. I was not and am not uncoachable. No one wanted to learn to ski better more than I did. It was simply a question of who gave me the hall pass and who didn't.

Ernst got me immediately. He understood that I needed my freedom. Other coaches worried about discipline and control, but all Ernst worried about was results. As long as I performed on the hill, he didn't care what I did off it.

I finished forty-third in my first downhill under Ernst, and as the 1992–93 season progressed, my results improved steadily: thirty-first, twenty-second, seventeenth. In the middle of January, we rolled into Cortina d'Ampezzo, a centuries-old village in the Italian Alps, for a two-downhill event. I finished twenty-second in the first race, but the second one ended up being postponed due to weather. We spent two weeks in Cortina, and Ernst and I made the most of them. Called "Olimpia delle Tofana," the Cortina course had every element you could ask for: steep pitches, basketball side hills, rolling terrain, technical turns, jumps, blind corners, and speed. The snow conditions changed somewhat from day to day, but for two weeks I skied the same course over and over again.

During those two weeks, Ernst taught me a crucial lesson. He showed me that I could instinctually find the fastest line on a course, that I didn't need a coach to point it out. He'd say, "Where do you want to ski the section? What line do you want to take through here?" And I'd tell him. If I was wrong, he'd correct me; if I was right, he let me go. And usually I was right. In a sense, Ernst put my career in my own hands. That lesson was a bookend to Tamara's vision, and once I grasped that, my confidence skyrocketed to a new level. *The sky's the limit,* I thought. *Nothing's going to stop me now.*

I started forty-fourth in the second race at Cortina, while Hilary Lindh, the veteran, started in the top thirty. At the end of the day she was fourth and I was eighth. Cortina instantly became my favorite course, and it remains so to this day.

From Cortina, we traveled to Haus, Austria. I finished seventeenth, and Hilary injured her knee and was out for the season. I cried when it happened. It was lousy timing, only a week before the World Championships in Morioka, Japan. Hilary and I weren't close, but she had worked so hard, and it seemed so unfair.

But that's what I was discovering about the World Cup. The grind took its toll. It was a war of attrition. We lost girls for a lot of reasons—injury, burnout, homesickness. Gibson LaFountaine left the team to find herself, and three years later I watched Wendy Fisher battle burnout and depression. She couldn't eat or sleep and felt sick all the time. Wendy had become my friend, but there was nothing I could do. She was sent home to "rest" and never came back. Wendy became an extreme skier instead.

The World Cup was like living in Triumph: unforgiving. You stepped up, or you got left behind. I may have been loud and uninhibited and more than a little rebellious, but those are the very traits that helped me survive.

By this time I had my first agent: a nice guy with a beard from Lake Tahoe, named Chris Hanna. Several agents had been sniffing around, but I signed with Chris because he knew the ins and outs of the ski industry. He had worked for a ski company before branching out into athlete representation, and I was one of his first clients.

I was still that ski racer with a memorable name but forgettable results, so most of my endorsements came from within the ski industry: Rossignol (skis), Lange (ski boots), Marker (bindings), and Swans (helmet, goggles, and poles). Chris also wrangled an endorsement deal with Ski USA, a marketing firm that lured Europeans to ski in the States. Chris told the owner, a jovial guy named Bernie Weichsel, that for a mere five thousand dollars I would display the Ski USA logo prominently on my headband during the 1992–93 World Cup season. They finally agreed on one thousand dollars. A month after my eighth-place finish in Cortina, Bernie's small investment paid off in a very big way.

The 1993 World Alpine Ski Championships were held the third week of January in Shizukuishi, a ski resort near the town of Morioka, 320 miles from Tokyo. It was my first time in Japan, and I loved it. What shocked me most was how clean the cities were, despite all the people and all the buildings. When I'd helped my mom clean those big houses in Sun Valley, I loved to vacuum myself out of a room and then stand back and admire the spotless carpet. That's how Japan was: as if some giant household god had gone over the country with a vacuum.

The rudest thing about Japan was the weather. During the Worlds the wind blew, the snow fell, and the rain followed; temperatures plummeted and soared and fell again. It was sort of apocalyptic. The six-day event stretched into twelve. The course workers toiled around the clock. Rain, snow, wind, whatever—those men were out there, shoveling and moving the snow around. They were amazing.

I went into the Worlds wanting nothing more than experience, to get the big-event jitters out of my system. I was skiing the combined, two slalom runs and a downhill. The slalom was first. The snow on the course was deep, soft, and rutted. The weather was consistent for everyone on the first run: high clouds and flurries. I was fifteenth after the first run, which meant I started first for the second run since the order is reversed. As I lunged out of the start, a blizzard blew across the course. I wasn't the most confident slalom skier simply because I didn't train it very often, so I switched into survival mode and fought my way down the run. The wind was blowing sideways and snow was sticking to my face, but a slalom run happens so quickly that two gates into it the weather no longer mattered. The fourth turn had a big hole in the snow and a tricky line, and as soon as I maneuvered it perfectly, I thought, *I'm on. I can do this.* I attacked the rest of the course, bashing my way down, battling crosswinds. I crossed the finish line with such force that I lost my balance and fell on my back. I camouflaged my embarrassment by bowing deeply to the crowd, and the Japanese spectators went wild. That run earned me my nickname "the Tiger."

I finished fifteenth in the slalom and was sitting pretty for the downhill portion of the combined, since speed was my strength. The downhill was a fun little course. It peeled off the mountain and rolled down, leveling off at a couple spots into flat sections, which were big advantages for me. The trickiest element was a big roundhouse turn around a television tower about three-quarters of the way down. My love of the straight, late line had earned me a reputation as a glider, not a turner, and I knew if I could finesse my way through that turn as cleanly as possible, I was going to be able to keep my momentum.

The night before the downhill, Ernst and I were relaxing at the hotel after dinner. I looked at him and said, "I could win a medal tomorrow if I ski really well."

This declaration made Ernst nervous. In true Teutonic fashion, he didn't like to show his emotions, no matter how excited he felt.

"Yup," he said, squirming a little. "I mean, you'd have to have a really clean, good, solid race and put everything together. Clear that roundhouse turn around the tower and take a couple of risks on the bottom and, yeah, you could. But let's not think about that. Let's just focus on skiing the race that we want to go out there and ski tomorrow."

I ran second on downhill day, and I absolutely nailed that course. I came off a rip-rocking flat and over a jump down into a bowl-like compression. I worked the bottom of that bowl, nailed the big right-footed roundhouse turn around the tower, dropped off a little ledge on my left foot, made three quick zigzag turns—right, left, right—and flew through a series of three gates and around the last corner. I took the late, straight line, cutting that corner by a razor-thin margin and gaining a ton of speed. I caught huge air off the final jump and landed just before the finish, crossing the line on the back of my skis.

Paul was standing by the side of the course with an Austrian coach, and as I whizzed by, the Austrian said, "She's going to win a medal."

"No, she's not," said Paul.

"Yes, she is," said the Austrian.

Yes, I did. I won that race and took the silver in the combined. No one could believe it—except Ernst. He'd known it was only a matter of time.

This was my first exposure to postrace hoopla, and I loved it. I was used to getting my stuff and heading back to the car in the parking lot to take off my ski boots. Now I had obligations. The press was out in full force, and after the race, I did something like two dozen interviews in a row. The first question out of everyone's mouth was, "Where did you get your name?" After I finished explaining it two dozen times, I thought, *Well, the world will know now.*

I was floating a few feet off the ground, and so was Paul. He was flabbergasted and euphoric. He gave me a huge hug. All the time and energy he had put into me, all the times he'd gone to bat on my behalf, had paid off. He felt vindicated. He walked around the finish area with a glassy look in his eyes, and it took him a while to come down to earth. No one had expected me to medal, and I didn't even have the right outfit to wear for the awards ceremony. I had to borrow Ernst's vest.

Little did I know there was a whole etiquette to standing on a podium. Anita Wachter of Austria, the bronze medalist, took me under her wing and put me through "podium school." She showed me where to stand, how long to smile for pictures, even which shoulder to lean my skis on so I didn't block the person standing next to me: second place, right shoulder; third place, left. Miriam Vogt of Germany, the winner, could put her skis on either shoulder because she was in the middle of the shot. Anita told me to make sure my sponsors' logos were showing. I adjusted my goggles around my neck so the strap showed and made sure my poles weren't covering the brand name of my skis. The Ski USA logo on my forehead appeared in photos around the world. Bernie was a happy man.

Marc Hodler, head of the International Ski Federation and a member of the International Olympic Committee (IOC), put the medal around my neck. Afterward I thrust my arms in the air and gave an Idaho tomboy whoop. I had arrived, and it felt amazing. I could hold my own with the big girls. Ernst had taught me that I could win.

After the medal ceremony, I was driven to the bottom of the hill on a snowmobile, still holding my flowers. The snowmobile's siren was wailing, and everyone was waving and clapping and looking at me. They acted as if they'd never seen freckles before. For the rest of my stay, the Japanese kept approaching me to take my picture or give me a gift. I feel lucky that my first big victory took place in a country where the people are so cordial and genuine. A few days later, as our train pulled out of the station, a crowd of children ran alongside and waved good-bye.

Morioka was another milestone: my first big payday. Each of my endorsement contracts contained a "victory schedule," which listed every one of my races and how much I'd be paid for winning a medal at each.

I'd gone to the International Broadcast Center for some interviews, and I was sitting in the bus, returning to the hotel, when it hit me: *kaching!*

I called Mom and asked her, "Hey, Mom, how much money did I make today?"

"I haven't added it up yet."

"Well, add it up. I want to know. Can I buy a truck?"

"Oh yes, honey. You'll be able to buy a truck."

I think I made around thirty-five thousand dollars that day. *Damn*, I thought. *We're rich!*

I FOLLOWED UP MY PERFORMANCE AT THE WORLDS WITH A TRIFECTA AT the U.S. National Alpine Championships in Winter Park, Colorado: a first in the Super G, second in the combined, and third in the downhill. I was on a roll—and, thanks to the prize money, about nine thousand dollars richer. "Only the wild ones win," I told the press, and they ate it up.

I took my new motto to heart. After one run failed to meet my exacting standards, I slammed my pole into the ground as hard as I could, spewed a few curse words, and sulked. Television cameras captured the whole incident. Ernst yelled at me and even my Aunt Jean, one of my mom's sisters whom I'd never met, called me up and told me I "had to get a handle" on my temper. When I finally saw the footage, I was so embarrassed by my behavior that I vowed never to throw another public tantrum.

At twenty-one, I appeared on the media's radar. A *Sports Illustrated* writer interviewed me for a story about the Worlds and wrote, "Never a star, she has nevertheless acted like one sometimes." The *Los Angeles Times* devoted an entire article to me, headlined "Before Long, Picabo Street May Be a Household Name." The writer, Chris Dufresne, called me "the greatest name in American skiing and either the best or worst thing to happen to the sport in years." My name, my upbringing, and my rocky history with the ski team made great copy. In an article entitled "Peekaboo: 1994 Olympic Hopeful Hopes to Surprise Skiing World," the *St. Louis Post-Dispatch* called me the ski team's "resident free spirit" and quoted Paul, who said, "She's a radical personality, difficult to handle, like a McEnroe."

I was getting a bad-girl image. Sometimes it was deserved; sometimes it wasn't. Those reporters never failed to mention my bio in the 1991 *U.S. Ski Team Media Guide*. I'd written that my hobbies were "mud wrestling, 'American Gladiators,' and making whoopie with my boyfriend, Mike." The media had a field day with that one, and what makes me mad to this day is that it was all a mistake. I'd written those "hobbies" as a joke at the U.S. Nationals because the announcer wanted something goofy to say over the loudspeaker. Unfortunately, my attempt at humor ended up being published in the official media guide, which only enhanced my image as having, to paraphrase one of Paul's favorite media-friendly sound bites, "no filter between my brain and my mouth."

As far as I was concerned, the staid world of ski racing could use a little shaking up. I was commenting, talking, living. My attitude toward the media was, *The more I talk about myself, the more you'll know, and isn't that the point?*

Besides, I was getting the results to back up the bluster. As one paper put it, I was now an "emerging medal hope for the 1994 Olympics in the combined and downhill." Three weeks later, on March 13, 1993, I got a chance to prove just how big a threat I was.

A WORLD CUP RACE IS USUALLY HELD ON THE OLYMPIC COURSE A YEAR before the Games to give the skiers a chance to acquaint themselves with the course. The women's Olympic course was in Hafjell, about thirty miles from the host city of Lillehammer, and there was no doubt about how the women felt about it: they hated it.

They hated it because it was easy. The run was extremely flat, with very few turns. Paul was quoted as saying the first fifty seconds were "like a cross-country track." After Albertville, the best skiers had proved they could handle tough courses, and they felt Hafjell was a step backward. To underscore their feelings, thirteen of the top fifteen women boycotted the final training run. I considered the course too mellow, too, but Ernst wanted me to get every advantage I could. I was young and eager to ski. The course was well suited to my gliding skills, and I wanted to see how much speed I could milk from it.

A lot, as it turned out—I finished second in the race, my first World Cup podium. The medal elated me, especially since it was the best finish for an American woman in a World Cup downhill in seven years. Yet deep down inside I wanted a more legitimate Olympic course. So I was pleased when the International Ski Federation (Federation Internationale de Ski, or FIS) and the Lillehammer Olympic Organizing Committee announced that they would change the venue and hold the women's downhill on the same course as the men's at Kvitfjell, a ski resort thirty miles from Lillehammer. Anyone who medalled on that course would get more respect.

After the 1993 season, I was on the map. Chris got me a five-figure deal with Key Bank of Idaho, which had been looking for a winter sports athlete to sponsor leading up to the Olympics. Now I had enough money to pay rent at my parents' house in Hailey, where I crashed between trips. I bought a mountain bike, a pair of in-line skates, and a fishing rod. My big splurge was a truck—a one-ton Ford pickup, midnight blue. I ordered it with all the bells and whistles: a stereo, chrome hubcaps, the works. Having money was a blast.

Dad was so proud of me. He finally felt as if I was going to make it. After I got kicked off the team in 1990, he'd held his breath for the next few years, waiting to see what would happen. When I won those medals, he finally let himself relax. He became more supportive, less pushy and demanding.

So this is where the big "I'm going to the Olympics!" moment ought to come, but in reality the realization of my longtime dream was relatively anticlimactic. Barring an injury, I was on my way to Lillehammer, and Mom, Dad, and Baba started making plans for their first trip to Norway. I told *People* magazine that "whoever can learn the Olympic course the fastest and put their guts to it is going to pull it off." But I knew I needed more than guts. I had heard that Kvitfjell was an extremely technical course, and I'd been training GS whenever I could to improve my turning ability. I didn't want to be known merely as the person who could take her fat ass and put it in a tuck and beat everybody else on the mountain. I wanted a reputation as a legitimate ski racer.

The best turner on the circuit was Katja Seizinger, the daughter of a German steel magnate. She was a year younger than I was, but she had been the hottest downhiller on the World Cup for three years. She was known for her beautiful, dynamic turns and phenomenal poise in the air. Our relationship was competitive yet cordial; Pilla and I would hit the disco, but Katja would stay in her room and study her business texts. She had an aloof, queen-of-the-downhill posture, but I saw right through it to the sweet person she was. She knew she wasn't fooling me. Katja and I had a healthy competitiveness that pushed us to do our best against each other.

My favorite skier was a graceful Austrian named Ulrike Maier. I had admired her for years, since my first days in Europe when I'd catch one of her races on the TV in my hotel room. She was the best ski racer I'd ever seen. I spent a lot of time watching video of her races, breaking down her technique and trying to emulate her. I cheered for her. Her demeanor, the way she carried herself, the way she skied: Uli was perfect.

I finally met Uli when I hit the World Cup in 1992–93 and was thrilled when we both won medals at the Worlds in Morioka, only hers was a gold in the Super G. She was very cordial to me. She was reserved in a typically European way, but not aloof like some. She always said hello to me every time I said hello to her, but we never became more than acquaintances.

Uli had another thing that made her special: she was the only ski racer on the women's tour with a child. Her young daughter, Melanie, and her boyfriend, Hubert Schweighofer, a former ski racer, traveled with her. Uli had been skiing the World Cup since 1985 and caused a big commotion at the 1989 Worlds in Vail when she won her first Super G world title and later announced she had been three months pregnant at the time. She took a season off to have Melanie and then returned to the World Cup in 1991 and won two more World titles.

Melanie was a fixture at every race. She'd wait at the bottom for her mother to finish her races, in her father's arms or the arms of a friend, her cheeks painted red and white, the Austrian colors.

I suppose I should be politically correct and tell you I admired Uli's ability to juggle ski racing and motherhood. Frankly, I never felt comfortable with it because I knew how dangerous Uli's career was. Like all ski racers, Uli understood the risks yet never dwelled on them. She was extremely good at what she did. At twenty-two, I chalked it up as another level of respect I had for her as an amazing woman who was doing something I couldn't fathom.

Uli wanted the 1993–94 season to be her last. She hoped to do well in Lillehammer, then retire and marry Hubert. She wanted to go out by winning the World Cup overall title. To do that, she'd have to ski the downhill, but like Pilla, she was a little afraid of the speeds, and skied it only because she had to. Uli knew the risks, but she also knew how capable she was.

The second to the last World Cup downhill before the Winter Olympics was held in Garmisch-Partenkirchen, Germany, in late January. Uli was fourth in the overall standings and needed a good showing here to move up in the rankings.

January 29, 1994, was a cloudy day, with flat light on the course. The snow was strange. Race organizers had applied a snow-hardening chemical to firm it up, but then new snow fell, a layer of soft on hard. Overall the course was not difficult; the trickiest part was the last turn, which led into a narrow chute right before the finish, flanked by high walls of snow.

I believe my start number was in the early twenties. I crossed the finish line in first place. If it held this would be my first World Cup win, so I stayed at the bottom to watch the other skiers come down. Uli ran thirty-fourth.

At the bottom of most World Cup courses, there's a giant screen that allows spectators to watch a skier's race from top to bottom. The race was also being broadcast live around Austria. As I stood at the finish, I saw Uli coming into view, straight toward the camera. She was hugging the side of the course as she entered the narrows.

Suddenly Uli caught an edge. Her ski tip jammed into the snow at the side of the course and she spun around. Her head hit a large timing pole and then struck the ground with enough force to pop her helmet off. She bounced and flew through the air backward, her hands flopping and her shoulder-length hair flying.

She was small in the distance, but her accident was magnified many times on the giant screen: her head hitting, the helmet coming loose, her hair spread out like a dark wing.

Uli came to a stop on the snow. My eyes were riveted on her still figure, but Chris Hanna, who was watching the race on TV, later told me that the next image on that giant screen was my face, drained of color. I can imagine some TV producer shouting, "Go to leader! Go to leader!" and the camera panning to my face. The camera didn't know where to go; it went to me, it went to the crowd, and then it went to commercial.

Up on the hill, people were rushing to Uli, including her coach, Herwig Demschar. Panic filled the finish area. "How bad is it," I asked Katja, "how bad?" We watched as Uli's lifeless body was placed in a large bag and loaded into a helicopter. Finally, we headed for the parking lot, where we leaned against our team vehicles in disbelief. The race started back up thirty minutes later and was won by an eighteen-year-old Italian rookie named Isolde Kostner. I ended up seventh, which was fine with me. I didn't want to be anywhere near that podium. I didn't want that cloud over me.

After we got back to our hotel, Paul called a team meeting. He told us Uli had been pronounced dead at a local hospital. Press reports said the impact had torn the main artery in her neck.

Uli was the first woman ever to die during a World Cup race. I watched a tape of her last run over and over, trying to find a clue to her death. I think her ski edges were too sharp. I watched them catch all the way down, and then catch one final time.

The tragedy's aftermath got completely out of hand. Anonymous death threats were made against the chair of the race organizing committee. Uli's fiancé accused her coach, Herwig Demschar, of pushing her past her limits. Herwig received threatening phone calls calling him a "murderer," among other things. Herwig's image among the Austrian public took another hit when he pulled his team out of the next World Cup downhill in Sierra Nevada, Spain. Ironically, Hilary Lindh, who had recovered from her knee injury, won that race. It was her first World Cup win, but it was overshadowed by the controversy and mourning that had enveloped the circuit.

The case dragged on for years. In 1996, the two FIS officials in charge of the race were brought up on charges of "negligently killing" Uli because they had allegedly placed the timing post four yards in, narrowing the run. The men settled out of court by agreeing to put money in a trust for Melanie, who now lives with her father.

In the short term, Uli's death ignited intense debate about how much speed women could handle. Some critics said the women's downhill courses had gotten too dangerous, that our skis were too fast, and our ability too low. This criticism was especially ironic since Olympic officials had relocated the women's downhill to a harder mountain, and speculation started flying that the Lillehammer Olympic Organizing Committee had made a mistake. But there was no turning back. We would show the world what we were made of. Uli would have wanted it that way.

6

LILLEHAMMER

Norway was a Scandinavian icebox. It was so cold that spectators stood on pieces of cardboard or hay bales to keep their feet from touching the frozen ground. It was so cold I had to wear a face mask on the hill. It was so cold the snow creaked. Whenever I started thinking about how cold my hands were, I'd just rub them together and tell myself, *Get over it, girl. You're at the Olympics!*

The team arrived in Oslo on February 3, 1994, a couple days before the opening ceremonies. We stayed in a hotel by the airport for a night to get our uniforms, credentials, and goody bags. I remember coming out of the hotel restaurant to find the lobby mobbed with reporters. I asked someone what the hell was going on and was told that Nancy Kerrigan was in the hotel. A month earlier, Tonya Harding's cronies had bashed Nancy in the knee at the U.S. National Figure Skating Championships in Detroit, setting off a tabloid frenzy. The IOC was still trying to decide whether it should let Tonya skate in the Olympics. Nancy had arrived early to train, and I noticed she was in the briefing room and would have to pass through the crush of reporters to get to the restaurant. I was angry that the press had invaded the hotel. And as Nancy was smuggled into the restaurant through a back door, I pushed and shoved my way through the reporters, giving them dirty looks and telling them to give the athletes a break and generally making it harder for them to get to Nancy.

Once Nancy got to the restaurant, I could see she was upset. She sat in a corner with her mom and her coach, looking at her plate and not eating. I walked over to her and bent down and said, "You don't know who I am. I'm just a skier. But I know who you are, and I just want to tell you you're here for a reason, and it's because you're great. If you can, try to blow off what's going on around you, concentrate on your skating, and enjoy the Olympics. I know that's going to be hard, but you owe it to yourself to try."

Nancy smiled at me, looked down, and said, "Thank you." She had become tabloid fodder through no fault of her own, and I think she felt guilty about deflecting attention from the other athletes. I felt sorry for her, but at the same time it didn't seem fair. Nancy had a bruised knee. Uli had died, and it already seemed she'd been forgotten—by everyone but the other ski racers.

Uli's death was still hanging over the ski racing community. Kerrin Lee-Gartner, a Canadian and the defending Olympic downhill champion, wasn't sure she was even going to compete. And the Austrians, usually heavy favorites, were emotional wrecks. As for the Americans, we were sad but determined to carry on. No one was expecting much from us. On February 7, *Sports Illustrated* ran an extremely negative article about the U.S. Ski Team. The writer, E. M. Swift, said that the team had been lousy for ten years, and blamed everything from mismanagement to a lack of development money to the idea that our skiers were a bunch of pampered rich kids. Swift claimed that "all seven million Austrians and half the cows in Switzerland ski faster than the entire U.S. Ski Team." He called us "Uncle Sam's lead-footed snowplow brigade" and predicted we'd repeat the Calgary fiasco of 1988.

It's true that we hadn't exactly been burning up the World Cup. Hilary Lindh and Diann Roffe-Steinrotter (she had married after Albertville) were the only members of the 1994 U.S. Olympic Ski Team who had ever won a World Cup race, and Diann's victory had been nine years earlier. But Swift's article fired up the team, especially Tommy Moe. His attitude was, "Screw you. I'm gonna show you." I didn't care what *Sports Illustrated* thought, but I did feed off the heightened energy that was flying around. My goal was to experience the Olympics to the fullest. I walked in the opening ceremonies, traded pins, and stayed in the Olympic Village. I was slated to race in the downhill and the combined. I tried not to expect too much of myself, though I was pretty sure I could ski faster than a Swiss cow.

If Swift's goal was to fire up the Americans, he succeeded brilliantly. On day one Tommy went out and won the first gold medal of the Games, in the downhill. Then Diann shocked everybody by winning the gold in the Super G two days later. Tommy followed that with a silver in the men's Super G. Three races, three medals for the United States, two of them gold. So much for Swift thinking. The entire team attended Tommy's and Diann's medal ceremonies, and the glow from their victories radiated through all of us. I ratcheted up my expectations. *This is my chance*, I thought. *I'm not going to let it slip away.*

The women's downhill took place on February 19. Before their events, the American skiers would transfer from the Olympic Village to a lodge atop Kvitfjell, thirty miles away. The day after she won, Diann came up to me in the village and whispered, "Stay in the little cabin behind the main house, in the upstairs bedroom." I assumed she steered me there because the room had a nice view of the start. Later I discovered the real reason: both she and Tommy had slept in the room the night before winning their races, and she was hoping some of the good luck would rub off on me.

The training runs were our first introduction to the downhill. The course turned and dipped and twisted down the mountain's face. I sensed a nervousness in the air, which I chalked up to Olympic tension. But looking back, I believe it was a sense of concern about our safety following Uli's death. We would have to maneuver a series of jumps, turns, and side hills at very high speeds, and a couple spots were particularly risky. The Russi jump was a huge jump built for the men. The race organizers had originally planned to divert the women around it, but that wasn't possible. So they sent us right off it. As soon as you landed the Russi jump, you skied onto a short flat; then the ground came back up a little and as you started the next turn you were already airborne. You landed on a zigzag side hill and then dropped straight into a tuck. I called this the "crooked" jump. The better your position off the crooked jump was, the better your chances were of landing right and diving into the straight line. The first time I skied that section, I was so intimidated I stood up on the incline to keep my hips from falling back and my ski tips from going up into the air. But overall I liked that course. It was exciting and challenging, everything an Olympic course should be.

All my GS training paid off—or maybe it was the vibes from the "gold room," as we called it. I finished in the top three in all three training runs, and in the last one, the day before the race, I finished first. I told myself all I had to do was duplicate that run and I would win a medal.

That night we held a public draw, where the skiers seeded in the top fifteen got to choose their bib numbers. The bibs were hung on a wall in Lillehammer's town square, and we walked up and picked one. I chose Number 8, because that was the number Tommy had worn when he won. In numerology eight represents infinity; just turn it on its side and it goes and goes. Let everything come full circle.

Mom, Dad, and Baba had traveled over separately and were staying in a house with a bunch of ski journalists in Lillehammer. I only saw my family twice before the downhill, and the first time was at the public draw. I hadn't expected to see them there. I spotted them in the crowd. We hugged, and I found out that Dad and Baba had lost their luggage and had to borrow clothes. Then Mom handed me a big bag full of squares of poster board.

"What's this?" I asked. Mom told me that a friend in Sun Valley had tacked them up all over town, along with a pen, so anyone could come up and write me a message, yearbook style. Then the poster boards were collected and given to Mom, who crammed them into her suitcase to deliver to me in Lillehammer. I spent two hours reading the messages in my room. They were all supportive, and they ranged from personal messages from people I'd known all my life to random jottings from tourists who happened to be in town.

"Go for the gold, girl, you can do it!"

"Give it your best because your best is all you've got!"

"You don't know us but we're from Columbus, Ohio, and we'll be cheering you on from there!"

The messages brought me back to Sun Valley in my heart. How could I go wrong with all these people behind me?

I got maybe twenty minutes of sleep the night before the race. I was nervous and anxious. I kept staring at the log ceiling and fantasizing myself coming through the finish line and being pleased with my time and giving interviews, all in front of my family. I couldn't wait to prove to myself and the world that I was good enough to wear that medal around my neck.

The next day, I had just finished the prerace inspection and was buzzing over to the lift to head back up when I heard a familiar whistle. I had my Walkman on, but there was no mistaking it: the same two notes that used to call Baba and me in for dinner in Triumph. I looked up and it was my folks. I'd skied within a foot of them, and Mom had whistled at me to get my attention. I skied over to say hi. I said I hoped they'd be able to figure out how to get to me after the race, because I wasn't going to be able to get to them. They wished me luck and we hugged and then I had to go.

I was late to the start, but it wasn't my fault. For those of you unfamiliar with European ski lifts, a T-bar is pretty much what it sounds like—a series of T-shaped metal bars hanging off a cable. The lift attendant hands you one, you stick the bar between your legs so the crossbar supports your butt, and let the cable pull you uphill while your skis slide along the snow. Keeping your balance can be tricky, and just as I was about to get a bar, the skier in front of me, a novice who probably had no idea she was sharing a lift with the world's best ski racers, fell off the T-bar. For a few minutes, she floundered around like a landed bass, trying to get up. Meanwhile, my first Olympic downhill was scheduled to start in ten minutes. The lift attendant wouldn't give me a bar because he was afraid I was going to run over her. Finally, I looked at the guy and, hoping he understood English, said, "Look, buddy, I'm going to miss my start. Give me a bar."

By the time I got to the start, my ski technician was a nervous wreck. Cookie (that's what his grandmother used to call him) was paid by my ski sponsor, Rossignol, to travel with the team and prepare the skis of the team members who skied on Rossis. He'd set up shop with the other ski technicians in a hotel's basement or garage, where he'd spend hours preparing the skis, a cigarette dangling from his mouth. He was extremely tall and as flexible as Gumby and could bend over to load skis into a bag without flexing his knees. Cookie was about forty and a confirmed bachelor, which was good, since no wife would have put up with his travel schedule.

Cookie and I had had our ups and downs. We'd met three years earlier in Switzerland, when I was a young buck with a flaky reputation skiing in one of my first World Cup downhills. I was supposed to carry my race skis to the top of the course. I had a little time before the race, so I set them down next to the T-bar and went to take an extra free-ski run on my training skis. When I got back, my race skis were gone—someone had snagged them. When I told Cookie, he got in my face and said, "That sucks. I guess you'll be racing on your trainers." I thought I was going to die, if he didn't kill me first. As far as he was concerned, I couldn't even be trusted to get a pair of skis to the top of the mountain. As I grew up and started winning, Cookie's respect for me grew, though we always said what was on our minds. We'd flare up at each other and make up later.

Cookie and I were a team. Before a race, he would write motivational messages on pieces of masking tape and stick them on my skis ("Go get 'em, Tiger"), pat me on the butt, and send me off. He gave all my skis nicknames. He called my downhill skis for Lillehammer "Olys," short for Olympics.

Ski technicians are intensely possessive of their skis. Having a pair stolen is the equivalent of having a child snatched off a street corner. At Kvitfjell, the ski techs had set up shop in a converted cow barn at the foot of the mountain. The night before the race Cookie woke and sat straight up in bed. The barn was on fire in his dreams and the skis were burning. He got out of bed, dressed, drove to the barn, put my skis in his car, drove them back to the house where he was staying, put the skis in his room, and went back to sleep. I had no idea. All I knew at the time was that when I finally got to the start in my first Olympics, Cookie was there as usual, holding my Olys. He looked like he was about to jump down my throat. I shot him a look, and he backed down.

The start area was buzzing with pent-up adrenaline. I was so jacked up I didn't even feel the cold. When I was younger, I used to hyperventilate before a race to the point where I'd almost pass out. I'd grown out of that habit, but the anxiety was still overwhelming. Here I was, twenty-two and in my first Olympics. Some racers go off and throw up in the woods before a race. I only *felt* as if I was going to puke. I had the same nauseous, out-of-control feeling I used to get when I'd stayed out all night and knew my parents were going to kill me when I got home. Skiers have different ways of overcoming the jitters. Some mess with other people's heads. Some try to pretend it's not happening. Some embrace the situation entirely. That's what I tried to do: stand up with a big chest to the pressure and just square my shoulders and say, *Fine. I own this.*

There were seven skiers out of the gate before me, including Katja Seizinger and Hilary Lindh. By the time I entered the start house, Katja was in first place and Hilary was in third. I stamped my skis, stretched my muscles, reined in my focus.

"All right, Peek, rip it, baby; come on," Cookie said behind me, and then the countdown commenced. I clicked my poles together over the start wand, took a deep breath, and said to myself, *You have nothing to lose and everything to gain—and the whole world is watching.*

I blistered through the top of the course and was seven-tenths of a second behind Katja at the split. I knew I could make up the time if I kept my skis on the snow and let them run, but I made a couple costly mistakes instead. As I ripped across the first flat in a full tuck, a gust of Arctic wind hit me and I thought to myself, *Oh, man, my hands are freezing.* I lost my focus briefly and got a little twisted on the next jump, losing valuable milliseconds. I started the next two turns too late and came into the crooked jump hauling so much ass I had to skid my skis a little to scrub some speed, and everything went sideways instead of down the hill. I opened up off a little roller on the last flat, squandering still more milliseconds. I crossed the finish line and was almost afraid to look at my time. Finally, I turned around and looked at the clock, and when I saw the time, 1:36:59, and the number two beside my name, I knew I'd pulled it off. I pumped my fists in the air and then thrust one fist forward like a boxer. Hilary was bumped to fourth, out of the medals. Then I stood and watched to see if the time would hold, and after the last girl crossed the line forty-five minutes later and I realized I'd won the silver medal, I started to cry and look for my parents.

Four events, four medals for the United States.

Someone must have fetched my parents because I turned and saw them making their way toward me through the crowd. I ran toward them. We met in an open area and embraced, cameras swarming around us. I wrapped them both in my arms, and I'll never forget that moment as long as I live. They were on the verge of crying, but Mom said, "Oh, don't cry. We're on TV." Dad said, "Congratulations, Boo. Wow, that was really great." Suddenly Baba was there, self-conscious in his borrowed clothes, and I hugged him, too.

I saw that Dad had an American flag tied around his shoulders. He had made good on his promise to Billy Baybutt and brought the Stars and Stripes to my first Olympics. He had been waving it during the race, but as he moved through the crowd he was afraid he was going to drop it. And he needed to free his hands so he could help Mom, who had been having trouble with her knees in the cold. He'd tried to find a place to put the flag, then finally draped it over his shoulders and tied it around his neck, like a cape.

Coaches can have a hard time speaking at times like these. Ernst said nothing. He just hugged me and looked at me with paternal pride, laughing his funny laugh. "Ha!" Pause. "Ha!" Paul just shook his head and said, "Jesus Christ, you did it. I can't believe you did it."

That was the greatest day of my life. Katja Seizinger won the gold, which was okay with me. If I had to lose, it might as well be to a friend. I wasn't stupid enough to think I could beat Katja—yet. Isolde Kostner, the young Italian who'd won the race in which Uli had died, got the bronze. There were a few falls, but everyone walked away in one piece.

While I was doing my doping control and interviews, my family was holding court in the finish corral. The press swarmed over them like bees to honeysuckle. I didn't read the articles until much later. Dad with his ponytail and beard, Mom in her fox fur coat, Baba in someone else's wool army pants: we weren't your typical ski racing clan. The media painted us as '60s throwbacks—the *Boston Herald* wrote that "the spirit and vitality of Woodstock Nation are alive and well at the Olympic Games." Baba showed them a scar near his eye where I'd thrown a cup at him during an argument over chores. Mom calmly explained how I'd gotten my name and called my medal "cosmic."

But Dad got most of the attention. Reporters look for colorful stories, and they hit the mother lode with Dad. The next day a photo of him wearing that flag appeared in newspapers around the United States, along with news stories about me and my colorful family. Like me, Dad didn't censor himself. He started talking story, just like those nights around the woodstove in Triumph. He admitted he was a "pot head" and talked about how he'd done LSD with Timothy Leary in San Francisco. He confessed that he'd protested the Vietnam War and said that my Olympic medal made up "for all the times I wasn't proud to be an American." Some people interpreted his wearing of the flag as a desecration, and Dad says he got death threats after they got back to Idaho.

It never occurred to Dad to be anybody other than who he was. He didn't dwell in that middle zone between candor and inhibition, where you censor and second-guess yourself. His behavior epitomized the way I grew up: keep it real. Not only that, but he wasn't going to give anyone the chance to dig up any dirt on him. He just flopped it all out there. It was also his way of protecting me, to some degree. Now reporters wouldn't ask me stupid questions like, "Your dad has a ponytail, so does he smoke weed?" because he'd told them himself that he did. But Dad was so beside himself with joy that he probably doesn't remember half the things he said.

I'd told a CBS commentator that I'd had a good run, but by the time I got to the press tent, I'd rerun it in my mind, replaying all the mistakes. When a reporter asked me what I thought of my run, I answered, "Actually, I'm really bummed because I skied like a dirt bag compared to everybody else. But I guess I had a lot of luck."

The media loved my honesty. I was called "a breath of fresh air" amidst the Tonya and Nancy mess. The fact is there were a lot of breaths of fresh air. I just happened to be the one they noticed. The media missed a lot of uplifting stories because they were too busy hanging around the ice rink in Hamar, trying to catch Tonya and Nancy glaring at each other during practice.

The medal ceremony that evening was incredibly dramatic. I was transported to the stage in a horse-drawn sleigh on a snowy road that wound through a vast crowd of spectators. The Norwegian speed skater Olas Johan Koss had won that day, so what seemed like two hundred thousand of his fellow countrymen showed up to see him receive his gold medal. I was one of seventeen athletes getting a medal that night. It was like an assembly line, and we went sport by sport. Alpine skiing was first because it started with an A. As the German national anthem played for Katja, I sang "The Star-Spangled Banner" to myself and swore I would never stand on an Olympic podium and listen to someone else's anthem again.

After the medal ceremony, Mom, Dad, Baba, Chris Hanna, and I were taken to the International Broadcast Center for another press conference.

We had to wait in a small, overheated room before entering the studio. Chris looked dazed, Baba looked downright giddy, and my parents just looked happy to be there. It was our first chance to process what had happened. We'd known this day was coming, yet at that moment we seemed stunned by its arrival. We'd just gotten the very thing we'd worked toward for years, and as my family sat there looking at one another, a question hung unspoken in the warm air: *now what do we do?*

AFTER LILLEHAMMER, I LEARNED A LOT OF LESSONS ABOUT BEING FAMOUS. I learned that I was good at it. I learned that fame opens doors. I learned that I had a story to tell and that people wanted to hear it. And I learned that like a lot of people who become well-known, I dragged the people I love into the spotlight with me, whether they liked it or not. My fame affected me in ways I never imagined, and my family in ways I never wanted.

I didn't celebrate much the night after the Olympic downhill because I had another race the next morning: the combined downhill. My run was ragged and unfocused, but I still managed to finish second. I skied poorly in the slalom the next day and finished tenth overall. (I never really stood much of a chance; after the 1993 Worlds, the scoring rules had been changed to favor competitors with strong slalom skills.) But Pilla Wiberg won the gold, which was fantastic—maybe my downhill pointers had something to do with it.

That night I hit the town with Baba. We stood in line in the deep freeze outside Lillehammer's hottest nightclub. Suddenly Baba had an idea.

"Go on; tell them who you are and maybe they'll let us in."

"Hell no, it was only a silver. They'll let us in in a minute."

Baba kept goading me, and I kept refusing. A few minutes later the doorman pointed me out.

"Hey, you!"

"Who, me?"

"Aren't you that American who won the silver in the downhill the other day? What are you doing standing in the line? Get up here!"

Baba elbowed me in the rib cage so hard I almost doubled over. "See? I told you."

I knew my life had really changed when flight attendants started being nice to me. After I left Norway, the royal treatment began to flow. Everyone knew who I was. I'd turn around and someone was congratulating me and offering to help me with my bags. On my way home to the United States, I got upgraded to first class and was fawned over all the way across the Atlantic. When I arrived in Salt Lake City, guys in red blazers were waiting to escort me to the Red Carpet Club, where I could hide out before catching the puddle jumper to Sun Valley. As I walked through the airport, people turned and stared and shouted, "It's Picabo Street!" Sometimes they'd even start applauding.

I sneaked into Sun Valley on February 21 and hibernated at home for three days. I spent those days watching the rest of the Olympics and the closing ceremonies on TV, trying to get a glimpse of my folks, who were still in Norway. The competitive ski circuit was still continuing; I had only a few days until the next World Cup, a downhill at Whistler, British Columbia, and I wanted to spend them alone. The "Late Show with David Letterman" had tried to book me right after the Games, but I didn't want to spend two of my free days flying back and forth to New York. Besides, Letterman made me feel insecure. I'd been too busy traveling the world to keep up with what was happening in it, and I was afraid I'd come across as a dumb jock. I did end up on one of his top ten lists, however. "Picabo Street" was number six on the list of "Ten Most Singable Names" between Abe Vigoda and Efrem Zimbalist Jr.

On March 2 I flew to Las Vegas for an appearance with Tommy Moe at a ski industry trade show. We were mobbed for autographs, and people called us the "future" of ski racing in America. I had been transformed from the ski team's bad girl to its great white hope. I was more than happy to fill that role. I wanted everyone to know how great skiing was, especially kids, and was willing to do my part to promote the sport that had done so much for me.

I met Steve Wynn, the casino tycoon, in Vegas. Steve was a big fan of ski racing. He arranged for Tommy and me to be on "Larry King Live" and then threw us a party at his new hotel, the Mirage. When I first met Steve, he stood very close to me and kept touching my arm and back. It made me a little uncomfortable. Later I found out he suffered from retinitis pigmentosa, a degenerative eye disease that was stealing his eyesight.

He was standing close in order to see me. But at the time, I thought he was hitting on me.

I met a lot of famous and powerful people that year, but Steve became a good friend. We really hit it off. The Mirage has its own dolphin habitat, and not long after we met, Steve called to tell me that one of his dolphins, Darla, had given birth. Could he name the pup after me? "Only if I get to swim with her," I said. And I have, and she's gorgeous. Her name is Picabo, but they call her Peek. She's a lot like me. She's wild, and she swims really fast.

I wouldn't stand on the World Cup podium for the rest of that season. I finished eleventh at Whistler and fourth the following weekend at the World Cup finals in Vail, Colorado. Katja Seizinger won that race, as well as her third consecutive World Cup downhill title. Unfortunately, Pilla's dreams of the overall title hit the skids when she flew into a safety fence and was taken to the hospital. I ran to the stretcher as she was being put in the ambulance. She'd only bruised her ribs, but going to the ER is no way to end a ski season.

I would have preferred to medal, obviously, but as I told a reporter for the *Los Angeles Times* that day, "I have to pay more dues to get up on that podium. Once I get there, I'll be there for a long time."

I flew to Sun Valley for my official welcome-home party on March 18. That arrival was a little more dramatic. As my plane taxied to a stop, fire engines shot great arcs of water over the runway. Reporters mobbed the arrivals area. My homecoming, called "Picabo's Party," was held at the Sun Valley Lodge. What seemed like the whole town showed up. Two U.S. Ski Team greats from the late '60s, Terry Palmer and Kenny Corrock, both of whom had coached me in Sun Valley, carried me to the stage on their shoulders. Idaho's U.S. congressman, Mike Crapo, was there, and Governor Cecil D. Andrus sent a representative who proclaimed March 19, 1994, "Picabo Street Day." The mayor of Sun Valley gave me the key to the city. Even the mayor of the tiny town of Picabo showed up. He said that the postmaster, who happened to be his wife, had been inundated with letters from people who just wanted their envelope stamped with the name "Picabo." Rupert House, my old Triumph neighbor who'd become a local politician of some note, got up and said I was the "only one to get some silver out of that lead in Triumph."

Suddenly everyone wanted to name things after me. The towns of Ketchum and Hailey each named a street after me—called, you guessed it, "Picabo Street." Sun Valley management named a trail on Baldy after me, just as they had for Gretchen Fraser and Christin Cooper. They called it—right again—"Picabo's Street." They gave me three trails to choose from—easy, medium, and hard—and I chose the toughest one. I didn't want my name on some pansy ski run.

It would be easy to think of my triumphant homecoming as revenge of the kid from Weirdsville, but that's not how it was. More than anything I was overwhelmed by the show of support and admiration. I made a short speech and thanked my parents and Baba, who were sitting on the stage behind me, and that's when the tears began to flow. My family belonged up there just as much as I did.

Meanwhile, appearance requests kept pouring in. "CBS This Morning." The Women's Sports Foundation's annual hall of fame banquet. Opening day at Yankee Stadium. Grand marshal in the Twin Falls' Western Days Parade. Grand marshal of the Hanes 500 NASCAR Winston Cup auto race. A Lion's Club luncheon at Sun Valley. Interviews for feature stories in national magazines such as *Outside* and *Men's Journal*. Autograph sessions for Rossignol and Key Bank in Boise. Guest ski star at the Women's Sports Festival in Denver. The list went on and on. I logged at least three hundred thousand air miles that year.

People approached me everywhere I went. I was thrilled that total strangers wanted to have a conversation with me because it meant I was someone worth talking to. They'd come up to say hello, and I'd end up telling them the story of my life. I'd go to the grocery store and get home three hours later.

I won't bullshit you, I liked being a big wheel. Who wouldn't? My personality made me well suited to fame. But I've never treated celebrity as a one-way street. If I was at a ski shop signing posters, and there were one hundred people in line, then I'd stay until one hundred people walked away with a signed poster. If someone wanted my autograph I couldn't just say "no problem" and sign my name. I'd have to *connect* with them: "Hey, what's up? Where are you from? What are you into?" My attitude was, *Look, I've given you something. Now you give me something: information, energy, an exchange.*

Dad taught me that. As a kid I'd watch him start up a conversation with a complete stranger, and in three questions he'd know where that person's passions lay. Before you knew it, they'd been talking for an hour and I'd be thinking, *How the hell did he do that?*

I can count the number of days I was home that spring on my hands and toes. My agent didn't want to turn down too many opportunities, so I traveled here, there, and everywhere. Dad felt I was overextending myself. He grumbled that I was spending too much time on the "rubber chicken tour" and that my time wasn't being managed efficiently. At one point he got so annoyed he bought a calendar and put an X through the days I was going to be home. There weren't a whole lot of Xs. I think Dad was angry because he had lost control of the family agenda to some extent. He was a big reason I'd made it this far, and he didn't want to become irrelevant.

As usual, Mom was stuck in the middle. She was wearing a lot of hats, trying to keep everything tied together. She was the liaison between Dad and my management group. She had to weed through the requests that came directly to us, deciding which to accept and how I was going to fit them into my athletic schedule. Because I had to make the ski team happy, too. Suddenly there were so many people I had to keep happy. It was a tough spot for everybody.

The family struggled with how to manage my time, my image, and especially my income. I was twenty-three and making a lot of money, but even I didn't realize how much. I liked buying little things for my family and myself. People I barely knew asked me for loans, and I had a hard time saying no. Even Baba weighed in. He'd yell at me about how much money I'd spent on Christmas presents the year before, which made me laugh, since the figure he cited was about half what I'd actually spent.

My allegiances and my energies were being pulled in a dozen different directions. It was just like the old days, when my parents would fight over me, and I felt guilty all over again. Only this time the issue wasn't how much money I was costing the family. It was how much I was bringing in.

I'm going to write this next part, not because I want to, but because I feel I have too. The last thing my parents want is the most painful episode in our family history, an incident we've worked hard to put behind us, exposed again to the light of day. What happened is nobody's business. But unfortunately it became a matter of public record, and after this book comes out, I don't want someone to say, "Picabo, if you have nothing to hide, why didn't you talk about what happened to your family in the spring and summer of 1994?"

As I said, my parents had been fighting a lot that spring. I can't say that my sudden success was the only reason, but it was a major contributing factor. The tensions came to a head in early May. Dad's temper got the best of him and he hit Mom. She fled to a friend's house, and on May 9 Dad was arrested and charged with misdemeanor battery. I was at a dry-land camp in Salt Lake City at the time. When I heard what had happened, I drove five hours straight, arriving home at three in the morning. Baba had bailed Dad out of jail and taken him to his apartment in Ketchum. I was so mad I didn't even want to see them, but Mom asked me to come and I did. Baba and Dad almost got in a fight. It was the saddest, scariest day of my life.

Dad pleaded guilty. He was sentenced a month later and ended up paying a $150 fine and performing fifty hours of community service. He and Mom also had to attend counseling sessions. The community rallied around my parents. It would have stayed a private matter if some reporter from Twin Falls hadn't come up soon after, nosing around the police station, looking for stories. And if I hadn't been Picabo Street, Olympic silver medalist, maybe he would have passed over the incident. But he didn't, and pretty soon my father's arrest was in the newspaper. The story went out on the AP news wire, and several national newspapers picked it up. *Sports Illustrated* mentioned the incident in a story about me in December 1995.

I was learning what a lot of celebrities know all too well: that the famous live two lives, one public, one private. And no matter how painful the private life, you have to wear a smile in public. The discord between my parents played out all summer, but I had to continue with my appearances. In a way, I didn't mind. They were a welcome distraction.

In late May I flew to Los Angeles to compete on "American Gladiators." I used to watch the show when I was a teenager on the U.S. Ski Team and living with my parents in Hailey. I'd get home from a trip abroad and, still on Europe time, find myself up in the middle of the night watching TV. "Gladiators" would always be on. With my athletic ability, I knew I could do well on that show. I wanted to know if those big, muscle-bound girls with names like Ice were as cool as they looked. After Lillehammer, Chris Hanna made the call, and the producers said yes. They said I'd fit right in with their upcoming "Olympians" segment.

My opponent was figure skater Debi Thomas, the 1988 Olympic bronze medalist. That detracted from my experience. They wouldn't put us in any events, such as jousting or running the gauntlet, where the margin for error was too narrow. I'd really been looking forward to doing the football basket dunk. Baba and I used to practice this as kids. You stiff-arm and spin off of your opponent and slam the football into the net before your opponent touches you. Debi didn't want to get hurt. I ended up doing stuff I wasn't crazy about, like the spider crawl, where you crawl along a ceiling while hanging upside down from a harness. I hate hanging upside down. But it ended up being a great day. I'll let you guess who won.

I piggybacked my "Gladiators" gig with an appearance at a fund-raiser for the Pediatric AIDS Foundation on June 8. It was a power picnic at a Brentwood estate in Los Angeles, and the place was wall-to-wall Hollywood actors. It was like Sun Valley at Christmas, only warmer. I have to admit I didn't share Dad's blasé attitude toward famous people. Jack Nicholson was there, having a drink and eating peanuts. He wore a Hawaiian shirt and tinted glasses that you could barely see his eyes through. Joe Pesci was there, smoking a cigar and looking like a wise guy straight out of his movies. Danny DeVito was an absolute sweetheart. Jeff Bridges was tall and handsome; Dustin Hoffman was short and wiry. In his Teva sandals and Patagonia shorts, Hoffman looked like a little kayaker from Sun Valley. He grabbed me around my waist and said "Hi!" Most of the stars were just normal people.

Most of them knew who I was, too. Kim Basinger actually trembled when she shook my hand. She was pregnant at the time and told me she and her husband, Alec Baldwin, had watched me during the Olympics and were considering naming their daughter after me.

"What do you think?" she asked me. "Do we have your permission?"

"By all means," I told her. "But I have to tell you that it's a horrible name for a little girl to grow up with. If you've got anything else in mind, you should go with that."

They took my advice. They named their daughter Ireland instead.

I met O. J. Simpson that day. I'd never watched him play football on TV, but Baba had admired him when he was younger. O.J. was cordial to me, but a little preoccupied. The event was winding down and he wanted to leave, but he couldn't find his car. Yet O.J. was attentive when he needed to be. He smiled at the camera when our photo was taken, and he shook my hand and looked into my eyes when he left. He reminded me of myself in ways: we were both top athletes, and the role model thing seemed to come naturally to him, just as it did to me. Our encounter was brief, and I didn't think anything of it at the time.

After the picnic and "Gladiators" I flew from Los Angeles to Salt Lake City. Mom picked me up at the airport. While Dad was at work, she had packed our stuff in my blue pickup and left Hailey. We stayed with her sisters in Salt Lake for a while. I couldn't believe what was happening. My parents were on the verge of divorce, O. J. Simpson was in a white Bronco being chased by the police on TV, and everything had gone crazy.

To make matters worse, things with my boyfriend, Mike, had gotten rocky, too. In July I flew up to see him in Alaska, but I couldn't spend as much time with him as I used to. Things weren't the same. Actually, it had nothing to do with my newfound fame; he was supportive and not at all envious. We were young, that's all, and like most young couples, we'd made mistakes (Michele, the French ski racer, was one of them). I got tired of not being the only girl in his life. Our relationship was like a broken vase that we had glued together and put back on the mantle, but we couldn't see past the cracks. By the fall it was over.

I wasn't happy with my private life, but I was thrilled about appearing on "Sesame Street." I wanted to reach kids, and this seemed like a direct route. Growing up without television, I didn't see the show much as a kid. But I'd catch it occasionally when I got older, and I really liked the fact that it wasn't meaningless entertainment, like some brain-dead cartoon. Kids were learning to count, and they didn't even *know* it. Personally, I had no idea Elmo was such an endearing character. When I started telling people I was going to do a skit with him, they'd freak out and say, "Oh my gosh, you're going to meet Elmo!" He seemed at least as famous as Dustin Hoffman.

I flew to New York to tape the show in the fall. Elmo was actually a six-foot-tall guy named Kevin with a really deep voice. He taped the script to his thigh and rolled around the floor on a tray with wheels, like a mechanic's dolly, moving the puppet and saying the words. The skit was cute. Elmo thought I'd gotten an Olympic medal in the game of peekaboo, so I had to explain my sport to him. Then we played peekaboo, which made him feel better.

If only making my family feel better was that easy. I tried to escape our troubles that summer. I spent a lot of time training in Salt Lake. But eventually I realized I had to help my parents solve their problems. Baba and I started calling family meetings, where we'd sit down and hash out the future. I told my parents that we hadn't come this far only to see it all fall apart.

We also figured out our roles in managing my career. I had become a small business, and my parents decided to run me the same way they'd run the rock business for fifteen years. We even adopted a name for our business: Team Street. Mom had been running the office at an engineering firm, so she understood how to communicate, set an agenda, meet a mission. Her bookkeeping skills made her a natural to manage my money. (She eventually turned my finances over to a professional in 1997. I had to learn the words, "My accountant has control.") Baba, who had joined Dad in the quarry business, would contribute opinions and advice. Dad would be my business liaison. Once in a while he'd put on a tie and come to meetings with potential sponsors. He wanted to make sure I was treated correctly. If he felt I wasn't, he'd get on the phone and set them straight. We started to call him Rude Ron. "I've got one daughter," he used to say. "She's not gonna end up in a goddamn double-wide trailer with five acres around it. She's a star, and she deserves the best."

My dad struggles with his demons. So do I. So do we all. But he has always been behind me, and that's why I couldn't give up on my parents. The family bond is like a knee: it can weaken and tear, but it can also be rehabilitated. Like an injured joint, my family healed itself. It was a slow, painful process that took almost a year. But we did it, and I consider it a great victory for all of us.

We rarely spoke publicly about that time. The closest we got was in a *USA Today* story in November 1996. The reporter, David Leon Moore, came out to Beaver Creek, Colorado, for a training camp, and the subject came up. Mom told Moore that when it came to getting her and Dad back together, "It had to be everybody. We've always done everything together, so it was only natural we'd do this together, too. We realized, in the end, that it takes all four of us.

When I needed a passport, my parents decided it was time I had a name. I was three.
© The Street family

Mom and I beside her amazing garden. That's Porfrey Peak in the distance. © The Street family

I just lost to the boys on the BMX track. Boy, did I ever hate to lose.
© The Street family

At an early ski race at age eight on Baldy. The run behind me was later renamed Picabo's Street. © Idaho Mountain Express

My biggest rival as a kid, Muffy Davis. I was usually first; she was usually second.
© Idaho Mountain Express

I skied all four disciplines as a teenager. Here I am ripping up a slalom course. © The Street family

Proudly displaying some of my medals from the 1991 North American Ski Trophy Series (Nor-Am). I won the overall title two years in a row.
© Idaho Mountain Express

Training with the ski team at Moab, Utah, in 1993. I never did like running.
© Sports File/Tim Hancock

My first big international finish: a silver at the 1993 World Alpine Ski
Championships in Morioka, Japan. I was a nobody—but not for long.
© Brian W. Robb

My time of 1:36:59 during the downhill won me a silver at the 1994 Winter Olympic Games in Lillehammer. © AP Photo/Diether Endlicher

On the podium at Lillehammer. I swore the next time I stood on the Olympic podium, I'd listen to my national anthem, not someone else's.

© Sports File/Tim Hancock

I cleaned up pretty well for a tomboy from Triumph.

© The Street family

Hilary Lindh and I made nice for the camera in December 1994, just as our historic season was beginning. © Allsport/Ian Tomlinson

Alberto Tomba greets his fans while the "female Tomba" (me) looks on. © Sports File/Tim Hancock

Ernst Hager, my speed coach, and I after I won the World Cup downhill title at Bormio, Italy, in March 1995. He was as happy as I was.
© Sports File/Tim Hancock

Celebrating after winning the World Championship downhill title in Sierra Nevada, Spain, on February 18, 1996.
© AP Photo/Michael Probst

I led the protest over a dangerous downhill course at Sestriere, Italy, January 1996. Here I'm huddling with other racers. © Brian W. Robb

My parents and I at the 1996 World Alpine Ski Championships in Sierra Nevada, Spain. We had a great time, even if I did pull a hamstring muscle. © Sports File/Heather Black

Watching the World Cup races with Dr. Richard Steadman on December 7, 1996, three days after blowing out my left knee. He operated a few days later.
© Allsport/Mike Powell

Muffy Davis, who was paralyzed at age sixteen, ended up making the U.S. Disabled Ski Team and becoming a world champion.
© Nathan Bilow

I spent all of 1997 getting my knee (and myself) in shape for the 1998 Winter Olympics. I spent hours a day at Nike's Bo Jackson Fitness Center. © Allsport/Mike Powell

On course to winning the gold in the Super G at the 1998 Winter Olympic Games in Nagano, Japan. My tiger was burning bright.
© AP Photo/Diether Endlicher

Celebrating the big win with my coaches and teammates.
© AP Photo/Rudi Blaha

On the podium in Nagano, February 11, 1998. I belted out "The Star-Spangled Banner" as loudly as I could.
© AP Photo/Paul Sakuma

Moments before my terrible crash in Crans-Montana, Switzerland, on March 13, 1998. © Brian W. Robb

World Cup officials and medics came to my aid. I was in a lot of pain and felt real fear for the first time in my life.
© Brian W. Robb

My left femur was crushed and the cartilage in my right knee was badly damaged.
© Brian W. Robb

My Bride of Frankenstein scar. © Nathan Bilow

My first World Cup race in almost three years: a Super G in Val d'Isère, France, on December 7, 2000. I finished thirty-fourth.
© AP Photo/Alessandro Trovati

On the podium after beating the world's best on the Olympic course at Snowbasin, Utah, March 15, 2001. The 2002 Winter Olympic Games in Salt Lake City are less than a year away.
© Nathan Bilow

In June 2001 I broke the sound barrier in an F-16 fighter plane. Can't go much faster than that. © AP Photo/Douglas C. Pizac

"Picabo was torn," she went on. "She couldn't see losing one or the other. She still can't. That won't work for her. I really think she'd rather break her leg than see something happen to one of us."

SPORTS HISTORY IS LITTERED WITH ATHLETES WHO FOLDED UNDER PUBlic scrutiny, who let fame blunt their competitive edge. After Lillehammer, some people wondered if I would become a flash in the pan, ski racing's equivalent of a one-hit wonder. There was a lot of pressure on me going into the 1994–95 season. And the ironic thing is, most people had no idea what I was really dealing with behind the scenes. In a way, that makes what happened next all the more amazing.

7

UNBEATABLE

HISTORIC SEASONS OFTEN HAPPEN BY ACCIDENT. I STARTED THE 1994–95 World Cup season with a nerve-racking crash in Colorado and ended it with an unexpected win in Italy that left the international ski racing community shaking its head in wonder. No one could have predicted what I would achieve that winter, myself included, especially after the difficult, whirlwind summer I'd had. But I couldn't have done it alone.

The winter after the Olympics, my goal was simply to win my first World Cup race and to snag as many top five finishes as I could. To Americans, the Olympics are the only ski race that matters. To many Europeans, it's just another competition. I had risen to the occasion at Lillehammer, but could I excel in the day-in, day-out grind of the World Cup? Consistency: that was the true sign of a champion. That was what earned you respect on the circuit.

After the Olympics, Paul Major was promoted from head women's coach to the U.S. Ski Team's Alpine Director. Basically, he was in charge of the whole shebang. That spring he announced his replacement as women's head coach: Herwig Demschar, the former head coach of the Austrian team who had gotten so much criticism after Uli Maier's death. He had left the team and was vacationing on the beach in Australia, his wife's native country, when his cell phone rang. It was Paul, offering him a job.

When Herwig arrived, the slalom and GS squads were in shambles, riddled by retirements and injuries. But on the speed side, Herwig had inherited two of the best downhillers in the world, Hilary Lindh and myself. Unfortunately, we were barely on speaking terms.

Hilary and I had both won silver medals in Olympic downhills, but that's about all we had in common. Our personalities were polar opposites. I was chatty and extroverted; she was studious and self-contained. I thrived on chaos and action; she preferred order and discipline. I used my position to spread the gospel of skiing to as many people as possible, but Hilary shied away from the spotlight. The media dubbed us "fire and ice." From the moment we met at Rowmark Ski Academy in 1985, we'd never hit it off, though I can't point to any particular incident that was the root of our mutual dislike. Once we were on the U.S. Ski Team together, I believe she saw me as a threat. She was twenty-five to my twenty-three, the older, wiser skier who was on track to be the United States' best downhiller ever, and I was the loud-mouthed kid who swooped in and took the title from her without ever really wanting it.

Hilary and my relationship had taken a nosedive in September 1993. The team was at its customary summer training camp in South America, this time in Portillo, Chile. Hilary was coming off the knee injury she'd suffered in January, and I was coming off my first big year, having won the silver at the Worlds and three medals at the Nationals. One afternoon at our hotel, the team's sports psychologist, Sean McCann, was leading us through team-building exercises. We sat in a circle, and each team member had to describe how she honestly felt about everybody else. I went first. I told Hilary that I had cried when she blew her knee out in Haus, Austria, earlier that year. I knew how hard she'd worked, and it was so unfair.

I expected Hilary to appreciate my show of empathy, but her response shocked me. She laughed. She let out a big, you're-full-of-shit "Ha!" I was stunned. I felt I was being genuine and open, yet was getting mocked in return. It really fried me. From that moment on, I wouldn't speak to her, ride the lift with her, or even sit at the same dinner table with her.

Looking back, my reaction might have been extreme and, I'll admit, a little immature. But that's how I was: all or nothing. I felt Hilary had disrespected me. And the ironic part is she didn't even know it at the time. She simply interpreted my anger as a mysterious escalation of our longtime cold war.

As the 1993–94 season got under way, we were still not speaking. Our feud was characterized by icy silences and drop-dead stares, but we kept it civil. After I bumped her out of the medals in Lillehammer, I told her I was sorry. She said something like, "Don't worry about it. It's all good. It's racing," and walked away. Our brief conversation was caught on camera, and it typified out relationship: curt, cool, distant.

Herwig had to manage two racehorses on the same team, and he knew he had to nip the tension between Hilary and me in the bud before it escalated into all-out war. Personally, I was thrilled to have Herwig as my new coach. Under his guidance, the Austrian women had become an Alpine juggernaut. In 1993, Anita Wachter had won the overall title and the team had taken the Nation's Cup, which goes to the country with the most World Cup points, by a landslide. When a reporter asked me what I thought of Herwig, I said, with typical bluntness, "He's a square head." Yet I soon discovered that Herwig wasn't your typical tight-lipped, inflexible Austrian. He expressed his emotions easily, and his approach impressed me right off the bat. The first thing he did was meet individually with every athlete, from the A team on down.

I spent April 1994 making appearances in New York City and blew into Oregon for a ten-day training camp in May. That's where Herwig and I had our first heart-to-heart about my relationship with Hilary.

"You guys have two options," he said to me. "You can keep fighting each other and spend so much energy that you're going to be too slow for ski racing. Or you can learn to live with each other. You guys don't have to get married. But you can draw on each other on a professional level. Don't forget: we're here to ski race, and nothing else."

What I really wanted to talk about was Uli. What did they discuss before that final, fatal race? I needed to know all the details. Herwig answered my questions honestly and directly. He said that Uli knew she had to run downhills to win the overall; the field was simply too good to think she could pull it off by winning technical events alone. "You have a young daughter," he'd said. "Are you willing to take the risk?" He and Uli had made a pact: if she ever had any doubts she could pull out at any time, and he would understand. All she had to do was give him the sign. That she hadn't was the one thing that gave him peace of mind. He had handed the responsibility for her own fate to her, and I told Herwig that I would want him to do the same for me.

Herwig had the same goal as every coach who'd come before him—to whip me into top physical condition. And he made no secret of his intentions. "Picabo can learn to work more," he told the *Denver Post* in September 1994. "She is learning that great skiing is not just talent, but plain hard work as well."

It took Marjan Cernigoj to bring out my best. Marjan was a top Slovenian skier before coming to the U.S. Ski Team in the early '90s as a coach and trainer. Marjan worked hard to get me to like working out. He took the sports I loved most—volleyball, obstacle courses, gymnastics—and incorporated them into my training regimen. He went out of his way to help me, creating one-on-one minicamps in Park City. I'll never forget our first session. I was dragging my heels through the workout, grumbling and beset by phantom aches and pains, when Marjan suddenly stopped, turned around, and threw my bad attitude back in my face.

"This is for *you*, you know," he said angrily. "I don't give a shit if you do this. But I'm telling you that if you do, you are going to make it. I don't understand why you're having such a hard time getting that. This is all you have to do to be fast. You'll be hard to beat."

Something about Marjan's passion struck a chord in me. Contrary to what he'd said, I knew he did give a shit, so the least I could do was give a shit back. *He's right*, I thought. *I've got to do this.*

My appearance schedule eased up in September, after the "Sesame Street" taping, and I dedicated the rest of the fall to preparing for the upcoming season. Some switch had been flipped in my brain. I knew what I had to do. I started lifting weights with a strength coach in Salt Lake City and put on about ten pounds of muscle mass. During the team's preseason on-snow camp in November, I skied with aggression and power. By the time the World Cup opener rolled around in early December, I was charging.

The World Cup traditionally kicks off in North America. That year the first downhill and Super G were held in Vail, Colorado. After Vail, we headed north of the border, to Lake Louise, Alberta, and then flew to Europe for the rest of the season.

That season's speed team was a small group. Besides Hilary and me, it included Megan Gerety and Krista Schmidinger. We'd all known each other for years. Megan and I were the same age. She was a shy blond from

Anchorage, Alaska, and she and Tommy Moe had been dating since they were teenagers. I'd competed against Megan at the Junior Olympics in the mid '80s, and she had evolved into the team's most consistent Super G skier. Krista was twenty-four, a year older than I was. She and her twin sister, Kim, a technical specialist, were from the East, but they'd attended the same 1984 training camp at Mount Hood as I had. Both girls had made it to the U.S. Ski Team, and Krista had finished eleventh in the combined and twelfth in the downhill at the 1992 Winter Olympics. Like many identical twins, the Schmidinger sisters were extremely close, and after knee problems grounded Kim's career in 1993, Krista struggled to continue without her sister. Krista felt lonely, frustrated, and, I think, a little envious of my star status on the team.

We'd talked about it that fall, at a training camp in Europe. The whole show had started to revolve around me, and it made me feel uncomfortable. I told Krista I didn't want to feel special, that what I wanted was for everyone else to win, too. "I want you to step up," I said. "I know that you can."

Team chemistry is a matter of luck more than anything. You can work hard to get along and overcome differences, but sometimes it just doesn't happen. That was the case with our team that season. Take three relatively low-key people, add one high-voltage personality, and stir, and the results can be explosive.

December 3, 1994

Vail, Colorado

The first World Cup of the season is like the first week of school. Everyone comes into the new year with new uniforms, new haircuts, new hair colors, new personas. Bodies change; boyfriends change. It's a time to renew old friendships and gauge old rivalries. It's also the time when you establish what kind of competitor, what kind of person, you'll be for the next four months.

There was a lot of expectation and speculation surrounding Hilary and me. Could we limit our rivalry to the hill? Would it affect our performances? At Herwig's prodding, we were trying to present a united front, but the media insisted on perpetuating the rivalry. In the days before that first World Cup, the *Denver Post* portrayed me as the spotlight-hogging extrovert and Hilary as the camera-shy introvert who resented the fact that my Olympic silver medal paid off more than hers.

There's no denying I was the star. I must have spent hours signing autographs and talking to people. I found out later that riding the chairlift during a training run, Hilary saw a banner that read "World Cup Race, Featuring Picabo Street." I'm sure that got her going.

An American World Cup is a nice way to start, if for no other reason than it forces the Europeans to cope with jet lag and strange food for once. It also makes it easier for your loved ones to watch you race against the best in the world. Mom and Dad came to Vail, but I wish I could have put on a better show for them, especially after all we'd been through. I've never skied particularly well at Vail, and the 1994–95 World Cup opener was no exception.

American mountains tend to be rounder and flatter than the knife-edge Alps, so U.S. courses have a reputation for being easy. But Vail's International is challenging and long. The most difficult parts come at the bottom, when you're tired: a series of three knolls nicknamed Huey, Dewey, and Louie, followed by a huge headwall called Pepi's Face that plummets practically into the finish line. The turn off the top of Pepi's is very tight and precise. One false move and you're out for the season.

On race day I pushed out of the gate to a huge roar from the crowd. My run was going well until I approached a side hill that fell at a brutal pitch under a chairlift. The snow looked nice and smooth, and I decided to run my usual straight, late line. I rolled hard into my next turn but failed to set myself up well for the next jump. My left knee dropped and I was off balance at the launch. The mountain flung me into the air; I landed badly and couldn't recover. I caught the inside edge of my left ski and started spinning like a top. Then I caught the outside edge of the same ski and smashed hard into the ground, taking out a gate as I tumbled downhill at fifty miles per hour.

I knew Mom had probably seen my fall on the big screen at the finish, and I struggled hard to arrest my slide. *Shit! Mom's gonna think I'm hurt. I gotta get up.* I clawed at the mountain to stop myself, the snow flying. Ernst ran toward me as I slid to a stop. I looked around for the camera, found it, and mouthed the words, "I'm okay, Mom!" hoping she would see them.

We have a saying in ski racing: "You've got to get your one crash out of the way." You're bound to have at least one bad fall a season, and it's good to get it over with, walk away from it, and move on. That fall got everyone's attention—the first race of the season and the big gun goes down—but I walked away with nothing more than a torn ligament between the last two fingers of my left hand. I got it taped up and went back out and watched the race with Ernst. My pride was hurt more than anything—especially since Hilary won that first downhill. But, I'd gotten that first fall out of my system.

All the attention I'd received in Vail had disrupted the team's schedule. It was hard for me to walk away from fans and leave them disappointed, so on the flight from Colorado to Canada, I devised a strategy with one of the coaches, Andreas Rickenbach. Everyone called him "Gnarly," a nickname he'd earned as a young racer when he wore a straggly beard and a perpetual scowl. In fact, Gnarly was a total teddy bear. He had been a speed specialist on the men's team before moving over to coach, so I already knew and respected him. His strong yet tranquil personality had a mellowing effect on me, and I attached myself to him immediately. We agreed that if I was mobbed and needed to leave, he would come rescue me by saying, "I'm really sorry. I've got to take her away; she has a meeting." I felt that sharing our plan with my teammates would seem like bragging, so we kept it to ourselves.

December 11, 1994

Lake Louise, Alberta

By the time we rolled into Lake Louise, I was fired up. There were two downhills and a Super G on the schedule. The night before the downhill, the top-seeded racers gathered in the lobby of the Chateau Lake Louise for the public draw, where we picked our start numbers.

I knew I'd have a hard time getting out of there afterward, so I reminded Gnarly of our plan. Sure enough, I found myself surrounded by autograph seekers and well-wishers. I kept looking around for Gnarly, but he never showed. He'd forgotten to come get me, and by the time I got to the team meeting, I was ten minutes late and Krista Schmidinger was fuming.

"Perfect," she said sarcastically. "The queen has arrived. The meeting can start."

I looked at her in total disbelief. "What?"

"You heard me."

We exchanged a few choice expletives, and finally Herwig came between us like a referee prying two boxers apart. But the damage was done. As far as I was concerned, Krista was just taking up space.

Lake Louise wasn't Norway-caliber cold, but it was close. Our staff wrapped us in blankets, and our breath hung over the start area like exhaust. Since frostbite could attack any patch of exposed skin, we tore off pieces of duct tape to put on our faces for the subzero trip down the mountain. My taped-together fingers felt cold and immobile, so immediately before entering the start house I ripped off the tape, jammed my hand back into my thick glove, and went for it.

The course at Lake Louise was full of energy and life. It had a lot of elements, and it made you step up and play your whole hand. Flats with turns. A turn into a jump. A big, blind turn onto a steep pitch into a big, fast C-turn that generated such powerful G forces it felt as if you were being pulled toward the center of the earth. My run was fast, furious, freezing, and fun. Hilary was in first place when I left the gate, but I crossed the finish line almost three-quarters of a second faster. She took the runner-up spot.

Here it was only the second event of the season, and I'd realized my dream of winning my first World Cup race. Herwig felt proud and relieved. After what had happened to Uli, it had been hard for him to come back and coach a women's team, particularly downhillers, who risk more than anyone else to win. Our one-two showing in Lake Louise confirmed he'd made the right choice.

I stood proudly on the top step of the podium with that medal around my neck and thrust my fists into the air, ecstatic. I liked the feeling of being a winner. I wanted more.

Hilary and I were capable of brief verbal exchanges, and after winning I said to her, "It's your turn." The next day she went out and won the second downhill. I finished ninth.

"Wait a minute," I said afterward. "I was only kidding."

I ended up getting third in the Super G behind Katja Seizinger, which meant I had a better weekend than Hil did. That made me feel a little better.

"This'll work," I joked to Hil. "We'll just trade off wins all year long."

"Sounds good to me."

Hil and I had won the first three World Cup downhills of the season, and we were sitting one-two, respectively, in the standings. It was the best performance ever by American downhillers, men or women, and even *Sports Illustrated* was paying attention. Like most of the reporters we spoke to, the *Sports Illustrated* reporter wanted to talk about the rivalry. Hilary was quoted as saying, "I've always disliked people who are over-bearing, people who have to make an impression by being loud. Classy. That's how I want to be defined. A class act." This came across as a not-so-veiled reference to yours truly, though I'm not convinced she meant it that way.

"We haven't worked all the little thorns out," I told *Sports Illustrated*. "We still have the sandpaper out, smoothing away stuff."

THAT DECEMBER THE NORMALLY SNOW-CLAD ALPS WERE BROWN, WITH A pathetic ribbon or two of manmade snow passing for a racecourse. The World Cup schedule was in upheaval. Races were postponed or scrapped altogether, and our season soon devolved into a fatiguing game of geographic connect-the-dots that tested what little team spirit we already possessed.

We stayed in the United States longer than expected. The A team skied a Nor-Am in Montana to stay sharp (our presence was a little bit like the Yankees showing up at a Little League tournament) before heading to Europe. On our way to the airport, a cop pulled us over—and I wasn't even driving. It turned out Herwig, who had flown to Europe ahead of us, had called the local police to track us down and tell us not to come because our race had been canceled. So we went home for a long Christmas break instead.

Ten days in Hailey and Sun Valley were just what I needed. My first World Cup win and the team politics and the hoopla had me all amped up, and being home with my family helped me regain the equilibrium that would set me up for the rest of the season. Mom and Dad had surprised me with the news that they were getting me a dog. An Oregon-based breeder of Australian cattle dogs had sent them a video of a recent litter, and I picked out the puppy I wanted, a male with a black mask across his eyes.

Christmas was anything but white in Europe, so our departure was delayed yet again. Ernst wanted us to get our ski legs back after the long break, so the entire A team, including Tommy Moe, headed to a Nor-Am in Sugarloaf, Maine, one of the few eastern mountains tall enough to accommodate a regulation speed event. Hil and I picked up where we left off, trading Super G wins. Afterward, we headed to New York and caught a flight for Munich.

I went abroad with a mission: to win my first World Cup in Europe. I wanted to show the Euros that Americans could win on their home turf. I was also looking ahead to the end of January, to the 1995 World Alpine Ski Championships in Sierra Nevada, Spain. This was my year. I could feel it.

January 13, 1995

Garmisch-Partenkirchen, Germany

Our first stop in Europe was a Super G on the same course that had claimed Uli's life a year earlier.

It was tough for Herwig to be there, tough for us all. Uli was on my mind the whole time. The training runs were emotionally taxing. I would ski through the narrows, past the same spot where her ski tip had hit the snow wall, and feel my stomach flip over. I felt uneasy and out of place, as if I shouldn't be there.

Ironically, I ended up leading the race again, just as I had the day Uli died, and once again it slipped away. If your time is still standing after twenty skiers cross the finish line, chances are you'll win because the back of the pack tends to be slower. So after the twenty-fifth skier came down, I was sure I'd bagged my first World Cup gold in Europe. The celebration was premature. Florence Masnada of France, the twenty-ninth skier out of the gate, sneaked across the finish line four-hundredths of a second faster than me.

I was disappointed and angry until Florence came up to me, gave me a hug, and said, "That was for Uli." Then I knew it was all good. Later, at the awards ceremony, I asked for a moment of silence in her memory.

I wanted the other racers to see what kind of person I planned to be that season: a fierce competitor on the hill, a compassionate person off of it.

January 21, 1995

Cortina d'Ampezzo, Italy

Ah, Olimpia delle Tofana. It was my favorite course, the place where I'd finished eighth as a World Cup rookie two years earlier. *I'm on the top step in Cortina*, I thought. It didn't go quite as planned.

Two downhills were scheduled, and I thought I had the first one. I finished first ahead of Katja with a time of 1:24:75, and was already celebrating when Michaela Gerg-Leitner of Germany skied out of thirtieth place and beat me by two-hundredths of a second. I'd lost another World Cup at the last possible second, and it enraged me. The stage was set for a blowup.

A storm blew in that night, heavy with fog and snow, and we spent the next day cooling our heels in the lodge until the second downhill was postponed for a day. By the time we piled into the team van to head back to the hotel, I was so pissed off I couldn't see straight. Krista tried to sit next to me in the van, but I wouldn't let her. I was still mad at her because it was easier than feeling sorry for her. I exploded and threw a full-out tantrum. I don't particularly want to repeat what I said, but it was bad enough for Ernst to demand I apologize to the team. If Mom had been there, she would have washed my mouth out with soap and sent me to bed hungry.

Afterward, Herwig sat us down for a talk about team dynamics. "Look," he said. "You have a lot of potential as a team. Don't let it go down the drain just because you're hung up on individual personalities." He told us that if anything, we were playing right into the Europeans' hands. They expected us to be cranky, tired, and teed off at one another. The way to get their goats was to act as if we were getting along.

It was a tall order. Our team dynamic was pretty dysfunctional. If Hilary's skis were on top of mine in the van, I didn't take them off and give them to her to get to mine; I waited until she took them off. We didn't go out of our way for each other.

I went out the next morning and demolished the field. I now had two World Cup golds in my back pocket. I was now only thirty-one points behind Hilary in the World Cup downhill standings. The roar and the hype had begun.

Both Hilary and I were expecting to do well at the upcoming Worlds in Sierra Nevada, Spain. She'd won her first World Cup on that course a year earlier, and I was on a hot streak.

Sierra Nevada is Europe's southernmost ski area—you can actually see Africa from the top of the mountain—and it had been gripped by a terrible drought. Even the lake that provided the water for snowmaking was dried up. The training runs were called off due to a lack of snow, so we got a few days of R&R at Marbella, on the Costa del Sol. I was kicking back in a foam beach chair when the word came down that for the first time ever, the World Alpine Ski Championships had been canceled. There simply wasn't enough snow to ski on. FIS officials had rescheduled them for January 1996, a year from now.

Suddenly I had two weeks on my hands. I worked on my tan for a few more days and then headed to Hailey. I wanted to see my new puppy, jet lag be damned. A reporter for the *Los Angeles Times* came out for an interview. When he asked about my feelings toward Hilary, I answered, "Hilary is kind of an introverted and coldhearted person, and everything that she does is for herself, which is fine with me."

I wasn't trying to be mean, just honest. I was genetically incapable of anything less.

The tension came to a head in mid-February. I met the team in France for a Europa Cup at Pra-Loup in southern France. But the race was canceled, so Ernst decided to keep us there to train. Hilary and I were interviewed by David Leon Moore for a feature story in *USA Today*. Moore called me first. When he asked me about the roots of my animosity toward Hilary, I told him about Chile in the fall of 1993, when Hilary had laughed at me. When he asked Hilary the same question, she said she didn't know why I disliked her. He told her, "Well, it's a very distinct moment for Picabo," and he told Hil what I'd said about Chile.

Later that night, I was relaxing in my room when a knock came on the door. It was Hilary. She stood in the doorway and said, "We need to talk."

"Cool," I said. "When?"

"How about now?"

"Sure." I threw on my coat and we went outside, neutral territory. The weather was dreary, with slight flurries gusting through. We faced each other in the fading light, hands jammed in our pockets. Hilary spoke first.

"I'd like to start by saying that I didn't realize that what happened in Chile was the reason you became so uncomfortable in our relationship." She went on to explain that my comment about crying for her had thrown her so off guard she hadn't known how to react. Her laughter was out of embarrassment, not cruelty. "I'm sorry I hurt your feelings."

I stepped back and just looked at her. She went on.

"I know you're going to find this hard to believe, because I know how you feel about me. But that's the truth. That's what happened, and I think you should know. Maybe now we'll have a chance to be on honest ground. If we can use each other to become better ski racers, then we owe it to each other."

That conversation was a turning point. We hugged and cried and talked for an hour and found a common ground. I admitted that I respected her work ethic and drive; and she said she respected my fierce will to win. We resolved to work together, to feed off each other's competitive energy.

In downhill, familiarity breeds success; the better you know a course, the better your chances of winning. The next four downhills took place on courses I'd never skied before. But nothing, it seemed, could stop me that season. Hil had a lot to do with my success. After our détente session in France, we became collaborators. Off the mountain we went our separate ways, but on the mountain we pushed each other to ski the line no one else could find, to take a risk no one else would take. We pushed the envelope, and it paid off.

February 17, 1995

Åre, Sweden

The team flew from Geneva to Copenhagen to Östersund, then drove another two hours into the cool blond heart of Sweden. Having been to

Norway several times, I wanted to see the other side of Scandinavia. The two countries acted like such rivals. What made them different? Besides, I was excited to see Pilla's homeland. Everyone was friendly, just like Pilla, and the sun hung around until almost midnight.

The course at Åre was too short and fast for mistakes. You dropped into your tuck right out of the start, got up to speed, made a few turns, and then it was over. Marjan figured out a secret that gave me an extra half-second on the field. I took one turn a little wide and went up on a low embankment, sucking some extra juice off the backside. I beat Katja by six-tenths of a second on a minute-eighteen course. Katja was leading in the Super G standings, but so far Hil and I had kept her off the top step in the downhill.

A year ago Katja had been the gold standard. Now the tables were turned. Katja came up to me after the race and told me something I'll never forget. "Picabo," she said, "I think that you are unbeatable for me this season."

"No, don't throw in the towel," I urged her. "Come on, Katja; keep fighting." But I could feel her slowly slipping away, pulled out of contention on a riptide of frustration. She was giving it all she had, yet it wasn't enough.

I dedicated the race in Åre to Tomas Fogdoe, a Swedish slalom star who had been paralyzed the week before when he hit a tree during a training run. I bought a blank guest book and asked all the girls to sign it, then delivered it to his hospital room. I admit I was thinking of Muffy Davis at the time. After being paralyzed she had distanced herself from all her old skiing friends, and we hadn't spoken in years. I would redeem myself by doing for Tomas what I had never done for Muffy: show that I cared.

March 4, 1995

Saalbach, Austria

Ski racing is a national obsession in Austria, and I arrived to find I was more famous there than in my own country. Everyone was expecting big things from me. The press was out in force, and the spectators flocked to me as if I were a rock star. They called out my name, reached over fences to touch me, thrust bits of paper in my face to sign. My every training run was accompanied by a chorus of clanging cowbells, the Alpine equivalent of holding a Bic lighter up at a concert.

This was also the first time Herwig had stepped foot in his home country in almost a year, and I knew he'd like nothing better than to shove a victory in the faces of his fellow Austrians. Herwig had become my friend as well as my coach. We talked about everything, and he was always reminding me not to let my success go to my head. "I've worked with more famous skiers than you," he'd say. Only Herwig could get away with statements like that, and I wanted to deliver the win for him.

That course had one turn. It had my name all over it. I crossed the finish at 1:37:87, squeaking out a win over Katja by two-hundredths of a second. Hilary finished fourteenth, and we swapped positions in the standings. I was first, and she was second. Katja was third.

I waited patiently in the finish area for Herwig to get off the mountain. "Thank you," he said, wrapping me in a huge bear hug.

"You're welcome," I answered.

Hilary was now comfortable enough with me to crack a joke. "You know," she said, "you're not sharing very much."

"I'm skiing as fast as I can," I responded. "Are you?"

But the thing I remember most about Saalbach is that for the first time in my career I made a better turn than Katja. I was in the video room analyzing my footage after the race, and I said to Ernst, "Hey! She didn't get me in that turn because I went in straighter and I held a tighter line and I came out faster."

Ernst agreed that I had come into my own. After my win in Saalbach, he told the Associated Press, "You can't really say this is her kind of course because with four wins, they're all her kind of course. She's become so good in the turns and such a good glider, and she's so very consistent. She makes so few mistakes on the way down, which is key."

That was high praise, coming from Ernst.

A World Cup win comes with more than bragging rights; it comes with cash. After each victory I received prize money in the local currency, which translated into anywhere from ten thousand to fifteen thousand dollars. By now my wallet was stuffed with foreign currency, so I asked some people for advice. They suggested I open a Swiss bank account. Since the team flew in and out of Zurich all the time, I could withdraw money from my account when I arrived in Europe and deposit my winnings into it before I left.

Being a winner meant a whole new set of logistics. For example, my hotel phone would start ringing off the hook once the local media and fans found out where I was staying. I'd put a block on incoming calls, but finally I got a cell phone. Everyone in Europe had one, and in the long run it turned out to be cheaper than a landline. After every race I got on my cell and phoned home. "Mom, I won again!" Each time I said those words I got more excited, though I worried the message was becoming monotonous. But at three-thirty in the morning, "I won again!" was probably all my parents wanted to hear.

I was also discovering the truth behind that old adage "It's lonely at the top." I would look out from the top step of the podium and see Cookie and my coaches. But unless Hilary was in the top five, I never saw my teammates. If I saw them at all, it was their backs as they walked away.

I dealt with the snub by reminding myself that I had never cared what my teammates thought about me. I loved what I was doing, and victory made the discord bearable.

I was having the time of my life. Every time I won a training run, every time I stuck a jump, my confidence swelled. I radiated such intensity that it reached the point where I was winning the race before it even began. When a winner is determined by hundredths of a second, skill isn't the issue. Everyone has skill. The contest is in your head. If you don't believe you can beat someone, you won't. If you believe you will beat your competitors, then it's just a matter of time until you're standing on the top step of the podium.

I began to believe what Katja had said: I was unbeatable. My domination began in the start area. The rest of the field did not exist for me. I was a world of one. I'd retreat into my headphones, grooving to the music and running the course in my head, putting my whole body into the visualization of my success. Then Cookie and I would go through our tried-and-true routine, and by the time I entered the start house, everyone else had accepted the inevitable.

Normally other teams take their cues from the front-runners; now I was the one everyone was watching. I had a bull's-eye on my forehead, on my back, on my ass. Everyone was looking to my coaches and me for answers. We had to determine the fastest line and choose the perfect start number. We had to figure out which skis to use. I was the one whose training runs were being videotaped by the other coaches and studied in the hotels at night.

I wanted to prove to the European ski racers that Americans could win, but more than that, I wanted to show them that it was okay to express themselves. If I felt like boogying to a song on my Walkman in the start, I did. If I felt like dancing a jig at the finish line, I did. If I felt like celebrating a win by kicking off my ski boots and cracking open a beer, I did. The European press loved the action, the fire, and the emotion I brought to the scene. Every time you picked up a newspaper to read about a race, there I was. In France I was nicknamed "La Picabo," in Switzerland, "Ein Verrucktes Huhn" (One Crazy Red Hen), in Austria, "Sommersprossiger Dusenjager" (the Freckle-Faced Jet Fighter Pilot). The headlines, the pressure, the tension, the triumphs: every single element was just another stick of kindling stoking my competitive fire.

I also wanted to prove to the United States that ski racing was worth paying attention to. The media certainly was. On March 7, after my Saalbach win, *The New York Times* ran a twelve-hundred-word story in its sports section about me. The headline read "The Mouth That Keeps Roaring: An American Free Spirit Overwhelms the Downhill Scene." The reporter, Christopher Clarey, described my influence on the World Cup, both as a competitor and a personality. "Seldom has she met a topic she didn't want to exhaust, a stranger she didn't want to befriend, or a façade she didn't want to bring crashing down," Clarey wrote.

The press often compared me to the World Cup's other larger-than-life personality, the Italian superstar Alberto Tomba. We both played with the crowd and embraced the pressure. You'd find us in the disco two out of five nights. His nickname was La Bomba. I was La Bombette.

We were both having great seasons that year. Tomba was unbeatable in the technical events. He was on track to win the overall World Cup title without competing in a single speed event. That's how dominant he was.

Tomba had burst onto the scene at the 1988 Winter Olympics in Calgary, a handsome playboy with a powerful build and a head of tight, black curls. He made headlines by winning gold medals in the slalom and GS and for his very public pursuit of Katarina Witt, the beautiful German figure skater. I met him at a party at a karaoke bar during the 1993 Worlds in Japan, hosted by our ski sponsor, Rossignol. I ran into him again that summer at Mt. Bachelor in Oregon. I was training and he was doing a photo shoot for a clothing company. One night he invited me and a friend to a dinner party. Tomba had a couple Ferraris parked in his garage back home in Bologna, but after dinner he asked me for a ride home because he wanted to hear my big stereo in my big blue truck. He climbed into the passenger seat, with my friend sandwiched between us.

So I was tooling along a two-lane road, Megadeth blasting on my big stereo, when flashing red lights popped into my rearview mirror.

Damn!

I pulled over and the cop got out of the car. It was a guy.

"What's the problem, officer?"

"Your tires are riding over the yellow line, and you're missing a taillight."

"My tires are too fat to fit on the road, so it's either off on the dirt there or ride the yellow line here. Which would you prefer I do?"

The cop stooped to get a closer look at the chick who was giving him so much lip. He asked for my license. I wasn't that famous yet, but he must have been a ski racing fan because the name on my license gave him pause.

I motioned with my head toward the passenger seat as if to say, "If you think I'm impressive, check this out." And the world's most famous skier, who had been scrunched down in his seat, leaned forward and gave a little wave.

I watched that cop's jaw drop to the general level of his gun belt. "Uh, well, okay, just be careful," he stammered. "And you can get your taillight fixed at that gas station tomorrow." And he let us go.

Tomba and I soon discovered we were soul mates. When he was younger he'd skip curfew to visit a girlfriend. He loved to eat and drink, and he struggled with his weight. People called him Bert, but his family called him Albie, and so did I. At Rossignol parties we would be seated next to each other on purpose, to galvanize the room. The men's World Cup usually travels a different circuit than the women's, so we spent most of our time together at meals. Eating was a ritual. Tomba made sure I had three different wines in front of me at a meal, and if he wanted me to taste something, he'd put a bite on a fork and place it gently in my mouth.

Tomba would often invite a friend to these dinners, and the friend would invariably bring along several hot girlfriends. Tomba usually ended up going home with one or all of them, and he'd invite me to come, knowing I'd decline. I remember one evening in Sestriere, Italy. One of his babes showed up, gave me the once-over, and asked haughtily, "Who are you?"

"She's the female Tomba," the real Tomba said. That shut her up.

But his girlfriends had nothing to worry about. Our relationship never went beyond flirting. I just didn't want to end up on that list, and besides, I wasn't his type. Tomba would put his hand on my leg and say, "Peekie, you're just too much for me."

"I know, Albie."

March 11, 1995

Lenzerheide, Switzerland

By the time we reached the Swiss Alps, I knew that the World Cup downhill title was mine for the taking. If I won Lenzerheide and Hilary and Katja finished out of the top five, I could clinch. All I could think about, and all Herwig, Ernst, Marjan, and Gnarly could think about, was the title.

The course basically had two turns. It had a rocking start, super fast and steep. You'd come ripping off the top and across a flat, meander through a few turns, scream around a side hill, bang out a big double turn, zigzag a couple singles off this big jump, maneuver a couple rolls, and then bang out another double, finally working the terrain into the finish. I crossed the line at 1:50:57, six-hundredths of a second faster than Russia's Warwara Zelenskaja.

I'd won my fourth race in a row and had become the first non-European to ever win a World Cup downhill title. I drank more champagne than anyone in the history of that hotel, or so they say. I don't remember, having passed out by 6:30 P.M.

By this time, the team atmosphere had calmed down somewhat. I knew that my nonstop energy exhausted Krista and Megan, and I tried to tone it down around them. I roomed by myself, and when Megan asked me not to bring my cell phone to the table while we were eating, I obliged. Krista and I were at an impasse, but Megan and I could discuss our differences and get past them. Krista didn't come back the following season, and Hilary retired in 1997. Megan and I are still competing, still going strong.

March 15, 1995

World Cup Finals, Bormio, Italy

The entire World Cup tour, men and women, showed up for the last races of the season. Tomba and I were the main attractions. I was there to get my sixth win and extend my winning streak to five. Tomba, who hadn't lost a slalom all season, was on the verge of clinching the men's overall title, the first Italian to do so in twenty years. He was from Bologna, only two hours to the south, so the Italian fans were more manic than usual. They packed the bars and thronged the cobblestone streets and the race-course, faces painted like Italian flags. A giant banner was strung across one street that read, "Picabo e Tomba: Belli e Invincibli." Beautiful and invincible.

Always a showboat, Tomba outdid himself in Bormio. He took a slalom run wearing shorts and a tie. One woman reportedly took off her shirt and asked Tomba to autograph her breasts. That's when I realized there was a line I drew in being the female Tomba.

I was glad Tomba was entertaining the troops because, frankly, I wasn't overly excited to be there. The motivation to win had subsided. I had clinched my title and was feeling complacent. Besides, I didn't like the course. Called "la pista Stelvio," it was icy and twisting and completely unforgiving. At one point, you'd come flying around this television tower and hit a jump that spit you sixty feet through the air. You'd land to the left, down and out, and there was nothing you could do about it. You'd be catching air on this jump, no matter what. And you'd better be forward when you hit it: if you sat back on the landing, your ACL would be history. I heard that jump had claimed six or seven knees the season before. Then you'd come hauling ass into this rip-roaring bottom pitch, the ultimate in downhill: a leg-burning, seventy-mile-per-hour thrill ride. You had to really buck up and embrace its intensity.

That course mystified me. I couldn't figure out the line. My training times were terrible—eighteenth and fifteenth. I hadn't seen a double digit next to my name in six races. *Whoa*, I thought, *what's going on?* To make matters worse I hit a gate with my hand and broke my left pinky. The injury was just another war wound, more of an inconvenience than anything, the pain like a fly buzzing around my head. The buzz in Bormio was that I was going to take it easy, coast.

The night before the race, I gave myself a talking to. *Are you going to ski half-assed tomorrow, or are you going to step up?*

Hilary had more to lose than I did. I had clinched my title, but she was still battling Katja for second place in the downhill standings and needed to beat her to get it. Later that evening I said to Hil, "I'm stepping up. Are you?"

"Yeah. Let's go out in style."

That night we analyzed our video together for the first time. The video room was this big space in the back of the hotel. We sat in front of the TV, two chairs apart, breaking down our training runs with our coaches: slow motion, fast motion, putting the line together. Katja was my friend, but Hil was a fellow American, and I wanted her to win.

Despite the pressure she was under, Hil pulled off an amazing run. She beat Katja's split time in the turny section and crossed the finish line ahead of her. Hil had stepped up. Now it was my turn.

When I race, I talk to myself the entire time. My inner monologue on the last stretch of la pista Stelvio went something like this: *Hang on; try to get in your tuck. Fuck that! Oh, forward. Okay, tuck. Oh, God! Get out of your tuck. It's not gonna happen. You press that shit! Come on; you can handle it. No way, that's too bouncy. Okay, God! Get back up. Fuck!*

And I remember thinking how fast it was and how tired I was and it was the end of the season and my legs were doing it all and had been for months and I was ready for a break. But I was loving it at the same time, and that's the crazy thing: I was running raw downhill and just eating it up, and I crossed the finish line with a time of 1:38:41 and won. I'd pulled it off. Fist pump. Relief. Exhaustion. Elation.

It's funny, if you look at footage of the finish in Bormio, the Italian spectators are going off, but the people who travel with the circuit—the ski company reps, for instance—just look bored. *There she goes again. Chalk up another one.*

I had won six out of nine downhills, the last five in a row. It was the longest single-season World Cup winning streak in more than twenty years, second only to Annemarie Moser-Proell's eight straight races in 1972. Add in Hilary's two wins in North America, and we had won every downhill that season except one. It was a show of speed unmatched in the history of U.S. skiing.

My coaches were beside themselves. Ernst kept saying, "I love it. I love it." Paul came up with a shit-eating grin on his face and pulled me into a hug. "You little shit. I can't believe we actually pulled it off." Herwig was relatively calm. He was used to winning titles. I think he enjoyed watching us celebrate because it was our first.

The World Cup trophy is the ultimate paperweight, a lead-crystal globe on a pedestal that must weigh about twenty-five pounds. When it was handed to me in the finish area, I planted a wet one on it and hugged it to my chest, tears streaming down my face.

Afterward Hil came up to me and asked shyly, "Can I hold it?"

I let her hold it as long as she wanted. We were proud of ourselves. We had figured out how to compete together and use each other in a positive way. I had pushed her to be a better ski racer, and I felt she recognized that and was all right with it.

Katja accepted defeat with grace. She told me she'd had fun competing against me and invited me to her wedding. The European coaches just stood there, looking stunned. "We can handle one American on the podium," an Austrian coach told Ernst later, "but two is unacceptable."

What really scared them was the fact that Hil and I would be back the next season. I remember how at one point Nathalie Bouvier of France sidled up next to me like a French double agent and whispered, "If you have a secret, tell me."

"I don't have a secret."

"*Merde.*"

I HAD TO LAY OFF THE CHAMPAGNE BECAUSE THE SUPER G WAS THE FOL-lowing day. I felt good the next morning, but the snow, which had been hard all week, softened overnight, making for treacherous spots. Six gates from the bottom, as I skied out of a shadow and into the sun, my outside edge danced underneath me as I was switching from one foot to the other. My ski shot out from under me, and I was instantly struck by two simultaneous revelations: I was about to take a big, bad crash, and there was a course worker with a shovel standing directly in my way.

I was going to take him out; it was only a matter of which part of my body I'd take him out with: my chest or my back. I chose the latter. I cocked my right shoulder and rolled. The outside edge of my left ski arced underneath me and sent me spinning. I went ass over teakettle and knocked him flat, which must have felt like being struck by a cement truck.

The course worker was okay, but I wasn't. I tried to get up, but the pain in my back where his shovel had struck me was excruciating. The rule with a back injury is to stay immobile, so I just lay there, praying I hadn't done any serious damage. Paul, who had been standing near the accident scene, comforted me while we waited for the helicopter.

"Paul," I said firmly, "I've got to call Hil on the radio. That's a really shitty spot and she needs to know about it."

"I'll tell her, Peek; don't worry."

"And hurry up and get me the fuck out of here because they're holding up the start."

Fifteen minutes later, the medics arrived and put me in a neck brace and loaded me into the chopper. I went out in style, all right, on a stretcher, nagging Paul the whole time: "You've got to tell Hil about that spot! Promise me you won't forget!"

Five thousand miles away a phone in Hailey, Idaho, began to ring. Mom was visiting her mother in Missouri, and Dad was home solo. It must have been two o'clock in the morning Idaho time. The answering machine picked up and Dad heard my agent's voice saying, "Picabo fell, and it's really bad. They're taking her to the hospital. I'll call you later when I know more." Dad was on the move in his skivvies, but he got to the phone just as Chris Hanna hung up.

Thirty seconds later, in a gear bag at the finish area in Bormio, Italy, my cell phone started to ring. It was Dad, desperate to find me. No one in the finish area thought to answer the phone.

I spent two hours at the hospital in Sondalo, and for two hours Dad was trying to get to me, and Mom was a basket case in Missouri, trying to figure out what the closest hospital to Bormio was. Finally, with the help of a tenacious international operator from Sprint, Dad was patched through to my hospital just as I was being wheeled out of my last test.

"Peeky, it's Dad. Are you okay?" He was panicked, breathing hard and crying.

"I'm fine, Dad. I just pulled a back muscle and bruised my hip. I'll be here for another day. I'll call you when I get back to the hotel and tell you what's going on. Tell Mom not to worry."

The doctors shot a painkiller into my ass and sent me back to my hotel. I got there just as the rest of the team was packing to return to the States. They helped me to my room and wished me well. I lay in bed all night and the next day, taking Tylenol 3 and eating room-service spaghetti in bed. My crystal globe was on the nightstand next to the bed, and when I felt the need for a little exercise, I'd heft it like a barbell. On the flight home my coaches schlepped all my luggage except one piece: the bag with my trophy. I carried that on the plane.

After I got home, I signed an endorsement deal with Sprint, so my cell phone addiction paid off. Dad accompanied Chris and me to the meetings, where he told the story of how the Sprint operator had helped him get to me. Dad likes to think that story helped seal the deal.

The U.S. Nationals were in Park City in late March, but I was too wrecked to compete. I drove there with my parents to watch the event. Sprint, which eventually sponsored the entire U.S. Ski Team, hired people to hand out ten thousand prepaid phone cards with a photo of me skiing on them. As usual, I was hard to ignore.

One afternoon a slender woman with dark, curly hair approached me and introduced herself.

"Hi, Picabo, I'm Sue Levin. I'm the woman you've been expecting."

When my agent had told me that the head of Nike's women's division was coming to Park City to meet me, I'd thought, *Nike wants to talk to me?* I knew that Sue wanted to know more about me, that nothing was set in stone. She took my parents and me to lunch. We didn't talk about money or deals; we were just having a nice meal, getting acquainted, talking story. Sue and I had a lot in common; I liked her, and so did my parents. When she shook my hand and said, "I'll be in touch," I had a feeling my life would never be the same.

8

NIKE GIRL

WHEN I WAS A KID, THE BIG EVENT OF THE YEAR WAS SHOPPING FOR school clothes in Twin Falls. Everyone went to Twin for major purchases because things were cheaper there than at the tourist places in Sun Valley and Ketchum. Our annual trip to Twin was the only time I got something new, something that wasn't homemade or handed down from Baba or one of the Triumph gang.

Mom, Dad, Baba, and I would cram into the front seat of our little pickup for the two-hour drive to the big city. We'd have lunch at McDonald's or a pancake house called Elmer's. Then we'd hit the Blue Lakes Shopping Mall, but the mall was a little expensive, so we looked more than we bought. We purchased most of our clothes at JC Penney, Sears, or a department store called The Bonmarché. But my favorite stop was Payless, because that's where we bought new sneakers.

I loved getting new sneakers. Payless had rows and rows of them, set out like trophies at an awards ceremony. I'd try on a million different pairs. It was the typical tomboy dilemma: trying to strike the perfect balance between macho and girlie. I didn't go for the pink styles, so I usually ended up with a boy's shoe. I didn't care. At that age, feet were feet. Back then sneakers didn't have an athlete's name, flashing lights, or tiny computers that measured how high you could jump. The shoes didn't need any fancy stuff to make me want them. I didn't even care about the brand. It was all about the pure allure of the shoes themselves and the feats I would perform while wearing them.

My parents would pay for the sneakers, and the first thing I'd do once we got in the car for the drive home was take off the lid, stick my face in the box, and take a big whiff of those shoes. I'd breathe deeply of their newness, part synthetic, part natural: the leather, the nylon, even the glue. All the way back to Triumph I'd keep opening the box and smelling them. When we got home, I'd place the shoes ceremoniously on the closet floor, on the far right side, the space reserved for my sneakers. I almost hated to wear them because I wanted to make that new-sneaker smell last as long as I could. I lived in sneakers. At night you practically had to pry them off my feet. Hopefully they survived until spring, when I wore them to run track, even if they were bandaged together with duct tape.

My first Nikes were blue with a yellow swoosh and the original waffle sole. I believe they were hand-me-downs from Jamie Collins. I wore them to run sprints, relays, and hurdles (the hurdles being my favorite because they were the hardest). I wore them in the Blaine County Recreational Department Grade School Track Meet. Mom still has a yellowed newspaper clipping about that meet from the *Wood River Journal*, dated May 5, 1982. There's a photo of the field leaning over the finish line on the front sports page. That's me at the top of the picture, wearing my blue and yellow Nikes, leading the pack. So you could say I've been endorsing Nike products since the age of eleven.

Thirteen years later, in the fall of 1995, it became official. That's when I signed a contract with Nike, the world's largest manufacturer of athletic footwear and apparel. It was a three-year deal extending through the 1998 Olympic Games in Nagano, Japan. Print ads. TV commercials. Representation by Nike Sports Management, whose roster of athletes included pro-sports superstars like Deion Sanders and Ken Griffey Jr. (I was the only woman). And the best part: a sneaker with my name on it! Designed to my specifications, to do what I wanted it to do, in the colors that I liked. A Picabo shoe.

Those were heady days. With the exception of figure skaters, athletes who toil away in Winter Olympic sports tend to get the cold shoulder as far as endorsements go; their passions are simply too obscure. I broke the mold. I was the first winter-sports athlete to get a signature sneaker, the benchmark of an athlete's popularity. The signature shoe concept had taken off with the Air Jordans: take a famous athlete, put his or her name on a shoe, and watch it get snapped up by people who crave reflected glory through footwear. The *Rocky Mountain News* called me "the hottest female athlete in the country." This was before the 1999 Women's World Cup in soccer, the Women's National Basketball Association, and Venus and Serena Williams. The marketing of women's sports was still relatively young, and for a brief, brilliant moment, a girl from Triumph stood at the top.

At first I couldn't believe my good fortune. Being signed by Nike meant you were the shit. But usually you had to be a basketball or soccer player, a star in a sport a lot of people actually played. I was a *ski racer*, for God's sake. Almost nobody did what I did. In fact, Nike did not make one single product that I used in my sport.

Why me? It was a question I asked my parents and Baba over and over. The conversation went something like this: "What makes me so special?"

"You're not bullshit, you're for real, and they know that, and that's why they want you."

"But all I'm doing is being me."

"Being you is enough. Don't you get it?"

"No, I don't get it, because being myself isn't hard work."

"Actually, being you *is* hard work. You just don't realize it because that's the way you've always been. A lot of people struggle to be like you. You're a natural. Plus you kick everybody's ass."

So did a lot of women. What I had, and what sports marketing had come to depend on, was *attitude*. "We think she can transcend the sport of skiing and not just be a seasonal commodity," my new agent, Tonya Weibke, told the *Rocky Mountain News*. "She has the skill combined with the personality, which makes her all the more marketable."

I represented an idea of what women could be and do. I defied stereotypes. I could fly down a mountainside at eighty miles an hour one day and get all dolled up for a formal ball the next. I was independent, confident, outspoken, strong.

And that was exactly what I worried about. Was I too big? Too brash? Too mouthy? Too opinionated? I had begun to think about my image, and I watched how other athletes with outsized personalities handled it. Take Charles Barkley, for example. No matter how many times he ran his mouth on the court, everybody loved him. He was so passionate on the court, and so composed and enlightened off it. I realized I didn't have to change in order to go mainstream. I could remain true to the person I was. And if people didn't like me, then they weren't supposed to.

Nike liked me—before I signed a contract, they courted me like a French ski racer who wouldn't take no for an answer. They gave me a grand tour of the "campus," their headquarters in Beaverton, a suburb of Portland. A big banner reading "Welcome Picabo Street" was hung across the main entrance. I loved how big and manicured the campus was and how all the buildings were named after athletes: Michael Jordan, Andre Agassi, Nolan Ryan, Joan Benoit Samuelson. Sue Levin and her department had made a special video, splicing footage of me skiing between shots of their star athletes. I couldn't believe I belonged in that company.

When I met Phil Knight, Nike's legendary president and CEO, I felt as nervous as I had in the start at Lillehammer. Phil had a beard and glasses and the same coloring as Baba: strawberry blond hair and blue eyes. He asked me to sit down and told me to relax. I looked at him and said, "I'm sorry. I'm just really excited. This is a really big deal for me." He sort of giggled, as if he was enjoying himself. I'd told him exactly how I felt: *I'm really excited to meet you and I don't care if you know it.*

By the summer, we had a deal hammered out, and in early June I was officially introduced to the Nike sales force at a sales conference at Portland's Oregon Convention Center. I was driven onto a stage in a Hummer, one of those huge vehicles that looks like a tank. I popped out of the vehicle and then stood there and told those hundreds of salespeople the story I just told you, about how much I loved to get new sneakers as a kid. Some people in the company had been skeptical about me—"but Phil, Sue, she's a *ski racer*"—but after I finished, everybody stood and cheered and applauded me. Afterward they let me drive the Hummer back to the Nike headquarters. That was a big rig; I could barely keep it on the road.

I was a Nike girl. I'd arrived. This became my mantra: *Oh man, I've made it now.*

Sure, it was a sweet deal, but I don't sign on with just anybody. I've refused to endorse a dandruff shampoo because I don't have dandruff and an energy bar because I didn't like the taste. I had to feel good about the product and the company, and so did my parents, because the decision belonged to all of us. I felt good about Nike. It felt like an extension of my family. Sue and her husband became good friends, and I spent hours in her corner office in the John McEnroe building, absorbing the finer points of the Marketing of Picabo 101.

The way Sue saw it, I was the next phase in Nike's marketing initiative aimed at women. In 1993, Nike had signed soccer player Mia Hamm, basketball player Sheryl Swoopes, track stars Jackie Joyner-Kersee and Gail Devers, and a 6'3" beach volleyball player named Gabrielle Reece. Gabby had the works: awesome athleticism, a cool personality, the body of a Greek goddess, and a face beautiful enough to land her on the cover of *Elle*. Gabby's second signature shoe, the Air Patrol, had taken off in 1995, actually outselling Air Jordans briefly. "You could be the cold-weather version of Gabby," Sue told me.

Selling shoes sounded fine, but that wasn't what it was all about for me. I had a message. I wanted to make a positive difference for the next generation. I felt girls were getting shortchanged in a lot of ways, and I wanted to tell parents to get their daughters involved in as many activities as possible. Try everything: sports, music, art. Sign them up for choir, put them in drama, let them try a team sport, and let them figure out if they want to be an athlete. You never know where you're going to find your niche. I had found mine, and it changed my life.

"Picabo, you have the opportunity to influence the lives of millions of girls," Sue would tell me. "We can take everything you represent in terms of being strong and going for your dreams and put a spotlight on it. You've had tough times and worked through them. Yours is a message of perseverance and personal growth, and little girls should hear it from someone as big and strong as you are."

Be Like Peek. I could get behind that.

WHAT A WILD, CRAZY, WHIRLWIND SUMMER THAT WAS. IMMEDIATELY after the Nike sales meeting I flew to Budapest. The International Olympic Committee was meeting there to decide which city would host the 2002 Winter Olympics. Salt Lake City was one of the four finalists, along with

Östersund, Sweden; Quebec City, Canada; and Sion, Switzerland. The Salt Lake bid committee had asked me to represent the athletes' point of view, and I was eager to help convince the IOC to throw the Games to us. It was a chance to represent my country, in a way, and besides, I was curious. I really wanted to know whether or not the Olympics were as politically motivated as everyone said they were. I had to see for myself.

We flew to Budapest on a Gulfstream jet owned by Earl Holding, the chairman of Sinclair Oil. Earl owns Sun Valley Resort as well as Snowbasin Resort, which is about an hour from Park City in Utah. If Salt Lake got the Games, Snowbasin would host the downhill and Super G. Mom and I traveled with Earl and his wife, Carol; their two daughters and a granddaughter; and the governor of Utah, Mike Leavitt, and his wife, Jackie. It was my first flight in a private jet. It was a beautiful plane, totally decked out with white carpet, white leather seats, and gold trim. I didn't want to touch anything; it was so pristine.

Once we got to Budapest, we met up with Tom Welch and Dave Johnson, two Salt Lake businessmen, who had lobbied for years to get the Games to their city. We were all staying at a grand, five-star hotel called the Kempinski, and I spent most of the week schmoozing the IOC heavyweights and telling them how great Utah was and how everyone should go there. When a few IOC members told me they were worried about Salt Lake's conservative Mormon reputation, I made a point of saying that Park City was one of the biggest parties on the World Cup tour.

On June 16, the host-city candidates gave their presentations in a huge auditorium that looked like one of those multilevel legislative halls you see on C-SPAN. Several dozen IOC delegates sat down in front, and when it was my turn to speak, I told them, "The Olympics are about the athletes. The athletes need great facilities, and Salt Lake has already constructed its venues, whereas other cities only have theirs on the drawing board. So we're ready if you are."

Then all we could do was wait. I was sitting with a young girl named Cynthia Ruiz whom I had taken under my wing. She was only nine or ten, a promising young figure skater, who represented the youth programs the Salt Lake Organizing Committee had put in place as part of its bid.

Waiting for the IOC's decision was what it must feel like to wait for a jury to deliver its verdict at a criminal trial. I felt excited, anxious, and overly warm, even in my silk pants suit. I expected the deliberations to take hours, but only twenty minutes later the committee came back. It was the quickest decision in the history of the Olympic bid. When they said, "The host city for the 2002 Winter Olympics will be . . . Salt Lake City," I couldn't believe it. "Yee-haw!" I shouted. I jumped up on the table and pulled Cynthia up with me, and we started jumping up and down with joy. Suddenly the table's legs buckled, and it folded up like a clamshell, and we went down. Fortunately, the table landed on my leg, not Cynthia's. We picked ourselves up, unhurt and laughing.

We flew home in a celebratory mood. Earl and Mike had a meeting in the back of the plane while the women stayed up front and sang old cowboy songs a cappella. I came home thinking the Olympics hadn't been corrupted by special interests, that the IOC put the needs of the athletes and the well-being of the community first. I thought I was paying close attention to everything that was going on. But I missed it. The whole white envelope under the table thing: I missed it. Three years later, after allegations surfaced that Welch and Johnson had bribed the IOC, my faith in the Olympic system would be shaken. But that summer, all I felt was pride.

I HIT A NEW TAX BRACKET IN 1995. I PULLED IN A HEALTHY SIX-FIGURE income that year. Now that I had some real dough, I knew exactly what I wanted: my own house.

Living in Hailey had become inconvenient. Flying in and out of the airport was a pain in the neck because flights were canceled and delayed so often. I wanted to be near a big international airport. Portland was only ninety minutes from Mount Hood, where I could ski almost year-round, and where I did a lot of photo shoots for my sponsors. Portland was also closer to my new boyfriend, Joey Hoeschmann. He was from the little town of White Rock, British Columbia, and skied for the Canadian team. We'd known each other a couple years, but started seeing each other after I moved to Portland. Joey was sweet and shy and safe, and I was tired of being alone.

I wanted Mom and Dad to live with me. Both of them had health problems. Mom had had a hard time walking around in Lillehammer, and a few months after she got home, she was diagnosed with rheumatoid arthritis.

Dad had been struggling to manage his diabetes for years, and frankly he wasn't very good at it. He'd forget to eat or take his insulin, and before we knew it, he'd be going into diabetic shock. He'd become incoherent and catatonic. Sometimes all it took was a glass of apple juice to snap him out of it, but a couple times we had to call the paramedics. He almost died twice. I had this sixth sense for when it was happening. I'd be sleeping in a hotel in Europe when I'd wake and think, *Dad's bonking. I can feel it.* And I'd call home and be right.

Being a mason is strenuous and occasionally hazardous work, and Dad was having a hard time balancing his job and his illness. It caused him a lot of stress, and finally I asked him to retire and come live with Mom and me in Portland.

I was too busy to go house hunting, so Baba and my parents did it for me. They went to Portland in late July and looked at two dozen houses, winnowing the field to eight. Then I flew in and spent a day looking at them. I ended up buying the first one the real estate lady had shown me: a one-story ranch in a subdivision outside town.

The house had everything I needed, everything our Triumph house didn't—all the modern conveniences plus glass on the windows. No one had to share a bedroom. There was a room for me, one for my parents, and a guest room for Baba, who'd be visiting regularly. It had a finished basement and an attic big enough to shoot small firearms in. There was a whole acre of land for my dog, Duggan, to run around on. He'd become my travel companion, accompanying me on long drives to out-of-state ski camps. The house also had features that meant something only to me, such as a back door that led to a laundry area. That way I could come home after a trip to Europe and drop my laundry and my "show-and-tell" bag next to the washing machine on the way to my room. The show-and-tell bag contained all the souvenirs and gifts from my travels, stuff I couldn't wait to show my parents: "Check out this trophy. Here's an envelope full of money. What do you think about that? Hey, have you guys ever seen Italian lire before? Here it is, a whole envelope of it!"

We moved in that September. Not long after that, the contract with Nike was ready to be signed, and Mom, Dad, Baba, and I gathered in the living room of our new house. The contract was on the coffee table.

The media reported the three-year deal was worth $1 million. I can say it was more than Dad had made in a dozen years working in the quarry, more money than my family would normally see in a lifetime, in five lifetimes.

We all sat there, looking at that little stack of papers.

Finally I spoke. "Okay, guys, what do you think?"

Mom and Dad and Baba nodded their heads in unison, like those funny wobbly-necked dolls you see in the rear windows of some cars.

"We're stoked," they said.

I signed it.

BY THIS TIME, MY SIGNATURE SHOE WAS WELL UNDER WAY. IT TAKES ABOUT a year to produce a shoe, from concept to final product, and the man who oversees the process is Tinker Hatfield, the mastermind behind the Air Jordan phenomenon. My shoe had to reflect who I was and what I wanted. "If you could have the ideal shoe," Tinker asked me at our first meeting in the spring of 1995, "what would you be able to do in it, and what would it look like?"

I said that I hated jogging, so a running shoe was out. I said it would be an outdoor shoe, green and gray and black. He asked me what activities I did in the summertime. I told him all the things I did: trail running, dryland drills in the grass, mountain biking. I later realized that what I wanted was the ultimate tomboy shoe, the shoe I would have wanted as a kid in Triumph. Because that's what I was doing as a kid, cross-training, only nobody called it that in the '70s. I just called it having fun.

Once in a while Tinker would call and say, "We've got an early production model and I'd like you to come in and look at it so we can talk about it." I'd drive over to the Nike campus for a design session. I'd walk into Tinker's studio and there would be the latest Air Jordan shoe, the latest Gabrielle Reece, the latest Sheryl Swoopes. *Holy shit,* I thought, *this guy probably has Michael Jordan's cell phone number. He can just call him up and say, "Hey Michael, the black looks kind of cheesy so we're going to try the silver. What do you think?"*

I never imagined that before long I'd be meeting Michael Jordan in the locker room after a Bulls' game. Or sitting up on a dais at the grand opening of New York Niketown, trying to keep a straight face while Tiger Woods told me dirty jokes and Gabby Reece shot me "be quiet and listen" looks because Phil was speaking. What a ride.

THE FIRST WOMEN'S WORLD CUP SPEED EVENT OF THE 1995–96 SEASON was slated for Vail in the middle of November, and Nike's publicity machine went into overdrive. We held a press conference to publicly announce our deal. Sue had used her contacts to wrangle a story about me in *Vogue*, and it came out in the November issue. Newspaper reporters stood in line for interviews.

I was a huge star in Europe, but Sue wanted to raise my profile in the United States, and the way to do that was to put me in my own commercial. As the World Cup approached, I had to shoot the commercial and attend an on-snow training camp in Vail. The solution: do both at the same time. Nike sent a camera crew to Vail. They put two remote mikes on me and filmed a morning's worth of training runs, complete with heavy breathing. I remember skiing Pepi's Face, popping that lip, and catching extra air off it for that shoot. We spent the afternoon finishing up. I read the script over and over. It consisted of one line: "The wind howls because it knows it has to race me." Shooting that commercial was a blast. When I saw the commercial, I loved it, too. It was a moody, black-and-white spot, and I looked sort of savage and uncombed. And then that swoosh at the end, and the tag line, "Just do it." It was super cool.

The commercial started airing as the World Cup season began. I can only imagine what the Euros were thinking when they saw me on TV: *Oh great, now she's got a national commercial, too.*

I had been very fast in training, fast enough to beat most of the men's downhill times, including Tommy Moe's. On some sections of the course, I was faster than everyone. Just to hassle one another, the guys would highlight my times on a piece of paper and tape it on one another's hotel room doors. I didn't make any of them cry, as in the old days in Sun Valley, but it sure motivated them the next day. I was smoking my female teammates by two to three seconds in the downhill. Still, I knew how hard it would be to repeat my previous season's performance. For the first time I was the hunted, not the hunter, and I wasn't used to it.

I felt as if I had maintained my level, but the Euros had worked their asses off all summer. Katja Seizinger came in loaded for bear. You could tell she'd been training all summer, hungry for revenge. There were some real beefcake downhillers who came in that year with the attitude, "Let's make this more interesting."

Actually, "tumultuous" is the word I'd use to describe the 1995–96 season. The snow was terrible in Europe once again, and the FIS and some of the World Cup racers were feuding over rules. The FIS can cancel a race after it's under way if the weather or the course deteriorates to the point where it's deemed dangerous for the racers. The person who's in first place is shit out of luck. One U.S. downhiller, A. J. Kitt, had had two wins nullified the previous season and went so far as to accuse the FIS of corruption, of stealing his wins under pressure from European nations who didn't want their skiers to lose points. Even Tomba was arguing with the FIS in the press about some changes in rules in the slalom because he felt they handicapped the top skiers like himself.

I was already feeling enough pressure to repeat as World Cup downhill champ; the last thing I wanted to do was get sucked into that political quicksand. But I did, and now I'm glad, in a way. As Dad likes to say, by 1995 I was a winner; by 1996 I was a millionaire. But I became something else that year: a leader.

Sue had told me that a win at Vail, combined with the TV commercial, would really kick off their marketing efforts. Unfortunately I finished eleventh. Two Germans, Martina Ertl and Katja, were first and second, with Italy's Isolde Kostner in third. I was disappointed, but I also knew that it was only a Super G, so my downhill streak remained intact. Hilary didn't race. She had hurt her back in training, and the injury would hamper her all season.

Krista Schmidinger had retired, so that left Hilary, Megan, and me on the speed team. Occasionally Ernst would bring in some young one to test her out, but we were the core group. Hilary and I were respectful to one another. She was twenty-six now and starting to see the end of her career. But we were still pushing each other, our coaching staff was solid, and there was no reason for her to walk away yet.

We rolled into Lake Louise the first week of December for the first World Cup downhill. I knew I was going to take that race, and I did, but I'll admit I got lucky. A storm was dumping on the mountain, and I was in thirteenth place in a downhill that was later canceled because of bad weather. The storm cleared long enough to rerun the race the next day, and this time I won, beating Katja by almost four-tenths of a second.

That was six wins in a row, and the press started asking me if I was going after Annemarie Moser-Proell's record of eleven consecutive races over two seasons. I told them I had no idea there was such a record, that I didn't read record books. They kept bringing it up, which annoyed the hell out of me. I knew how hard it was to perpetuate that kind of dominance in this generation. Twenty-three years ago, Moser-Proell simply hadn't had as much competition.

My streak came to an end in St. Anton, Austria, on December 16, 1995, and it was broken, fittingly, by Katja. There wasn't enough snow to cover the entire course, so the race was changed to a sprint format. Basically, you ski half the course twice, and the fastest combined time wins. I hate sprint formats. They're so half-assed, so unsatisfying, like getting served half a portion of a meal and being left hungry.

Confidence is a fickle commodity. One season you're brimming with it; the next it comes and goes. My inner tiger, my sense of invincibility and energy that had been so dominant in 1995, decided to take a catnap. I took one look at that course, with its twisting top section and slick, icy man-made surface, and knew I wasn't willing to take the risks necessary to win. I seemed to forecast my own defeat. "The possibility of me not winning is very high," I told *The Times* of London the night before the race. "All kinds of elements could come into play."

Each run lasted about sixty seconds, leaving no margin for error. I made two. I had a bad start and then, halfway down the first run, skied up on some snow banked against a safety fence. Katja won, Hilary was fourth, and I was sixth. I walked off without commenting, and the press noticed. It was the first time in six downhills that I hadn't stood on the top step, which was enough to piss me off. Not only that, I didn't want to answer questions like, "How do you feel, missing the record?" Because all I wanted to say was, "I don't give a shit, and I never did."

A second downhill was held the next day. The Austrians swept the first three spots, not surprising since they trained at St. Anton all the time. Ties are rare in downhill skiing, but I tied for third with Renate Goetschl at 1:36:52. The announcer mistakenly said I was in fourth place, and Alexandra Meissnitzer, a hot young Austrian who had finished second, grabbed the mike and corrected him, saying I'd tied for third. The resort was very apologetic and offered me a free week at St. Anton, which I never used. But I appreciated Meisi's gesture, and by the end of that season we were buddies. We were very similar. She was candid, energetic, outspoken, and she loved to party.

The first downhill after Christmas was in Cortina in mid-January. I asked Mom to come. I would always talk about how much Cortina meant to me, about the scene and the crowds, but having never been there, she couldn't picture it. Also, she wanted to see me getting the respect in Europe that I wasn't getting in the States. My results were printed in the newspapers—as long as I was winning—but my races weren't televised live here. Nothing I did would ever take precedence over the NBA; if I was lucky, I was a highlight on the local news. I had a following in the States, but in Europe I was a hero. Mom wanted to see the people who made big signs for me and screamed for me for a whole week straight and told me they loved me. She was feeling healthy enough to travel, and she wasn't working for anyone but me. She knew that if she was going to get there, now was the time.

Dad stayed behind. He and I shared too much intensity to spend two solid weeks together (we couldn't exactly share a room), and the last thing I needed was for him to bonk in a foreign country the night before a race.

Mom met me in Germany the first week of January, and we traveled to Italy together. We were in Cortina for almost two weeks, and other than a nagging case of altitude sickness, Mom had a great time. The FIS officials told her that if she needed anything, to just ask. She was treated like the queen mother. We stayed in the same room and sang together on the chairlift, "Here Comes the Sun" and "Mr. Man in the Moon." Mom enjoyed seeing how supportive the Italian fans were of me; one guy had made a big heart-shaped sign that read, "Picabo, I love you." Our entire stay in Cortina was one big valentine.

I placed first, second, third, and fourth in training runs and won the race, beating Pilla by half a second. Isolde Kostner was third. She spoiled my hopes for a two in a row, beating me the next day by nineteen-hundredths of a second. A first and a second in two days—Mom was my lucky charm. She had seen me win, at the top of my form, and that meant everything.

Mom's visit seemed to rouse my inner tiger, which was fortuitous, since I was about to do a lot of roaring.

Our next event was in Sestriere, Italy, in late January. It was a big event, with speed and technical races for both men and women. Sestriere had just announced its bid for the 1997 Worlds and wanted to make a good impression by presenting its hero, Alberto Tomba, with a perfect skiing surface. If Tomba didn't like race conditions, he let the world know it, and the last thing Sestriere's race organizers wanted was Mr. Big badmouthing their slalom course and spoiling their chances of hosting the Worlds.

The women's downhill course did not seem to be a priority. Called Kandahar Banchetta, it was a new track that had never been skied by World Cup racers. I'd sit in the hotel at night with my teammates and watch the course workers through the window, slaving over the slalom for Tomba, which wasn't being held for a week. Meanwhile, the women's downhill, which was set to go in two days, was a disgrace. "When are you guys going to prep our downhill?" we'd ask. Snow would fall and no one would be out there grooming and packing it down. One gate was set in a dangerous spot. The snow would go from hard to soft, steep to flat, uphill to downhill. The snow wasn't packed down against the safety fences, leaving a soft spot between the edge of the course and the fence; get a ski caught in there and it would rip your leg off. The margin for error, never great, had become extremely narrow.

It was potentially a killer course, and all the women knew it. Training runs kept getting canceled due to bad weather. Racers usually ignore each other in the days before a race, but in Sestriere, everyone was making eye contact. On the chairlift, in the lodge, during inspection—I would see women giving each other worried looks, which telegraphed something was wrong.

This isn't normal, I thought to myself. The day before the race I ran into Pilla standing at the bottom of the course, and I saw fear in her eyes.

"You're afraid. Why?"

"Look at this fucking thing."

"I know," I said gently, "but listen, they're not going to let us go if it's not safe. And besides, you can always pull."

"But the points . . ."

"Points? What about life, health?"

She turned to me and said, "We need to do something about this."

Pilla was my friend, and when she got this worried, it was for a good reason. I couldn't leave her out in the cold.

"I'm ready when you are," I said.

Pilla started talking to the other racers and soon found out we were all on the same page. That afternoon we held an emergency meeting in a hotel conference room. Everyone was there except the German team, which opted not to come. Several of their athletes were still trying to get enough points to qualify for the Worlds, which were one week away. They wanted that race to happen, no matter what.

There were about twenty-five women in that room, speaking five different languages, all saying the same thing: "We can't ski that course. We won't." Someone had to go to the FIS officials with our concerns.

"I would do it myself," Barbara Merlin, an Italian, said to me, "but this is my home country. So I'm asking you to do it for us."

We took a quick vote with a show of hands. The decision was made: "Picabo speaks for us."

That vote meant more to me than any gold medal. Those women in that room trusted and respected me, and I didn't want to let them down. Three years earlier, in Norway, I had not stood with the others when they threatened to boycott. This time I would lead the charge. I believed in our position, and I wasn't worried about how it would affect my image in Europe. The papers could write whatever they wanted about me; I didn't care. I couldn't read Italian or German anyway.

Besides, standing up to the guys was my specialty.

Ernst wasn't thrilled about what I was about to do, but he respected my willingness to stand up for the other girls. Later he brought me to a seed meeting at the hotel, where World Cup officials and team coaches decide on the next day's starting positions. Before the meeting Ernst said, "Picabo has something to say."

I didn't mince words. "Sestriere has done a lousy job of preparing and managing that course," I said. "And I'm here on behalf of the whole women's World Cup to tell you that you'd better get it done and get it done tomorrow, or else we're sitting down, just like the men have done two or three times. Well guess what, girls have brains, too. We know what feels dangerous, and this is it. We're not going to ski it, and we're not going to let you push us out there."

Kurt Hoch, the director of the women's World Cup, and Jan Tischhauser, an FIS race official, looked almost relieved. They knew the course was borderline, and the threat of a boycott took some of the weight off them.

"We agree that safety is our first priority," Kurt said. "We'll do our best to get a safe race off tomorrow. Thanks for your time and your concern." I left the room to report to the others.

Saturday, January 27, was race day. The officials scheduled the morning for training followed by the race that afternoon. As usual, my coaches were stationed at various spots on the course. The dangerous gate was placed above a jump near the top of the course, and that's where Marjan stood. I was wearing Number 12. Renate Goetschl was Number 11. She went around that gate, flew off the jump, landed on her butt, and sprained both her knees. I didn't know that at the time, and I pushed out the gate. Marjan turned to Kurt Hoch and said, "Flag her." I came around a corner to find Kurt standing in the course, flagging me to stop. I slowed down and skied up to him and started giving him a piece of my mind about the course.

Our conversation was aired on the big TV screen at the bottom of the course. Miriam Vogt of the German team was watching the screen and thought I was telling Kurt to call off the race. Miriam became furious because she was winning the training run. She got on the chairlift to come up and see what was going on.

Meanwhile, the rest of the field had skied down to me. The officials had walked off to discuss whether or not to cancel the race, and the other girls kept urging me to go over and tell them we were pulling out. "No, calm down," I replied. "It's better for them to make the decision. Let's see what happens. If they ask us to go, then let's make our move, and not until then."

The next thing I knew Miriam was in my face telling me in heavily accented English that I didn't speak for everyone, especially the Germans.

I looked at her and replied, "If you had come to our meeting last night, you'd know that I do speak for everybody. We're not going to risk our lives so you can qualify for the World Championships. Sorry."

That's when Barbara Merlin stepped in and said something that translated roughly into, "Actually, Miriam, she does speak for all of us because we asked her to. She just got flagged. So get your fucking facts straight before you get in her face again."

Practice was suspended and the race was canceled, but not because I demanded it. Officials didn't have time to reposition the dangerous gate, inspect it, have a training run, and race all in one day. Time had run out. The press, on the other hand, made it sound as if I'd demanded the cancellation, and the Germans called it a conspiracy to prevent Katja Seizinger and her teammate, Martina Ertl, from winning the overall title. "She can speak for us on our behalf if she consults us before," Katja told a reporter for the *Deutsche Presse-Agentur*. "But it is not as if she speaks for us without asking our opinion."

For once I was the diplomatic one. "Friendships have their ups and downs," I told the same reporter. "Katja deserves to win the overall World Cup. I love watching her ski."

Katja stormed into the next event in Val d'Isère, France, as if hell-bent on exacting revenge for the entire German nation. There were three races, two downhills and a Super G, and she swept all three. I was leading in the first downhill until I dragged my hand in the snow on a big, roundhouse turn and squandered valuable milliseconds. Katja actually showed her glee at beating me, a first for her, and I was so furious I refused to smile during the medal ceremony that evening. I was mad about a lot of things. Mad that I'd dragged my hand. Mad that Katja had won. Mad that the team wasn't doing better. Herwig and Ernst considered this unprofessional behavior, and afterward they sat me down.

"You are an American, and you represent America when you're on a podium."

"I don't care. I got second. I'm not happy. I can't smile."

"You'd better find a way."

"Look, man, I'm the only skier anywhere near that podium representing this country, and you have the nerve to give me shit about how I behave up there? You should just be happy that I'm there!"

I couldn't believe I was getting reprimanded for showing my emotions. I was mad for the rest of the week. I went into the Worlds with a head full of steam, my tiger roaring, burning bright.

At that time, no American had ever won the downhill at the World Alpine Ski Championships. I intended to be the first. I put in a call to John Blackman, the football coach back at Wood River High in Hailey. He was also the art teacher. I'd gotten tired of having a boring helmet, so a couple years earlier I'd hired John to airbrush pictures on my helmets. The first explained my name. John painted the Idaho mountains and my name across the front, along with the words "shining waters." The second had ram horns symbolizing my astrological sign, Aries, ram power. I'd been skiing in that one all season. But I wanted something special for the biggest event of the year.

"John," I said, "I'm going to the World Championships, and I'm going to win. I need a helmet that befits the occasion." I told him to surprise me.

The whole family met me in Sierra Nevada, Spain, for the ten-day event. Baba brought his girlfriend, Lauren Feinman, an artist he'd known since high school, and my boyfriend, Joey, came, too. It was like a family reunion. "We have something for you," Mom said, and she handed me a box. I opened it and gasped, "It's beautiful!" I pulled out my new helmet. John had painted it like a globe, complete with all the continents and oceans and the Arctic Circle on the top.

The Veleta course at Sierra Nevada was right up my alley: relatively flat with very few turns and a huge jump called Geronimo. It was a glider's paradise. I won the first downhill training run on a fog-shortened course and took the bronze in the opening race, the Super G (I wore the ram power helmet for that one). I shocked everybody, including myself, because it was only my second top-three finish in a World Cup Super G. I'd never been so happy to stand on the third step. The next day, Valentine's Day, Baba asked Lauren to marry him, and Nike Sports Management finalized a deal with Spyder Skiwear for my own line of ski clothes. The Street family was on a roll.

The combined downhill was held on the morning of February 16. The downhill would be running at the same time two days later, and my coaches and I decided to use the combined downhill as a training run for the regular downhill because it would give Cookie a better idea of the snow conditions. I hadn't fallen all season—on a racecourse at least. That was another streak that was about to come to an end.

It had snowed heavily for two days, particularly the night before the race. By the morning of the combined downhill there were two feet of fresh snow over a layer of ice. To get to the top of the course, I had to take a gondola, followed by a chairlift and then a T-bar. It was 8:00 A.M. and the resort was practically deserted. I was in race mode, my training skis on my feet, my race skis on one shoulder, and my backpack on the other. I was skiing down to the T-bar on a nice groomed path of snow when the grooming stopped and my left ski hit a bank of fresh powder. I caught an edge, and my ski darted out from underneath me. I felt my left hamstring muscle go *twang* like a broken guitar string. I came down on my elbows and smashed my face on the rock-hard surface beneath the snow, knocking myself out cold.

I don't know how long I was out. I woke up, and there was no one around. I lay there blinking, thinking, *Oh, shit. What happened?*

I sat up and shook my head and realized the race skis I'd been carrying were missing. I panicked. I got back in my training skis, grabbed my backpack, and rode up the T-bar, checking my face and head and lips, which were swollen and bleeding. I got to the start, completely traumatized. Gnarly and Cookie were there, and Cookie said, "Where are your skis?"

I burst into tears. "I just packed it in, and I don't know where they are. I think someone stole them, or they're lost." Meanwhile Gnarly was peering into my eyes to see if my pupils were dilated. "What town are we in?" he asked.

"Spain."

Then Gnarly got into his skis and made a beeline for the T-bar to look for my skis. The course inspection was starting, and I had to go. I did my best to keep my shit together, but my eyes were bugging out, my body was stiffening, and my hamstring was throbbing. The team's physiotherapist, Stephanie Siry, put a heat pack on my muscle to keep it warm. Thank God Gnarly showed up with my skis before the race. He'd found them under eighteen inches of powder on the other side of the T-bar. Steph strapped my thigh down with an Ace bandage. The race started, and my leg hurt so badly I cried in the start.

I won that race, but by the afternoon word had gotten out that I'd been injured. My parents were staying in a hotel at the foot of the mountain, about a quarter mile away. At the finish area I ran into Dad, who needed to get back to the hotel. If my opponents thought I was weak, they'd think they could beat me, and I couldn't have that.

"Come on, Dad. I'll give you a piggyback."

"No, man, what about your leg?"

"My leg's fine. Get on."

He hopped on and I skied him down to his hotel, in agony but refusing to show it.

Stephanie spent the next two nights working on my hamstring, so I could ski the downhill: massage, ibuprofen, heat, and ice. Outside I seemed strong. Inside I was in a lot of pain and full of self-doubt. I liked winning every day, and I hadn't been able to re-create that magic. The night before the race, Mom and I had a heart-to-heart.

"Mom, this season seems like such a failure compared to last year," I said. "I was unbeatable. What happened?"

"You're looking at the glass half empty, Peeky," she said. "A bad year for you is an excellent year for anyone else."

She was right. On race day I woke to blue skies and perfect snow. I put on my globe helmet. I had the world on my shoulders and my family in the finish arena, and I was going to put on a show, sore hamstring be damned.

I became the United States's first world downhill champion that day. My jumps could have been better, but otherwise I skied a nearly perfect race. I gained a lot of time in the turns and glided well on the flat, rolling sections. My leg was wrapped, and I didn't even think about it except to wonder whether people could see the bandage on TV. Katja (who had learned the truth about Sestriere and apologized) was second. Everybody stepped up that day; Hilary was third and Megan was fifth. It was the best single-race showing for American skiers in World Alpine Ski Championship history. I posed for photographs with one foot on my helmet. I was on top of the world.

WITH TWO WINS, TWO SECONDS, AND A THIRD, I WAS A NEAR LOCK FOR A second straight World Cup downhill title. I needed one more win, and I practically had to go to the North Pole to get it.

On a map Norway's western coastline looks ragged and frayed, as if a dog had chewed on it. Somewhere along that coast lies Narvik, a small industrial port city. It was as if the FIS had said, "Let's find the most remote, inconvenient place we can and try to hold a race there." The team slept on a ship, and I was worried about getting seasick.

A snowstorm blew in the morning of the race. That course was a sheer ice wall; you practically needed crampons to get down it. The race was held in a two-run sprint format, which made it even worse. I made no secret of my dislike for the course. I thought it was dangerous, a battle for survival all the way down. I wanted the race canceled. The organizers came close, but decided to proceed at the last minute. I had twenty minutes to pull myself together and go.

I stood in the start house, adjusting my goggles. Suddenly, they snapped and broke. Cookie rushed to get another pair from my gear bag, and I pulled them on and went. They didn't fit right, and at the first turn I put my pole under my arm and fixed my goggles. I finished behind Russia's Warwara Zelenskaja by eight-tenths of a second. I beat her on the next run for the fastest combined time and clinched my second consecutive World Cup downhill title. One of the things I'm most proud of was my ability to get my shit together and win my third race of the season. Little did I know it would be my last World Cup win.

The World Cup finals were in Lillehammer. I was pooped and just couldn't pull another Bormio-style surprise out of the hat. I finished sixteenth. Katja finished second. She won the overall title and I placed sixth, not bad for someone who didn't run a technical race all year. But I had won the downhill title, and as I hefted that crystal globe, I felt proud, yet not as deserving as the year before when I'd been so dominant.

I flew from Oslo to Zurich, made a deposit to my Swiss bank account, and headed home.

I TURNED TWENTY-FIVE THAT APRIL, AND BY FATHER'S DAY JOEY AND I had broken up. It was hard at first, but it made sense. Joey was an old-fashioned kind of guy who believed that the man brings home the bacon and gets to make the rules. I was raised the same way; in my household, money equaled power. I watched Mom put up with a lot more than she should have simply because Dad earned more. I had started to pride myself on the fact that I didn't need a man to take care of me financially, but it takes a boyfriend with a resilient ego to handle that. It hurt Joey's pride that I paid for everything: the trip to the Worlds, the toys, the vacations to Maui and Cabo San Lucas. Joey felt powerless, which as a Taurus wasn't his natural inclination. He ended up marrying his high school sweetheart.

I was beginning to face the same issues that confront any single, successful, headstrong career woman; my career just happened to be risking my neck. I had a healthy bank account, my own house, and a signature sneaker in the works, but that didn't guarantee success in the romance department. I've always gravitated toward "normal" guys because I can relate to them—eccentric guys demand too much energy—but normal guys have a hard time keeping up with my jet-set lifestyle. A relationship has to be on my terms, or I don't need it.

The breakup with Joey wasn't the only ordeal that June. My feet had been giving me trouble since St. Anton. All those years of wearing ski boots had splayed my little toes out and caused bone spurs to grow. In June I flew to Houston, where Dr. Donald E. Baxter, a world-renowned foot and ankle surgeon, fixed my feet. He cut the fifth metatarsal away from each foot, shaved off the bone spurs, then pinned my little toes into their new positions. For two weeks I had to sit around with my feet in the air. Then I made some down booties, which felt like sleeping bags on my feet, and walked on my heels everywhere I went for about three weeks. I had crutches if I needed them, but I used them only when I had to get around quickly. I wasn't crazy about the crutches. They made me feel like a cripple.

My shoe was coming along. I missed the spring and early summer conditioning camps, so I had lots of time to devote to its completion.

Mom and I started kicking around names for the shoe. We wanted it to resonate with Triumph, and we wrote a long list of all my nicknames from my childhood: Peek, Peeky, Boo. Squeak, Squeakers, Squeakerbuns.

The Air Squeakerbuns. Hmm.

Skeekers, Skeekaboo, Skeek.

The Air Skeek. Ski and Peek. It made perfect sense. Tinker and his staff and the Nike marketing folks agreed. It was memorable—just like me.

The shoe was due to hit stores at the end of the year, and Nike wanted to create a new ad campaign to go with it. I had a few meetings with Nike's ad agency, Wieden & Kennedy. I told them I really wanted to reach the younger generation, and they came up with Sister Slope, a cartoon superhero version of myself. Sister Slope battled an evil villain called the Overlord who embodied all the bad karma in the world. Sister Slope's ski poles turned into deadly lasers, and she blew the Overlord away and restored the proper karmic balance to the universe. She would star in her own commercial and maybe even a comic book. You know you've made it when you become a cartoon.

Sister Slope was a babe. She had waist-length red hair, a tight purple suit, and long, voluptuous thighs. I was all woman. That's the way I wanted her. Her creator was a tall, African-American guy with long dreadlocks named Jimmy Smith. Jimmy would show me a sketch and I'd say, "I want her to have big boobies." And he'd laugh and say, "You got 'em! Cool!"

The Air Skeek was due to debut in late 1996. I saw a finished version for the first time in the summer of 1996. It was just what I'd wanted, a hardcore outdoor training shoe with lots of lateral support for side-to-side movements and a plastic arch support so that if you stepped on a log while trail running it wouldn't hurt. The tread was black rubber with an off-road dirt bike type pattern. The finishing touch: a black squiggle above the heel, like a tiny downhill course.

Sue and Tinker and the marketing folks gathered in a conference room in the Nolan Ryan building. Everyone was milling around and talking. I saw the box on the table, and when I thought no one was looking, I took off the lid, stuck my nose in the box, and took a deep whiff.

The new-sneaker smell was euphoric and resonant of the past. So many memories floated to the surface, all the times I'd spent in sneakers. It was the smell of ripping down the quarry road on a blistering summer day and of tackle ball on Billy and Jamie's lawn. It was the smell of cops and robbers in the old hotel and of pickle on East Fork Road. It was the smell of Triumph, the place I took with me wherever I went.

I looked up and everybody in the room was staring at me as if I were nuts.

"I'll be really honest," I told the room. "I can probably count the number of new sneakers that I've had in my whole life on my hands and toes. I was just smelling the newness of them. It's an old habit."

IN 1996, I MOVED UP TO YET ANOTHER TAX BRACKET. THE ENDORSEMENT deals were stacking up. That summer Rossignol, my ski sponsor, brought me to the factory in Burlington, Vermont. They gave me a video camera and told me I was their star athlete and how glad they were to have me on their skis. They said they planned to manufacture new skis with my name on them. We'd call them the Peak.

Rolex, the luxury watchmaker, came on board, and in July I drove to Mount Hood to do a photo shoot for a new ad. A bunch of kids approached me wanting my autograph, and I was signing when a slim blond woman in a wheelchair rolled up to me. "Hey, Peek." It was Muffy Davis.

I'd only seen Muffy once since her accident in 1989. It was the summer of 1994, after I won my silver at Lillehammer. I was still with Mike at the time, and I had come to pick him up at a gym in Sun Valley when he came out and told me Muffy was working out inside. I went in to say hi. I'd never seen her in a wheelchair, and to be honest it made me feel guiltier than ever. We hugged and she congratulated me on my medal. We made some awkward small talk; she told me she was going into her last year of pre-med studies at Stanford and was considering making a comeback as a disabled skier. She could go downhill by sitting in a mono ski, a pod-shaped contraption with a ski on the bottom. But what could I say? That I was the new star of American skiing? She already knew that, and it made me feel even worse. It was a brief, unsatisfying conversation, and we parted with so many things left unsaid.

Two years later, she was at Hood training with the U.S. Disabled Ski Team, trying to get a spot. When she wheeled up to me to say hello, I decided not to let another opportunity pass by. "What are you doing for dinner later in the week?" I asked. "Come to my place in Portland."

She came over two days later with a couple teammates, Matt Perkins and Paul Martin. Both of them were missing all or part of one leg. I had four steps leading to my front door, and I watched as they lifted Muffy's wheelchair over the obstacle. I showed them around the house, still limping a bit because of my feet, and then we went out back for a barbecue on the deck.

Muffy was nervous, and so was I. We had a lot of catching up to do. As we ate she explained that she had decided against going to medical school so she could try to ski again. Her goal was to compete in the Winter Paralympics, a competition for disabled athletes held two weeks after the Olympic Games. "After watching you in Lillehammer, I told my mom I had some unfinished business," she said. "So I decided not to go to medical school and to take up skiing instead."

She paused for a few moments and went on. "You know, it was great watching you win that medal. But to be honest with you, it was the hardest day of my life since I broke my back."

I closed my eyes to stop the tears from welling. "I knew it," I half whispered.

"You were doing what we'd always said we'd do, while there I was, sitting in California, so far away from my goal," she said. "I thought to myself, 'Muffy, there's a way you can go to the Olympics; it's just not the way you always envisioned you would.' I got the old dream back, Peek. I want to go and do what you've done."

That was a healing visit for both of us. As we hugged good-bye, I knew I didn't have to feel bad about what had happened to Muffy, and she knew she didn't have to resent my success.

That summer, my agents at Nike Sports Management were negotiating an endorsement deal with the nation's most popular brand of lip balm. You know those old "Suzy Chapstick" commercials with freestyle skier Suzy Chaffee? I would be the next generation. The Chapstick folks wanted to do a commercial with me, but they needed snow, and by the time I left for the ski team's annual summer ski camp they were still debating the locations for the shoot.

The ski camp was held in Australia that summer. It took two days to fly there. The camp wasn't very successful. I'd been unable to work out because of my feet, and I felt overweight and out of shape, and my feet still hurt when I skied. I was hoping to know where the shoot was happening before I left Australia so I could fly straight there. It didn't happen. I flew home to Portland, and two days later the word came down: they decided to shoot the commercial in New Zealand, which, as you probably know, is about a two-hour flight from Australia.

Doing the commercial would mean another exhausting trip, and by the time I got home I'd have very little time before the dry-land camp in Park City. All I wanted to do was stay home to recharge my batteries. But I agreed to do it. If something happened to me that season, if my feet weren't right or I got injured, I'd have that much more money to fall back on.

I WENT INTO THE 1996–97 WORLD CUP SEASON UNDER MORE PRESSURE than usual. For the first time, there was pressure on me to win in the marketplace. "Picabo Street" was now a brand, a name on a sneaker and a line of skiwear. Winning meant visibility, visibility meant sales, and sales made my sponsors happy—which was fine; I could handle it. I think I put more pressure on myself than anything. I had made no secret of my intentions to win a third straight World Cup downhill title. The 1998 Winter Olympics in Nagano, Japan, were only two years away, and I planned to solidify my status as the gold-medal favorite in the downhill.

The World Cup opened in Lake Louise in late November, and everybody was buzzing about a three-peat. I'd won Lake Louise two years in a row, but given my physical problems, I was hoping for a top-five finish. My feet weren't quite 100 percent. In September I'd started working out in Portland with a new trainer named Matt James. We'd only had a month together, so I'd have to ski myself into shape as usual. When I ended up fourth, I was happy with that. It showed I could contend, and there was a lot of season left—or so I thought.

The next race was in Vail. Mountains can be like people: no matter how hard you try, you can't get along. That's how I felt about Vail. That mountain just didn't like me. And on December 4, 1996, it delivered a karmic smack down of major proportions.

It happened during the first training run. I was a half second faster than the rest of the field as I approached Pepi's Face, the steep final drop into the finish, and the same place I'd filmed the Nike commercial a year earlier. I wanted to ski a tighter, straighter line above the lip than ever before. I was leaving myself little room for error, but I thought I could pull it off. I hit the lip of the headwall and launched.

I was in midair when I realized I wasn't going to make it. My weight fell too far back and I lost my bearings. This crash would claim a knee; it was just a matter of which one, depending on which way I fell. Left or right? I decided to sacrifice the left. It had been injured once already, after all. I landed hard on my left ski and fell backward, my left leg twisting under me. I heard the telltale pop of my ACL. I slid for about twenty yards on my back into a safety net. I lay there for a moment, stunned, one pole and a ski snagged in the fence's orange webbing.

I had fallen in full view of the finish corral, and Meisi was the first to reach me. "Oh, Peek, this is terrible," she said, cradling me in her arms. I was furious. I pounded my fist on the snow and shouted, "Fuck! This isn't what I ordered up! I wanted another downhill title, not a season on crutches!"

Ten minutes later, the medics were loading me onto a toboggan and skiing me down. I was out for the season. I knew it; the Euros knew it. When I got to the bottom, Hilary bent down and said to me, "I'll get 'em for both of us this year." I pulled the blanket over my face so no one could see me cry.

It so happened that Dr. Richard Steadman, the orthopedic surgeon who had fixed my knee in 1989, had moved his practice from Tahoe to Vail four years earlier. He had gone into a partnership with a shoulder specialist named Richard Hawkins, and the Steadman Hawkins Clinic was located on the third floor of the Vail Valley Medical Center, within walking distance of the downhill course.

An MRI confirmed what we all suspected. My knee joint was a junkyard, a tangled mess of torn ligaments and misplaced cartilage. My anterior cruciate and medial collateral ligaments (MCL) were completely detached, and other ligaments were torn as well, though less severely. The bottom of the femur where it meets the tibia was bruised. I had also ruptured my posterior capsule, the sheath of fluid that surrounds the knee joint, and my knee had swollen to the size of a small melon.

"The ACL held together for eight years, and did a good job for you," Richard said. "We'll go in there and tighten it back up and make it better than new."

Richard would have to rebuild my knee like an engine. He'd reconstruct my ACL by grafting on a piece of the patella tendon, then drill holes into the tibia and the femur, insert the ligament, and fix it into place with screws. My MCL was torn from the tibia, and he would have to stitch it back into place.

Sue Levin got the news by accident. She was in New York City negotiating a sponsorship deal with the fledgling Women's National Basketball Association. On the morning of December 5 she opened her hotel room door and looked down. A free copy of USA Today lay on the carpet, and on the front page was a picture of me, holding my knee and grimacing while Meisi comforted me. Sue remembers feeling worried about me. She also remembers thinking, *There goes everything we've been working on this year.*

The Sister Slope commercial never aired. The entire campaign was built around my kicking butt on the World Cup, and my cartoon alter ego couldn't be active if I wasn't. Sister Slope may have been a superhero, but she couldn't survive the realities of the marketplace.

I was all too aware of what my injury could cost me. "I screwed up," I told Herwig in the hospital. "I should have known."

I called my parents, crying. Dad asked me if I was okay. I said no.

"Oh, no," he said, "are you at Steadman's?" I said yes.

"What do you want us to do?"

"Just come. Please."

My parents dropped everything and flew to my side. They booked an adjoining hotel room to mine, and when they walked into my room, I was sitting with a bunch of my World Cup buddies. It looked like the Alpine equivalent of a United Nations summit. Their concern moved me to tears.

Steadman had to wait until the swelling went down before operating. I couldn't put any weight on my knee, so I wore a knee brace and crutched around Vail for a week, watching the World Cup races, being consoled by my friends, and moping in my hotel room.

One day the phone rang. It was Muffy Davis. She was in Vail for a ski camp and had heard about my accident. "Would you like some company?" she asked. It was good to hear from her. I told her to come around noon the next day; I had nothing scheduled.

When Muffy rolled into my room, I was lying on my bed, my knee elevated and iced, feeling sorry for myself. I do believe that my lower lip was literally sticking out. "Days of Our Lives" was on TV. Muffy said she'd gotten into watching the soap when she was in the hospital after breaking her back, so we sat and watched it together.

During a commercial I started bemoaning my bad karma.

"Peek, you're one of the strongest people I know," Muffy said. "If anyone can come back from this, it's you. It's only your knee. You've got great doctors, and it's going to heal and be as strong as ever, if not stronger."

I looked over at Muffy. She had suffered an injury that would never heal, and yet she refused to wallow in self-pity. So what was I crying about? Muffy was the strong one in the room, the superhero, as much a Nike girl as I was.

Muffy stayed until "Days" was over. Before she left, she told me she had a race in Breckenridge, Colorado, the following week and had nothing to wear. "You wouldn't happen to have an extra downhill suit laying around, would you?" she asked.

One week later Muffy competed in one of my U.S. Ski Team downhill suits. She went on to not only make the U.S. Disabled Ski Team; she became a champion. She won a bronze in the slalom at the 1998 Winter Paralympics, took the World Cup Super G title in 1999, and took the gold in the GS at the 2000 World Disabled Ski Championships.

Muffy says I inspired her to ski again, but I disagree. Muffy found that power within herself. She inspired me.

9

LOVE AND REHAB

WITHIN HOURS AFTER CRASHING ON PEPI'S FACE IN VAIL, I HAD A MISsion: to win a gold medal at the 1998 Winter Olympics in Japan. My knee had been badly hurt, but when Dr. Richard Steadman told me, in December 1996, that it could take up to two years to fully heal, I resolved to cut that estimate in half. The Olympics were fourteen months away. Time was a luxury I didn't have.

"How long until I can ski again?" I asked Richard.

"Six months," he answered. "At least."

I let the number sink in—six months away from what I loved, and much longer before I was up to speed. I would need determination and patience. I had a lot of the first, little of the second. I had to remind myself that this injury was a speed bump on the way to my dream. All I had to do was downshift, slowly drive over it, and keep going, hopefully better than ever.

Ski racing is like football—you keep beating up on yourself until your body cries foul. This was my body's way of telling me to slow down, to stop asking so much of it, to give it a rest—whether I liked it or not.

I had my surgery on December 11. A week later, after I arrived home in Portland, the first thing I did was draw the Olympic rings on a piece of paper and tape them to my bathroom mirror, just as I'd done when I was fifteen. Those rings were the first thing I saw in the morning and the last thing I saw at night, a reminder that my dream was stronger than ever.

I faced months of grueling physical therapy and more months of training to get back into shape. I knew I couldn't do it alone. I picked up the phone and called my trainer, Matt James, the man who would change the way I looked at my body.

I had met Matt four months earlier, in September 1996. I called the people in Nike's training department to see if they knew anyone who could spot me in the weight room. They recommended Matt, a local trainer who worked for Nike as a performance enhancement specialist. He was a former football player for Portland State who now ran camps and clinics for Nike and trained some of Nike's top athletes.

I hadn't been able to work out because of my foot surgery and was feeling really out of shape. Actually, I was feeling a lot of things at the time. I was feeling my age. At twenty-five I knew I couldn't keep asking this much of my body without taking better care of it. I wanted to have children someday, and I was even worrying if I was jeopardizing my ability to do that safely. And I wasn't happy with how my body looked. I wanted to get leaner, but without compromising my strength.

In my sport, bigger is better. The heavier you are, the faster you go. It's simple physics: mass times velocity equals momentum. I find I'm faster when I'm bulkier; in fact, one reason I was so dominant in 1995 is that I'd been doing a lot of weight training and had built a lot of muscle. I went into that season a dozen pounds heavier than usual, 176 versus my usual 164 pounds on my 5'7" frame. The word used most often to describe me is "solid." *Time* magazine called me a "human cannonball." A few years ago *Sports Illustrated for Kids* asked me, "If you built a snowman to resemble yourself, what would it look like?" I answered, "It would be powerful looking and packed as solid as a tree trunk—no arms or legs!" Richard called me "Miss Big Bones." During my knee surgery he had to drill a hole in the base of my femur to reattach the ACL, and my bones were so dense he had to change drill bits twice to get the job done.

I can't deny that my size attracts attention. Once in a while someone will come up to me and literally ask if he or she can touch me, as if I were some kind of flesh-and-bone monolith that has to be felt to be believed. People have said to my boyfriends, "Yo, man, is it cool, can I *touch* her?" I tell them, "Define *touch*. You want to shake my hand or squeeze my bicep or flex my thigh or what? What kind of 'touch' are you talking about?" I have to draw the line somewhere.

People assume that because women athletes are so physically gifted that we're somehow immune to the insecurities that plague many women: that we don't wish we were thinner or had smaller butts or larger breasts. For many years I'd been conscious that I didn't possess an ideal womanly shape, though it didn't bother me at first. In junior high I'd look at fashion magazines with Terri and Julie and scoff at the skinny models and the funny-looking clothes. "Ha!" I'd say out loud. "I'd like to see them try to do what I do with those legs!" I didn't want to wear those clothes, and I knew I would definitely never look like those models. But at that time I didn't really care. They could wear a size four, but I could jump and leap and fly.

I remember what it's like to be little. As a kid I was strong and tough, a real fireplug. I loved my body for the same reason I loved new sneakers: for what it could do. My body was my vehicle, and it took me everywhere.

In high school my body changed. Some Street-family largeness gene kicked in, and I started lifting weights. I became bigger, more muscular. My legs were particularly impressive, substantial and hard as quarry rock. I'd walk down halls and hear kids whisper "thunder thighs" and try to contain my anger. *Bottle it and use it on the course*, I told myself. *Bottle it and use it.*

My sole defense for being a big girl was my success as a skier, but my confidence on the hill didn't translate to my body image. I could slay the most dangerous downhill course, but I wouldn't wear a tank top because I felt my arms and shoulders were too big. I started looking at those skinny models with a new eye, thinking, *That's what guys are going to want, and I don't look like that. How am I going to pull this off?*

That's why appearing in *Vogue* in 1995 was such a big deal for me. When Sue Levin told me the magazine wanted to do a story on me I felt flattered, as if I'd jumped some sort of cultural hurdle. What an irony: I was going to be in the very magazine I used to mock. A big girl in a skinny girl's magazine.

It was my first high-fashion shoot, and I didn't care for it all that much. A huge crew—photo, art, hair and makeup, fashion—came from New York to Mount Hood in mid-July. The photographer had short gray hair, wire glasses, and a pinky ring. The fashion editors floundered around in the snow, and when the wind blew or a cloud crossed the sun, they shivered and complained about the cold. *Welcome to my world*, I thought.

They changed my outfit several times, and the photographer took a million pictures. In the one that was printed I'm holding a deep tuck. My hair is slicked back into a chignon, and I'm wearing big black glasses, tons of mascara, and a skintight white cat suit. Please. You have to weigh ninety pounds to look good in a skintight white cat suit. Sue Levin's point was that a woman didn't have to be scrawny to be beautiful; you just had to be fit, but I didn't quite see it that way.

"I look fat," I told Mom.

"Oh baloney," she scoffed, the way a good mom should. "You look beautiful."

Mom and Sue saw a big, strong, beautiful woman, but all I could see was the roll of fat around my midriff. The art department at *Vogue* could have helped me out with that. They could have airbrushed the fat away, the way they would a mole off a model's face.

Unfortunately, ski racing is no way to lose weight. Between all the rich food and all the waiting around, Americans tend to gain weight in Europe. (The Europeans, for some reason, tend to lose weight.) Skiing is also anaerobic. Getting your heart rate up for ninety seconds isn't long enough to burn much fat. Then you sit around in the lodge, trying not to eat pastries and french fries. What can I say? I like to eat.

Sometimes I get fed up with myself and start watching my diet. I'm no different from any woman: I finally get sick of having an extra roll around my midriff and I say to myself, *That's it. I'm done eating anything that's going to make me fat. Period.*

That's how I was feeling the first time I worked out with Matt James: fed up.

We met one September afternoon at the Bo Jackson Fitness Center, a gleaming temple to physical fitness on the Nike campus with every machine, fitness contraption, and sports facility imaginable. Matt was upbeat and so energetic that he walked on his toes. From the moment we met I felt as if he understood me. I started off by warming up on the stationary bike, followed by some stretches. Matt's specialty is speed, agility, and quickness—in other words, aerobic activities—all things I needed to work on.

And it showed. We started doing some drills, and two minutes into them I was out of breath. Then a strange thing happened: I broke down and started crying—full-out, uncontrollable bawling. All the feelings I'd been struggling with for so long simply bubbled over the top.

Matt led me to the bleachers and sat me down and asked me what was wrong. I confessed everything. I told him how I'd always hated working out. I told him I hadn't been taking care of my body, and here I was twenty-five and I still didn't have the gold medal, and the Olympics were a year and a half away. I told him how much I hated running and how tired I was of having to motivate myself. I told him how I hadn't trained a lick all summer and now I was having to play catch-up three months before the season started. I told him I was tired of being chubby, yet afraid of compromising my strength.

I was crying out of relief more than anything. I knew I'd finally found someone who was capable of taking me to the next level, which I apparently couldn't reach myself. Not only that, he wasn't a part of the U.S. Ski Team, so I didn't have all that baggage to worry about either. I knew Matt wouldn't judge me or think I was lazy. He knew me only as the person he was seeing at that very moment, and we'd move forward from there. He represented a fresh start to my physical fitness life.

Matt just sat there and listened. Finally I wiped my eyes and said, "Can you help me with any of that?"

"I'd be honored to."

Matty and I didn't have a lot of time together at first. He worked me out for about a month, and then I had to go ski. On December 4 I blew out my knee, and when I got home to Portland, I gave Matty a call. The Olympics were now a little over a year away, and I couldn't even put any weight on my left leg, let alone ski a downhill course. I needed him more than ever.

Matty knew how impatient I could be, so he devised a clever plan. I couldn't work my legs very hard until I'd completed six weeks of physical therapy, but as far as he was concerned, it was open season for my upper body. "Yes, we're inhibited in our training, but that's all we are," he told me. "There's 15 percent of your body we can't hammer on, but that leaves 85 percent of your body that we can work full out. That means we're not behind; we're ahead."

Matty called this "prehab." While my leg was healing, we'd strengthen the rest of me. Not only would this help prevent injuries down the road, but also I'd feel as if I was doing something besides waiting for my knee to heal.

Matt and I became joined at the hip. Every morning he accompanied me to my physical therapy sessions. I used two therapists, Rock Reid and Cheryl Kosta, though I finally settled with Cheryl because her office, at North Lake Physical Therapy in Lake Oswego, was more convenient. While Rock and Cheryl expertly moved and manipulated my left leg, Matt watched and learned the exercises. Then twice a day, at home or at the gym, we'd repeat them—tedious, often painful exercises designed to strengthen the muscles around the knee and increase the joint's range of motion. I'd do basic things like lie on my side and lift my leg straight in the air, sit in a chair and pull my foot toward my butt one hundred times, or lie flat on my back, put my socked foot on a wall, and try to slide my heel down the wall as far as I could. Every day I could slide it farther. Every repetition was one step closer to walking, to skiing, to winning.

It was disconcerting to watch my left leg waste away. My quadriceps softened and the skin sagged. "My quad is going!" I'd cry to Matty. And he'd just smile and tell me to stay positive and urge me to do another rep.

My injury forced Sue to scale back her marketing plans for the Air Skeek. My rehab would be the story. Matty and I would promote the shoe that spring by putting media types through the same workout I was doing. Instead of doing a commercial, Nike would run print ads in magazines of me in the gym and save its TV budget for the Olympics. A new version of the shoe was already on the drawing board, set to debut concurrently with my appearance in the Games. That only increased my determination to get to Nagano.

In the meantime, there was the billboard. Five days a week (Wednesdays and Sundays off) I'd drive to the Bo Jackson Fitness Center in Beaverton and pass a billboard with a huge picture of me racing down the mountain along with the slogan "There are no shortcuts." It was as if they'd put it up there just for me.

While we were babying my legs, Matt would exhaust every other body part possible. We worked the pushing muscles (chest, shoulders, and triceps) one day and the pulling muscles (back and biceps) another. Another day would be devoted to building core strength, the abs and lower back. We'd use weight machines, free weights, or some form of torture that Matt himself came up with. I'll use the towel curl as an example. I'd sit on a contraption called a preacher's chair, my triceps resting on the arm rests. Matt would wrap a towel nice and tight. I'd grab the middle of it, as if it were a bar, and Matt would grip each end. Then I'd curl it up while Matt pulled on the towel to resist my efforts. Once I got the towel up to eye level I'd lower it slowly with Matt applying more resistance from the other direction. We'd do three sets of ten to fifteen, depending on what I could take, and by the last few I'd be grunting my way through it, my eyes practically bulging with the effort. Sometimes my arms were so tired I couldn't crutch down the stairs, and Matt would have to carry me down on his back.

I hated the crutches. As my knee got stronger, I started using one, and then none, preferring to hop. I went from hopping to limping, limping to my usual lopsided gait. (My left leg is a half-inch shorter than the right.) After six weeks the crutches were history. I refused to wear a knee brace for support because I felt it made me look and feel weak.

I went to see Richard Steadman for my six-week checkup, and he said I was ready for weight-bearing exercises on my knee. Matt started very gradually, very gently. We worked out in the pool because there was no impact on my joints. I'd float on my back and make snow angels in the water or run in the deep end while wearing a special vest that helped me float in place. I spent up to ninety minutes a day walking on a treadmill (forward and backward) and pedaling on a stationary bike. I racked up so much mileage on that bike I started wishing there was such a thing as Frequent Pedaling Miles.

I learned the difference between good pain and bad pain. Good pain was the muscle soreness I felt after being pushed to my limits. Bad pain was the throbbing in my knee that signaled it was being overtaxed. It was a fine balance: work the knee hard enough to make it stronger but not so strong as to reinjure or inflame the muscles. One wrong move and my dream was on the ropes. If my knee flared up, we'd take it easy the next day, but we'd always do something.

There were good days and bad days, too. On the good days I'd feel strong and full of promise. On the bad days the slow crawl toward recovery left me deeply discouraged. I'd descend into dark funks, questioning my chances and myself. I wanted to be 100 percent again, and fast. I had all this pent-up energy and no outlet for it. I wanted to take a sledgehammer to an old car, smash the headlights, and demolish the windshield or take a BB gun and shoot out the windows of an old hotel.

I made a vow to myself: if I blew out a knee a third time, that was it. I was retiring.

When the storm clouds settled around my head, Mom came to the rescue. I had bought her a Steinway upright piano for her fiftieth birthday, and she'd play "The Star-Spangled Banner" while I belted out the words, determined to get the rhythm and the cadence perfect. Other times Mom would stage a "viewing." She kept my silver medal from Lillehammer in her office so she could show it to people, and on bad days she'd bring the medal out and put it on the dining room table where I could look at it and imagine it was gold. Once in a while she'd drape it around Duggan's neck and he'd trot out wearing that medal and a big, sloppy dog grin. I'd scratch his head and laugh. "Humor is the best healer," Mom would say.

NOTHING COULD DISTRACT ME FROM THE FACT THAT THE WORLD CUP was proceeding without me. The 1997 World Alpine Ski Championships were held in Sestriere, Italy, in mid-February. One year earlier I had been standing on top of the world. Now I wanted to be as far away from snow as possible, to try to forget where I wasn't. With Matty's blessing, I took a week off from training and went to Maui with Tiffany. There we met up with another friend, Jessica Williams-Kahae. I'd known Jess for a little over a year. Joey and I had gone to Maui on vacation, and I looked up my old boyfriend Steven Kahae, whom I'd met while rehabbing my knee in Maui in 1989. Jess was Steven's wife. She was a few years younger than I and was still in college, finishing up her teaching degree. She was originally from Reno and had been a ski racer herself. She couldn't believe that Steven had dated Picabo Street way back when. Jess had a round, pretty face and a feminine figure—the opposite of mine—with long, lean limbs and a narrow waist. Her best attribute was her sweet nature. We became instant buddies. My friendship with Jess outlasted my relationship with Joey.

When Tiff and I visited Jess in Maui in February 1997, the last thing I was looking for was romance. Then one night, the three of us went to a club in Lahaina. I locked eyes with a great-looking guy on the other side of the dance floor. *Wow, I thought; he's hot.* My next thought was, *No way, I can't go there. I don't have time.* We spent the rest of the night avoiding each other, as if the magnitude of our attraction was too much to face.

Later my friends and I went for a walk, and as we were heading back to our car, we saw the hot guy walking ahead of us. Tiff called out to him, and before we knew it, he'd agreed to go to Denny's with us. We introduced ourselves. "I'm J.J.," he said.

"I'm Picabo."

"Wow, cool name." He didn't seem to know who I was. I liked that.

J. J. Lasley turned out to be an ex–football player who'd just quit his job at an investment banking firm in San Francisco and was spending time in Maui with friends. I remember he ordered a chocolate-strawberry milkshake, which he'd later say symbolized us. I didn't talk about myself much, and as we were driving J.J. back to the house where he was staying, he said, "Your name sounds really familiar to me."

Jess looked over at him and said, "Haven't you ever heard of her?"

J.J. started to put it together (he was sobering up at that point), and he said, "Are you like an athlete or something?"

"Yup."

"An Olympic athlete?"

"Yup."

"Hey, you're that skier girl! My mom and I watched you on TV!"

J.J. asked for my phone number, and the next day he made me really happy by calling. He went to Hana for a couple days, and when he got back, he called me and we went to Moose McGillycuddy's, a restaurant and bar in Lahaina where Jess worked. J.J. didn't want to flirt or party or dance; he just wanted to talk. So we found a private corner and talked story and got to know each other.

J.J. was born in Detroit. His dad was African-American and his mom was white. When he was little, his mother took him and left the family and moved to Los Angeles. J.J. went to Stanford on a football scholarship, where he played wide receiver. He'd tried out for the pros but suffered a career-ending knee injury at a Vikings training camp. Bad knees weren't the only thing we had in common. We were both soul-searching, trying to figure out who we were away from our sports. Several of my Sun Valley teammates had ended up going to Stanford, so we knew a lot of the same people. He had one leg that was shorter than the other, just like me, and we even planned to be in Sun Valley at the same time that spring. J.J. was a snowboarder, but I didn't hold that against him. We took a liking to each other, and we knew we could hang out and have fun.

That's where our relationship stopped for the time being because I had to fly to Japan. As usual, the FIS was holding a World Cup downhill on the Olympic course a year before the Games, and Herwig wanted me to check it out. Even though I couldn't ski, I could see the course, absorb the environment, and take a mental picture of the place to carry around in my brain for a year. It was also my chance to congratulate Hilary, who had won the gold medal in the downhill at the Worlds. When we saw each other, I gave her a big hug and said, "I'm so happy for you. You deserved that win so much and I'm so glad that you got it. I'm just sorry I couldn't have been there to share it." I paused and added, "But I'm sure you probably enjoyed it just fine without me."

For a ski racer, watching a ski race and not being able to compete is like being a dieter forced to attend a chocolate convention. I caught up with old friends and watched the training races on the big screen in the finish arena. I took the gondola up to take a look at the top of the course, but it wasn't enough. One night at dinner I said to Gnarly, "I want to see the whole thing."

He nodded his head in agreement, not suspecting what was coming next.

"Do you think you could carry me down on your back?"

"Sure, no problem," he said without missing a bite. "Just let me put my stiffer boots on."

We got special permission to ski down the course after inspection on race day. I met Gnarly at the top; he had his good, strong ski boots on. He clicked into his skis, I hopped on his back, and away we went. He carried me down each section of the course, pointing out every terrain feature. I had a blast—it was like being a sightseer on one of those double-decker tour buses in London. Sometimes he'd let me off and he'd point out where the girls were running and the line they were taking. I got a good vibe off Mount Karamatsu. It made me feel comfortable, confident, and welcome.

On the way back from Japan I stopped in Maui for two days. I wanted to see J.J. again, and I had an appointment with Sapphire, an energy reader who lived up-country.

I am what you'd call a spiritual adventurer. Growing up in Triumph, I was curious about God, like a lot of kids. But my parents weren't big on organized religion, so in junior high I'd sneak off to church with a friend named Joy. I liked the singing part, but once I figured out what they were talking about, I lost interest. Hell sounded scary, and I wasn't interested in a message that came from fear, not joy. Maybe it was inevitable for someone who grew up in the unofficial UFO landing area for Blaine County, Idaho, but my beliefs evolved along a nonconformist path. I saw that good things happened and bad things happened, and that it all seemed to make sense in the long run, even the tragedies. So I figured there had to be a master plan, somebody up there steering, a higher power who decided which way the karmic seesaw would tilt. I believe in the power of astrological signs; I believe in the energy of the mountains and the land; I believe in reincarnation. Basically, I'm open to just about anything. Jess is, too, so when she suggested we visit Sapphire, I was all for it.

Jess met me at the airport with a couple sausage McMuffins and we drove inland. To test our spirituality, Sapphire had made the directions to her house intentionally vague to see if we could find our own way. "It's this road; turn down this one!" I told Jess suddenly. We drove along a rural road, all flowery and overgrown, came around a corner, and saw a woman in her mid-forties with sun-fried surfer hair sitting on the steps of a ramshackle bungalow, waiting for us.

I went first. Sapphire sat across from me, looking at my face, reading my energy field. Sometimes she'd close her eyes to see my spirits better. "Everybody has guides that are with us all the time," she said. "They're the ones who tap you on the shoulder and say, 'Hey, slow down, there's a cop around the corner.' And sure enough you come around the corner, and there's the cop."

My guides gave Sapphire an earful, especially about my previous lives. Sapphire said I had been a very wealthy English woman who played polo and was very generous with her money. I had been Amelia Earhart's best friend in one life and played some sort of strategic role in freeing the slaves in another. I had also been an East Indian woman with dark, shining eyes. Then she said she saw a dark man whom I'd known for seven life-times. Sometimes we were lovers, but usually we'd come together to accomplish some great mission and then split apart. This was our eighth lifetime together, our last chance to make love work. I knew she was talking about J.J.

"How'd you know that?" I blurted out. Sapphire just looked at me and said, "Oh, honey, it's all right here in front of me; I'm just trying to keep up."

Finally it was Jess's turn, but Sapphire had one last vision: "Oh, and your knees: keep riding your bike and swimming."

I SKI BETTER WHEN I'M NOT IN LOVE. LOVE IS DISTRACTING. YOU DON'T want to be in the start gate, missing your boyfriend back in the States, or thinking about that fight you had, or wondering what the hell he's up to while you're putting your life on the line. That's another reason I won so many races in 1995: not only was I twelve pounds heavier, I didn't have a boyfriend either. So it's a good thing I wasn't skiing when I met J.J. I fell so hard for him that I wouldn't have been able to win a Kindercup on Dollar Mountain.

When we first met, J.J. and I made a pact: no love. We were just hanging out. Neither one of us wanted to fall in love at that point in our lives. J.J. shared my spiritual beliefs, and when I told him about Sapphire's vision, we both got a little nervous.

The pact lasted about two weeks.

J.J. lived in San Francisco, but we saw each other as much as possible. He'd come to Portland and live at the house. My parents liked him, but he made them nervous, too. They could see how compatible we were, how self-confident J.J. made me feel. There was a fifth, very strong presence in our family, and that was tough for them and Baba, too. Dad thought we were going to get married, but I put his mind at ease. "No, we're not there at all. We're hanging. He's super supportive, and it's all good."

And for a long time, it was. We decided we were meant to be together, just as Sapphire had said. The timing was perfect—J.J. was between careers, and I was on a mission, so he poured all his ambitions and energies into me. It made him feel good to be supportive and empowering. On days when I couldn't get out of bed he'd say, "Get your ass up!" and get me moving. He and Matty hit it off—they had football in common, among other things—and J.J. would work out right alongside us.

For the first time in my life, the importance of physical conditioning really sank in. I was no longer a young pup who could stay out all night and race the next morning. I couldn't rely on my natural athleticism anymore. I had to work for it. I even changed my diet. Mom cleared the cupboards of potato chips and stocked the house with cottage cheese, fruit, and nonfat milk. I ate fewer M&M's, more fish.

My attitude toward my body changed as well. Despite all the ways I relied on it, I'd actually been neglecting it. I had come to think of my body as a high-performance machine, something to be fueled and trained and abused, rather than a gift to be nurtured and appreciated. Before the injury, my goal had been to be tough and invincible, and I'd lifted heavy weights for power and bulk. Matty, on the other hand, showed me how to sculpt my muscles. We focused on more repetitions with lighter weights, laboring over every muscle group. He helped me connect with the muscles deep within my body, all the little guys that were crying out to be noticed. Matt made me think about my body: which muscle groups I was using, how I could best strengthen them, how hard I could push myself. I was present at the creation of a whole new me.

By May I'd lost fifteen pounds. While no one would mistake me for Twiggy, my body was obviously changing shape. My muscles were leaner and more defined. I had to buy new jeans and a smaller belt. Matty didn't like to call it "losing weight." In fact, he didn't even want me to weigh in every day. "Muscle weighs more than fat, so you should judge by the way your clothes fit and by the way you look in the mirror," he said. When I looked in the mirror, I liked what I saw. I was falling in love with my body all over again.

J.J. did his part, too. When I'd fret about my size, he'd say, "Stop that, girl! You're not just running around the track worrying about some little head wind. You're going eighty, ninety miles an hour down a mountain. When you fall down and go boom, you need protection. You need some meat on that ass."

He talked me into buying my first tank top. "That's my girl!" he said after I put it on. He came up behind me, grabbed my shoulders, and gave them a big, healthy squeeze.

JOB ONE FOR ANY INJURED ATHLETE IS TO STAY BUSY, STAY IN THE PUBLIC eye. One minute you're a household name; one knee injury later you're what's-her-name. Nike Sports Management had been dissolved, and in early 1997 I switched to Gold Medal Management, a sports agency based in Boulder, Colorado, that specialized in Olympic athletes. Its star clients were Michael Johnson and Amy Van Dyken, both gold medalists from the '96 Games. I'd met Gold Medal's owner, Brad Hunt, at a U.S. Olympic Committee awards ceremony in 1996, and later that year he hooked me up with tickets to the Summer Olympics in Atlanta. I started working with a young agent named Nadia Guerriero. I liked her a lot. She was about my age, upbeat and efficient, with long blond hair and wicked cell phone and computer skills. That girl could get shit done.

The big social event of the summer was Baba and Lauren's wedding on a ranch south of Hailey. Otherwise, I was taking care of business. With Nike, Gold Medal, and the U.S. Ski Team, I stayed busy. I went to the World Cup finals in Vail and flew to trade shows to promote my new skis and skiwear. Gold Medal wrangled some new endorsements for me, including American Airlines and Mountain Dew. I was part of a sweepstakes, along with Shaquille O'Neal and Mia Hamm. The winner of the contest got to ski with me at Vail. In June, Matty and I flew to New York to introduce the Air Skeek to the media at Chelsea Piers, a sports complex on Manhattan's West Side. Despite the traveling, I stuck to my exercise routine. If I had a 7 A.M. flight, I got up at 4:30 to hit the gym first.

As the weather warmed up, we took it outside for dry-land training. Matty had these rubber gizmos called Sidewinders, which went around my ankles like shackles for resistance work. I rode my bike, in-line skated, played tennis, and swam. In early May Matty accompanied me to a ski team training camp in San Francisco. I was pleased to be spending time with J.J., and my coaches were pleased to see what good shape I was in. And when I went to Vail to get Richard Steadman's okay to ski, Matty was there too.

On July 7, 1997, seven months and three days after my injury, I skied again at Mount Hood. Jim Tracy, the new speed coach (Ernst had retired) made me poke along behind him down a flat sissy run. It was incredibly boring, but Jim wanted to ease me into it. "You're going to follow me for a whole run, and then I'll let you go," he said. After two runs I said, "I've got to take it out." I did a hop turn, blew right past him, and shot down the mountain, carving big, fat turns and squealing like a five-year-old on a new bike. I suddenly knew how a caught fish must feel when it's thrown back in a lake. By the end I was hanging it out, and I felt so good I upgraded my goal. "I want double gold in Nagano and I want my down-hill title back, pure and simple," I told *USA Today*. I was back.

Or so I thought. That's the tricky thing about comebacks: just when you think you're as good as new, your body reminds you who's in charge.

At the end of August I went to Chile with the team for more intensive training. We had a new coach/trainer named Chip White. Chip was running the team through its workouts, and my knee wasn't ready for it. He and I were just getting to know each other, and when I hesitated to participate in a volleyball game, he said, "Come on; just do part of it."

"No, you don't understand," I told him. "I don't half-ass stuff. You can't invite me to *sort of* play volleyball. I'm going to play all out." I wasn't about to let my teammates think I couldn't hang tough, so I went for it. I ran up and down stairs, did too many squats, and played a rowdy game of parking lot hockey and got knocked into a car.

The next morning my knee was extremely swollen and sore. The coaches had set up a GS course on the hill. I should have told them my knee couldn't handle it, but true to form, I went for it. I made it through about three gates when my knee started hurting so badly I skied off the course, collapsed in the snow, and broke into tears. This was bad pain, and I knew I couldn't push through it, that I *shouldn't* push through it.

A slalom and GS coach named Georg Capaul came over to comfort me. "You're asking a lot of yourself," he said. "I believe you can do it, but you have to accept that right now, this is too intense."

Three days into the camp, and I was done. I was diagnosed with tendinitis and spent the next week in my hotel room, crying and calling Mom and J.J. for consolation. I had been religious about physical therapy and training. I had been patient and optimistic. I'd done everything by the book for once, so why wasn't my body reciprocating? I had assumed I could will my knee to heal, that my body would simply glide into the slipstream of my gold-medal dream. Yet it wasn't going as planned. And the thought of not winning in Nagano literally made me sick to my stomach.

I also felt out of place. Hilary had retired, leaving Megan Gerety and me as the veterans. My role on the team had changed. There was a new hot rookie now, a shy twenty-year-old named Kirsten Clark from Maine. We called her "Clarkie." At twenty-six I was getting old by ski racing standards. The atmosphere at that camp was particularly silly that year, and I was the old lady, the grumpy grandma. I didn't want to get in a snowball fight with the Austrian team or get to know the new guys who raced for the Swiss team. I kept walking into the middle of water fights, and when someone threw snow in the pool while I was doing laps, I became furious. Everybody was playing like a bunch of kids, and I didn't feel like a kid anymore. I missed Matty, I missed J.J., I missed home, and I was seriously contemplating leaving the camp early.

The next dry-land session was a game of ultimate Frisbee in a snowy parking lot. It looked fun, but I didn't allow myself to play. I couldn't take the chance. Instead, I decided to build a snowman nearby. I constructed him with the passion of a Renaissance sculptor. He would be my masterpiece, a real monster of a snowman. I rolled and patted the snow into place, and while his body took shape, I kept one eye on the game. I put all the energy I would have expended playing Frisbee into that snowman, and pretty soon he was about eight feet tall and completely styled in hat, goggles, and gloves with ski poles for arms.

I ran inside to get my camera, and I returned a few minutes later to a tragic sight. Someone had knocked my snowman over and then split, leaving his body behind like snowy roadkill, the props scattered. I followed the telltale footprints in the snow back to a maintenance shed. I threw rocks and shovels at the door and shouted obscenities and made a huge scene. Then I stormed up to Herwig's room. He was sitting at a desk, doing paperwork.

"Some asshole knocked down my snowman!" I screamed. "I'm going home! I quit!"

It was all Herwig could do not to laugh in my face. He couldn't believe how upset I was over a snowman. At the same time, he realized what an emotional train wreck I'd become, and how easily I could dig myself an even deeper hole. Herwig knew I could be my own worst enemy, and he knew how to turn me around: reverse psychology.

"You want to go home?" he said nonchalantly. "Go ahead. I don't care."

"I know what you're doing," I said, glaring at him. "Well, screw you. I'll stay here and finish this fucking camp even if I can't ski."

"You'll just keep trying every day," he said calmly. "That's all you can do."

And at that I marched out.

When Matty saw my knee, he put his foot down. "I haven't done all this work with her just to see you guys blow her apart," he told Chip. "I'm too close to getting her there." From that moment on, Matty wouldn't let me out of his sight. My knee was so sore I had to pass on a ski camp in Switzerland with the team and stay behind to work with Matty. I'd developed scar tissue in my knee and had to endure daily sessions where Cheryl would dig into my knee to break up scar tissue, a painful process that brought me to tears. I was beginning to feel a little panicked. The recovery wasn't going as quickly as I'd hoped.

The first week of November I took a quick business trip to Seattle and San Francisco. I had to promote my signature skis and skiwear, which were just hitting the stores; attend a press conference where Charles Schwab, the brokerage firm, would announce its sponsorship of the U.S. Ski Team; and attend a black-tie fund-raiser for the ski team. David Leon Moore, the *USA Today* reporter, trailed me around for an article that ended up being titled "Aboard the Picabo Express." He wrote that I seemed "more determined than healthy." The World Cup opener was a Super G in Mammoth Mountain, California, on November 27, and I kept telling Moore I'd be ready.

Herwig wasn't so sure. While on vacation in Austria he told Moore in a phone interview, "The worst-case scenario is that this will be just a season to return to health, and that her next focus will be not the Olympics, but the World Championships in 1999 in Vail. The best-case scenario is that she wins a medal at the Olympics, but that's not a good bet. People in the U.S. need to get ready for the possibility that Picabo will not win."

Good old Herwig, the eternal optimist.

Our fall ski camp was in early November in Beaver Creek, Colorado, near Vail. I had to ski as much as possible over those two weeks to get miles on my knee. The World Cup opener in Mammoth was two weeks away, the Olympics less than three months away. I was running out of time. With every run my confidence grew; that vital connection between my knee and my brain strengthened. But by the end of the camp I wasn't there. Not quite. Not yet.

Herwig sat me down and told me he didn't think I was ready to compete. He said I should skip Mammoth and the first two downhills at Lake Louise the first week of December, targeting instead a downhill in Val d'Isère, France, on December 11. I was intensely frustrated and upset, but I knew he was right. My mind was ready, but my body wasn't. This was one of my lowest points. I realized I had to stop fixating on my gold medal and simply focus on each day as it came, working a little harder every day. I could look up once in a while at the horizon, but then return to the daily grind.

The pundits were pessimistic. A segment for the morning show on CBS declared, "Most observers say Picabo is simply running out of time to be a serious threat in Nagano."

Instead of competing I went into hiding. Right before Thanksgiving I spent five days at Vail with Gnarly working on Super G technique. I went home for three days for Thanksgiving break and then returned to Colorado for five days of speed training with Herwig at Copper Mountain. For two weeks all I did was ski, away from the media spotlight and doubters and nagging questions. By sunrise I was already on the mountain, and by 9 A.M., when the lifts started running, I'd already done six runs. I took run after run, going back to the top by snowmobile, making laps, logging miles, racing time. I ran gates and went fast on bumpy, ungroomed snow. Every day I'd wonder when my knee was going to start hurting, and every day it took longer to ache. Matty and my physical therapist were with me, and at the end of the day they worked me out and worked me over. The faster I got, the more confident I became, until finally one morning Herwig looked at me and said, "You're ready."

WHEN I SHOWED UP AT VAL D'ISÈRE THE SECOND WEEK OF DECEMBER, ALL my old World Cup buddies were thrilled to see me. I hugged Meisi and Pilla. Katja was beside herself. She had been unbeatable so far, winning every World Cup downhill, and she couldn't wait to kick my ass again.

But she had to wait. The European winter was unseasonably warm, and it rained in Val d'Isère. I spent the time sitting around the hotel, doing interviews, calling J.J., and cooling my heels. The first race was postponed and postponed again. I'd waited this long, what were two more days? Time, at this moment at least, was on my side: two more days for my knee to heal. I played volleyball with the team, showing the young ones I could still serve and block despite my advanced age. The Winter Olympics were two months away, and I felt good.

The downhill finally took place on December 17. I remember standing in the gate, butterflies playing rugby in my gut. All I wanted to do was hold my own with Katja and other big guns like Heidi Zurbriggen. As I glided down the course, all thoughts of my knee faded away and were replaced by the sheer thrill of competing again. I knocked off a few perfect turns at the bottom and finished tenth, ahead of Katja and Heidi. I couldn't believe I could be happy with a top ten finish, but I was. The next day I finished eleventh in the Super G, and Jim was ecstatic.

I didn't ski much for the next month. The next race in Europe was canceled, and at New Year's, I entered an event in Lake Placid, New York, called the Dash for Cash. The winner got ten thousand dollars. My competition was a few of my teammates and a bunch of up-and-comers. The race was delayed by fog for several days while J.J. and I stayed in a log cabin and pretended to like the rustic life. I decided I'd had enough of it as a kid. I won the ten grand on a fog-shortened Super G course. It wasn't a World Cup, but it was my first win.

I headed back to Europe, and J.J. came with me. I had made a deal with the team: J.J. and I would travel to races in our own car, but I'd stay in the same hotel as the team, train with the team, and attend all the meetings. J.J. got along great with the girls, but Herwig went along grudgingly. He wanted to keep me happy, and J.J. made me happy.

There were only three World Cup races left before the Games: Kitzbühel, Austria; Cortina, Italy; and Åre, Sweden. I'd agreed to keep an online diary for CBS's *Sportsline.com* leading up to the Games, and I phoned in my entry of January 7 while sitting in the Portland airport waiting for a flight to Frankfurt. "I know people might not be expecting a lot from me and I'm maybe not the favorite," I said, "but I'd like to be one of the people to beat. And I'm going to work my butt off to get there. I have nothing to lose."

At least my knee was feeling great. The only time I thought about it was when someone asked me how it was feeling.

Kitzbühel was rained out, and the venue changed to Altenmarkt. This was only my second downhill of the season, and I didn't crack the top five. The race didn't flow, and I finished tenth. I missed a gate in the next day's Super G and failed to finish. That was a bad day.

Next stop: Cortina, familiar ground. I remembered how magical it was to win with Mom there the year before, and I knew I'd do well. I felt like my old self. I cheered on my friends and my younger teammates and went fast in the downhill. When I looked at the scoreboard and saw the number four by my name, I started to cry. In the finish corral Katja, who finished sixth, tapped me on the leg with her ski pole to get my attention and said, "It's good to have you back."

The next day I finished eleventh on a tough Super G that overpowered ten of the top fifteen racers, including Katja. She was right. I was back.

After Cortina J.J. went home, so I headed to Sweden alone for the last World Cup downhill before the Olympics. I knew the course at Åre well, having won there three years earlier. I had the fastest time in training, but the night before the race I went to battle with Rossignol over which skis to use.

Ski manufacturers are always introducing new skis to the market and are eager to have the racers ski on them to give feedback on their performance and, ideally, get some good results. Rossignol had introduced a new ski called the Dualtec. The Dualtecs were completely different from the old-school skis I was used to. They were shorter, narrower, and made of fiberglass instead of wood and steel. Downhill ski racers tend to develop an affection for a particular pair of skis—it's not unheard of for someone to race on the same pair of downhill boards for ten years—and prying a ski racer from that lucky pair is like trying to separate a toddler from his or her security blanket. My favorite skis were a classic, old-school model. I had two pairs: my Olys, which I'd won the silver on at Lillehammer, and my Juniors, so called because they were the same skis as my Olys, only newer. Rossignol's race director, Jan Larsson, had been urging me all season to race on the Dualtecs, and all season I'd resisted. It can take months to adjust to new skis, and the last thing I wanted to do was throw another variable into my comeback program only weeks before the Games.

I had agreed to train on the Dualtecs, but at Åre, Jan put his foot down: he insisted I race on them. He called a summit meeting at our hotel with me, Cookie, Jim, and Herwig. Gnarly wasn't there, but he had made his opinion known. "Peek," he'd said, "to get your confidence back you have to go on something familiar. You have to know what's going to happen under your feet."

On the evening of January 30, we sat in a tense circle while Jan argued his case. He said Rossignol was going to discontinue my skis, and that if I was going to keep racing, I'd have to switch eventually. "Picabo, we're changing technology," he said. "We need you on the Dualtecs."

"Look, I'm not going to break in a new pair of skis right now," I argued. "I've got some skis that are rockets, and I'll beat everybody on them. Just leave me alone."

Cookie was caught in the middle, between his allegiance to his employer and his loyalty to me. We went way back, Cookie and I, and he knew how headstrong I was and how important it was that I be happy on my skis. He had Rossi in his face saying, "Push her for the Dualtecs," and me in his face saying, "I don't like them. I want my old ones." He sat there chain-smoking nervously, saying little.

"Look," said Herwig finally. "My priority is Picabo. If she's going to do well at Nagano, she can't be changing skis in midstream."

The next morning I entered the start on my Juniors.

The run was going well until I reached the steepest, most dangerous part of the course. I was in the middle of a seventy-five-mile-an-hour turn, all my weight on my left ski, when that ski, without warning, came off. The binding, which holds the boot to the ski, had malfunctioned and released the ski, the way a horse throws a shoe. I tried to recover. I switched my weight to my right ski and pivoted it sideways, hoping to go into a controlled slide down the pitch and come to a stop. I pivoted a little too far and spun around. Now I was going downhill at seventy-five miles an hour on one ski backward. At the bottom of the pitch I hit a low spot, caught the outside edge of my remaining ski, and went flying through the air as if ejected out of a cannon. I impacted the ground with my head and tumbled, tumbled, tumbled into a safety fence, hitting it face first. Between the initial impact and the fence I suffered a double whammy, as if a boxer had hit me on the chin and then come in for an uppercut. *Boom.* I was down for the count. When I regained consciousness thirty seconds later, I couldn't move my neck, and my head was throbbing.

I staggered to my feet and walked away crying, but not from the pain. The ski I'd lost had flown twenty feet through the air and landed badly, bending its tip. I'd broken one of my Juniors. It was as if the Rossi guys had put a curse on it.

"That's a bad thing," Herwig told *The New York Times*. "It was a very good ski."

I had only one pair of my favorite skis left, my Olys. Gnarly looked at the bright side. "Well, your knee held up."

I was airlifted to a hospital in Östersund, where I was diagnosed with whiplash and a slight concussion. The Olympic opening ceremonies were one week away.

I flew home to Portland for several days of physical therapy and R&R. On February 5 I arrived in Japan with J.J. and Nadia. We stayed a night in Osaka for uniforms and briefings, took the bullet train to Nagano, and hopped a bus for Hakuba as the opening ceremonies were in full swing. Baba and Dad were going to meet us there, but Mom had decided at the last minute not to come. Her own knees were bothering her, and she simply didn't feel up to it. Mom and Lauren would keep their fingers crossed in Maui, where we'd rented a big house for a post-Olympic family reunion.

I intended to bring a gold medal home with me. A month earlier I'd put in a call to John Blackman, the art teacher who painted my headgear.

"John," I said, "I'm going to the Olympics, and I need a new helmet. Make it a tiger."

10

NAGANO

SO MY STORY HAS COME FULL CIRCLE, BACK TO WHERE IT BEGAN: WITH A miracle. I shocked the world when I won the Olympic Super G on February 11, 1998. An almost mystical series of events and coincidences, large and small, culminated in a once-in-a-lifetime moment: seeing my brother by the gondola; the way the storm cleared out at the last minute, leaving behind blue skies and perfect visibility for the race; the fact that I was given the number two start position, when the snow was still firm and fast; the way the course was set, wide open like a downhill; and of course, the decision to race on my Olys, the last surviving pair of the downhill skis I loved.

I have my coaches to thank for that one. Herwig, Jim, Marjan, Gnarly, and Chip had skied the side of the course during inspection, and after reaching the bottom they'd looked at each other. "What do you think, guys?" Herwig had asked. "Downhill skis?"

"Oh yeah," they agreed.

The Americans weren't the only coaches who made that crucial decision; the top five finishers that day skied on downhill boards. The fact is I pulled off the run of my life. I wish I could explain how I did it, but that's the beauty of miracles: they're inexplicable. "I surprised myself a little," I told *USA Today*.

Somehow Gnarly knew. He and Chip stayed in the same house with me, and Gnarly would later say that all week he could see the confidence and determination in my eyes. On the morning of the race he said to Chip, "Picabo's going to medal today."

"No, she's not," said Chip.

"Yes, she is," said Gnarly.

Nothing about the way I skied in the prerace warm-up supported Gnarly's prediction. Several other coaches remarked on how rough my technique was. "Yeah, but she's taking it down the hill and going fast," Gnarly argued. "She's going to do well."

A lot of people doubted whether I could come back, but Gnarly always believed in me. He knew that when I set my mind to it, I could push the accelerator and just do it. And Dr. Richard Steadman knew, too. He'd come to Japan to see how his handiwork would stand up, and after I won, we hugged, tears in our eyes.

I was big news back home. *Newsweek* writer Larry Reibstein wrote, "Picabo Street achieved a kind of harmonic convergence that she's been seeking her whole life—and maybe a few of her previous lives too." (I had shared my Sapphire experience with Frank Deford in a pre-Olympics story, also for *Newsweek*, which only added to my reputation for "New Age honesty.") Reibstein dubbed me "America's Olympic poster girl." In a story headlined "Street of Gold—Legend of the Tiger Enhanced with Street's Victory in Super-G," Ron C. Judd, a columnist for *The Seattle Times*, wrote that "you get the feeling that after this, nothing is out of her reach. You get the feeling that when the downhill begins here Saturday, the eyes of the world will be on her. You get the feeling this is a very indefinable, serendipitous energy that charges Street's batteries. . . . She is a legend in progress, a plot waiting to climax, a story awaiting a moral."

The end of my Olympic story was supposed to be another gold medal, in the downhill, the moral being that a lot of hard work and a little harmonic convergence could make lightning strike twice. My Super G win made me the favorite to take the downhill three days later, but things didn't go as planned. If you believe *Sports Illustrated*, all the drama among what the magazine called my "entourage" affected my performance in that final race. But the reporter didn't get half the story, and what he did get, he got wrong. I lost much more than a race one month later in Crans-Montana, Switzerland, for reasons that have never been fully told until now.

My home during the Olympics was a spacious ski lodge called "Log Haven." It was owned by the father of a Japanese employee of Nike, and it had Western beds, toilets with heated seats, and those big, deep Japanese tubs. The lodge was within walking distance of the ski lifts. The owner's daughter, whose name was Nami, was on hand to help out. Healthy Choice, one of the ski team's sponsors, had provided us with two chefs, Pat and Nina, who whipped up anything we wanted on a moment's notice. It was one more perk of being a Nike athlete.

There were six other people staying at Log Haven: J.J.; my agent, Nadia; Chip; Gnarly; Dad; and Baba. But after my Super G win, the population of Log Haven seemed to double and then triple. People came and went at all hours, hugging and high-fiving. Sue Levin called, beside herself with joy, and I received reams of congratulatory faxes. The house looked like a florist's shop; Nike sent two bouquets that were so massive they filled up a window seat in the living room. I spent the next two days doing phone interviews with the American media and walking around with the shit-eating grin of someone who had won the lottery. In effect I had, since an Olympic gold medal can be parlayed into millions in endorsements.

Nadia's cell phone rang on the average of every eighteen seconds with interview and appearance requests, most of which she turned down because I was on hold to race the downhill. But there was one call I made sure to return.

Two days after I won the gold, Nadia's phone rang yet again.

"President Clinton calling for Picabo Street." Nadia gulped and told the White House person that I was on the hill training but would call back as soon as I got in.

An hour later the White House person called again, sounding like an impatient teenager. "Is she going to call?"

When I got home, Nadia gave me a message. "The president called. Twice."

"Oh my god, the president?" I called back right away. After a security check I was patched through to the leader of the free world.

"What's up, girl?" President Clinton asked. His informal tone took me aback a little.

"Hello, Mr. President," I said, trying to strike a more formal note. "How are you doing?"

"I'm well. I just wanted to congratulate you for doing such a fine job of representing your country and reaching your lifetime dream. It's a wonderful moment, and I hope you enjoy it. Do you have your family there? Are your colorful folks around?"

"Yes, my dad and my brother are here," I answered. And since the Monica Lewinsky scandal was in full force, I asked after his well-being, too. "How are you and Hillary holding up?"

"We're hanging in there, thank you very much."

Then the president wished me luck in the downhill and said he'd see me in April, when the U.S. Olympians would make their traditional post-Games White House visit. I never made it.

THE WEATHER HAD BEEN CHAOTIC. IT WOULD SNOW TWO FEET, AND THEN rain six inches, and then the gale-force winds would kick in. Over at the bottom of the race hill, Cookie and the other ski technicians were slogging through knee-deep mud wearing rubber fishing boots. The schedule was thrown into upheaval. The Alpine ski races were postponed again and again, leaving CBS little to televise except a lot of snowboarding and figure skating highlights. The downhill was originally supposed to happen before the Super G, but it got pushed to Saturday the 14. I had three days to keep my focus on my next goal.

Some athletes do everything in their power to wall off the world before a big competition, under the theory that outside distractions can disrupt the single-mindedness necessary to do your best. At Nagano, Michelle Kwan holed up in a hotel room with her parents for two weeks, leaving only to go to the rink to practice. I'm the opposite. I focus best when surrounded by activity and borderline chaos. I like to feel like a bee at the center of a thriving, buzzing hive—which is good, because there was never a dull moment at Log Haven.

Take Dad and Baba's trip, for example. They traveled over separately, and I was expecting them to arrive a day after J.J., Nadia, and I got there. But I got to Log Haven from training to find they weren't there yet. Worried, I asked Nami's father to drive to the train station and look for them. He got back and told me they were nowhere to be found, which worried me even more. The next morning, before I left for the ski hill, I asked

Nami's dad to please go back and try again. I was concerned they had lost their luggage, just as they had while traveling to Lillehammer, or that they'd got lost themselves.

It turned out that Dad and Baba's flight had been delayed for hours. Once they got to Tokyo they couldn't read the signs and missed their bullet train to Nagano. They finally got to Hakuba ten hours late, at 2 A.M. The town was deserted, and they had no idea how to get to Log Haven. Fortunately, a local guy who was on his way to work the early shift at a soy sauce factory took pity on them. He spoke English and called Log Haven for directions. By the time Dad and Baba reached the house they'd been up for two days. When I got home that afternoon, I peeked in their room and saw them on their beds, sound asleep. I was so excited to see them—and their luggage—that my eyes welled with tears. Finally, everyone was here, and I had one less thing to worry about.

That afternoon I went to play coed volleyball with some of my teammates, who were staying at a nearby hotel. Our opponents were members of the Swedish ski team. Volleyball is my favorite team sport, and I play all out. At one point, I jumped for an outside block and landed on the side of my right ankle. I pulled a ligament and was limping badly. The ankle swelled up and turn several shades of blue. My coaches held their breaths, and our physiotherapist got down to business. I wasn't worried. At least my left knee had held up.

Then, a day before the Super G, J.J. and I had a fight. On February 9 he, Dad, and Baba went to Nagano to watch a hockey game and to celebrate J.J.'s twenty-ninth birthday. I had training the next morning and stayed behind. Nami and I had made J.J. a cake and a card, and I'd asked Nami to write "happy birthday" on it in Japanese. I waited up to surprise him, but the three of them didn't get home until late, so our celebration was short-lived. I went to bed disappointed, feeling jilted. And since I'm lousy at hiding my feelings, I let J.J. know it the next morning.

In all fairness, J.J. was under a lot of pressure. He was a kind of an emotional jack-of-all-trades around Log Haven. When he wasn't running errands for Nadia, he was trying to keep me happy, Baba entertained, and Dad calm. This last duty wasn't easy. After my win Dad's molten temper started to bubble and roil. He wanted to help, to pitch in, to be part of the process, just like the old days. This had been our dream together, and now that it had been realized, he had a hard time just sitting back and watching the aftermath unfold without him. When I was younger, he had been the one supporting me, guiding me, goading me on. Now he felt lost among all the people around me and helpless that he couldn't support me in the same way he used to. J.J. bore the brunt of Dad's ranting and raving. He'd just sit there, absorbing Dad's fury.

On Thursday, Log Haven's population increased when a friend of J.J.'s, named Jonas, arrived. At this point my Olympic experience was beginning to resemble a slumber party. Herwig, who wanted that second gold as much as I did, was getting concerned. One day when we were riding the chairlift together, he said, "Picabo, you'd do yourself a favor by trying to clear your plate as much as you can. Keep your program simple." Paul Major was on the same wavelength. He faxed me his congratulations from Park City, and the last thing he wrote was something along the lines of, "Peek, you thrive on chaos better than anyone I've ever met in my life. But there comes a time when it becomes too much. So I would recommend that you simplify."

The downhill training run scheduled for Thursday, February 12, was canceled. Friday's training run took place, but weather shut down Saturday's downhill, and it was rescheduled for Monday, February 16. Three days had become five days, and possibly more, depending on the weather. I spent most of my downtime with J.J. and Baba. We took walks in the woods, soaked in traditional Japanese baths, went to movies with the team, and watched curling on TV.

But they were starting to get antsy.

On Saturday night the whole gang piled into one of Nike's Hummers and went to Nagano. John Hancock, a ski team sponsor, had asked if I would appear at a reception in Nagano for the U.S. gold medalists.

Sports Illustrated made the reception sound like the second coming of the Beatles, but it wasn't that big a deal. I did a couple interviews, was introduced onstage, and ate some food. The reception was televised, so Baba, Dad, and I looked into a TV camera and wished Mom a happy Valentine's Day. After we got back to Hakuba, Baba, J.J., and Jonas decided to go bar hopping. I had training the next day and went home to get some sleep.

J.J. got back to Log Haven at five-thirty on Sunday morning. He said nothing, just crawled into bed beside me.

I got up at seven, furious. I was upset because J.J. and Baba stayed out so late while I'd spent two evenings alone. I hadn't brought them to Japan to party; I'd brought them there to support me. And to be honest, I was also a little jealous because I couldn't have a good time right along with them. I was in the mood to simplify, all right, starting with my boyfriend and my brother.

Dad was up early too, and after breakfast, as he walked me to the ski room, I told him I'd decided to ask them to leave Japan. When I got to the hill, I pulled Jim Tracy aside and told him I was pissed off because Baba and J.J. had partied all night.

"Take a minute and figure out what you want to do about it," Jim said. "I suggest you tell them that if they can't keep their shit together, they should head out and meet you stateside when you get done."

Jim's advice calmed me down. I skied well that morning and had a nice moment when a local guy in a lift shack lent me his scarf so I could clean my goggles and then let me keep it. I tied it around my neck and skied with it the rest of the day. I had scoped out what I thought was a winning line on the course, and I was feeling confident.

I was home by lunchtime. I walked in the door, put my skis down, and unbuckled my boots. I asked Pat, the cook, to make me a ham sandwich and some apple juice for lunch. He said, "We have some real nice soup; would you like some?" I agreed to the soup.

I sat down at the kitchen table. Baba and J.J. were sitting there, hung-over and miserable, trying to swallow breakfast food.

I stared at them hard enough to drill a hole through their foreheads. "So," I said. They both looked up at me and then back down. "Did we get that out of our systems, or is this the program from here on out?"

"I'm fine," J.J. said. "That's all I needed. I'm sorry, but I needed to have a good time and vent. We kind of wanted to celebrate your win. I'm sorry that you couldn't come do that with us, but we went big and got it a little bit for you too." Then he added, "I'm done with it."

"All right," I said.

Baba agreed. "I don't want to feel like this again."

"That's not good enough for me," I snapped. "I don't feel sorry for you at all right now. In fact, will someone turn the music on real loud? Because that's how much I care about your hangover. I need a better answer than that."

"Nope, nope, I'm good, I just needed to vent a little bit, too, and celebrate a little bit for you. We won't do it again."

"Okay. The reason I'm asking is, I need to know if you guys are in the mood to stick this out until the downhill. I need people to be able to keep it together. If you don't think you're going to be able to or don't want to, no hard feelings, Maui's waiting for you. Mom and Lauren are already there."

No, no, no they insisted; they were in it for the long haul. In two minutes it was settled. We were cool.

The whole time Dad had been pacing in another room, expecting a knock-down-drag-out to happen. From what Baba and J.J. told me later, he'd been prancing around all morning, giving them a hard time, expecting me to send them packing when I got home. He hadn't made me mad, so he would get to stay, and it would be the two of us, just like the old days.

When it didn't turn out that way, he couldn't accept it. He kept poking and stirring, trying to perpetuate the tension. Finally I turned to him and said, "Dad, it's over. We've dealt with it, we've communicated, and everything's okay."

Then he lit into me. "Look, man, if you need somebody to be pissed off at, I'll gladly be that person!"

"Dad," I yelled back, "I don't need to be pissed off! I need every last ounce of energy I have to keep me strong, to make this happen!"

At that, Dad marched up to his room, got his jacket, and walked out the door—only to run smack into Tim Layden, a reporter covering the Olympic ski events for *Sports Illustrated*. What Layden was doing rolling around in the middle of the woods I don't know, other than looking for where I lived. So Dad ran into him, the filter between his brain and his mouth disappeared, and pretty soon Layden had the big scoop he'd been looking for.

While Dad was out, J.J. told me what had happened at the bar in Hakuba.

J.J. said that he was standing with his back to the bar when a couple guys who worked for a European ski team came up and started hassling him. They called J.J. a "nigger." They must have known J.J. was my boyfriend since he'd been with me on the World Cup. Maybe they figured they'd rattle my cage by rattling his. If they didn't know who J.J. was, then they were straight-out racists.

Baba felt that by disrespecting J.J., the Austrians were disrespecting me, too, and he wanted to do something about it. But J.J. wouldn't take the bait. He told his friends that any other time, in any other place he would have been in the Austrians' faces, snapping their necks, and teaching them a lesson. But he was in my sandbox, and he wasn't going to piss in it. He wanted to blow them off and have a good time. But the rest of the guys couldn't relax, and J.J.—who was the only person who had a right to be upset—finally said let's go. They hit one last bar before crawling home, toasted.

All my dad knew about the bar incident were tidbits he grasped by eavesdropping on J.J. and Baba that morning. He didn't have his facts straight. He couldn't believe J.J. had kept his composure after being called that name. Dad would have gone after the guy, just like he'd gone after John Majors in the trailer park fifteen years earlier. So he re-created the scene in his mind as he would have lived it and let it fly. I can imagine Layden scrambling to write it all down.

After Dad came back from his "walk," he went straight upstairs without saying a word to anyone and lay down for a nap, having gone without food since breakfast.

A week earlier the cooks had told the team they'd make us whatever we wanted the night before the big race. We said we wanted Mexican. This was the ultimate challenge in the land of dried seaweed and raw fish, but Pat and Nina went to town. They spent two days scouring the region for the ingredients to make Mexican food. That night they set out, buffet-style, the most delicious Mexican food I had ever had. There were two kinds of rice, three kinds of meat, beans, corn, guacamole, and handmade tortillas. At about five-thirty my teammates started arriving for dinner.

It occurred to me that I hadn't seen Dad since lunchtime. I went up to my room to get something when suddenly a strange feeling washed over me. I walked into his room and found Dad lying on his bed, sweating profusely and barely conscious.

I tried not to panic. Dad had done this before, and I knew what to do. I ran downstairs and pointed to my brother and said, "I need you in the kitchen. Now." He met me there and I told him, "Dad's bonking, and we've got to get him turned around. I need you to grab me sugar and orange juice and some water and a banana and some bread and meet me upstairs as soon as you can."

One of the dinner guests, a doctor on the U.S. Olympic Committee, sensed something was wrong. "Is there anything I can do?" he asked.

Dad was not a big fan of doctors. "I'm not sure, but if there is, I'll let you know."

"Mind if I join you?"

"I don't, but the man upstairs is going to as soon as he starts coming around." By that time I was running up the stairs.

"I'm ready for that," he said, falling in behind me. "What are we dealing with?"

"Diabetic."

"He goes low blood sugar?"

"Yep, borderline unconscious."

It took us an hour and a half to bring Dad around. The doctor monitored his pulse while Baba and I plied him with food. "Hi Dad, it's me. Come on; roll over; sit up; you've got to come around for me; you've got to get going." Finally we got Dad to change his shirt, brush his hair, and go downstairs for dinner, where I made him a plate and coaxed him to eat it. The doctor wanted to test Dad's blood sugar, but his monitor was broken. Nami said the next-door neighbor was diabetic, so she ran over there to borrow her monitor. It showed that Dad's blood sugar was only 28, and this was after eating. His blood sugar may have been in the single digits when I found him, in the lethal range.

Later Dad confessed. "Ran into Tim Layden," he said, a little too casually.

"Great. Am I going to read some things that will make me unhappy?"

"No, no," he insisted.

"I am, aren't I?" I was fuming. I knew my dad well enough to know that he had probably blown his top and told Layden way more than he needed to know. That was why he'd gone upstairs without eating lunch: He knew what he had done and was afraid I'd feel upset and betrayed, and that J.J. would turn out looking bad when the article came out. And you didn't want to get J.J. mad.

SOME PEOPLE MIGHT CALL THE EVENTS THAT TRANSPIRED IN LOG HAVEN distracting. I called them life as usual. It was raining the next morning, cloudy and cold, but the downhill was still on. Despite the dismal weather, I woke up feeling good about my chances.

The race organizers were playing catch-up with the schedule, and the men's Super G and the women's downhill were scheduled for that morning on two different courses. The lodge looked like the Tokyo train station at rush hour, packed with ski racers waiting to compete.

The men's Super G started first. It was won by Hermann Maier of Austria, who had taken a spectacular crash three days earlier in the men's downhill. He had flown through the air in a spread-eagle position, so high he seemed to sprout wings, and then took out two safety fences as he tumbled off course. If he hadn't landed in feather-soft snow, he could have been seriously injured.

While the men's Super G was in progress, the women were inspecting their downhill course. What I saw threw me for a loop. It was the same course as the Super G I'd won, only longer, but it might as well have been a whole different mountain. I'd scoped out an aggressive line on the top of the course during training, when the snow conditions had been perfect. But the heavy rain had transformed the course, especially the first three turns, into a bumpy, brutal mess. The snow conditions had changed so dramatically that my line had become unsafe. I was risking blowing out two turns into the race and tumbling into the safety fence. What was my plan of attack now? I felt as if I were looking at the course for the first time.

After inspection I decided to take a shortcut through the woods to the gondola. I shot along a narrow track behind the stadium toward the trees. I flew past someone trudging uphill, and two seconds later I realized it was Dad. I chucked my skis sideways and screeched to a halt and started hiking up toward him. He started running toward me, and when we met, he grabbed me in a bear hug.

"I'm sorry for all the behavior I've displayed this week," he said, his voice heavy with emotion. "It's been a really tough week for me. I feel really out of control. I don't know what I'm supposed to do. I want to be around you and give you everything you need, but you don't need anything because the ski team is taking care of everything. I feel along for the ride, and that's hard for me. I just want to tell you to go for it, be safe, have a good run, and we'll be here waiting for you when you get down."

"Thanks, Dad." We hugged intensely, and I took off.

I got to the mountaintop lodge and stripped down to my downhill suit. As I was leaving, I stopped to congratulate Jean-Luc Cretier of France on winning the men's downhill earlier that week. "It's your turn," he said.

Then something strange happened. It was a bad sign, the first of many. As I turned to walk out of the lodge, my tiger helmet slipped out of my hands and crashed to the ground. The face mask, the part his lower jaw was painted on, cracked in half near the bolt that attached it to the rest of the helmet.

I can't believe that just happened.

I got to the start and told Cookie I'd broken my helmet. He got out his roll of duct tape and patched it together, but my confidence was even more shaken as if it, too, had fallen to the ground and cracked.

Then another bad sign. I was running in sixteenth position. Isolde Kostner and Renate Goetschl went out in front of me, and both of them blew out of their bindings and crashed on the upper part of the course, delaying the race. I had too much time to think. I knew if I skied as aggressively here as I had in Åre, I would bend the ski so far that the toe piece on the binding could pop open and release the ski. I asked Cookie, "Do you think if I crank my bindings down harder for the upper part that my skis will stay on for sure?"

We tried to formulate a plan of attack. We decided I'd take it easy on the top part and try to make up the time on the bottom.

I got on course. Almost immediately everything that had been magical and mystical about my skiing dissolved, and I was left as the person I truly was: a skier with a rebuilt knee who'd raced only a handful of World Cups that season. I had my Olympic gold medal; I'd realized my dream. So why risk falling and hurting myself all over again?

I skied like a pussy on the top. My inner monologue went like this: *Oh God oh God oh God oh God oh God oh God oh God! Switch. I've got to tuck. Okay wait. Oh God oh God oh my God I almost fell down. Okay, I made it. I'm alive. Oh boy! I lost a lot of time. Let me see. What am I gonna do? Oh boy, I better tuck low. I better work this terrain. I better make this all happen.*

At the bottom of the pitch I tried to turn it on. I sped through the middle section and approached the first jump. I'd been having a hard time with it all week; it had been placed in the middle of the course and felt unnatural, as if it didn't belong there. My instinct when I'm trying to make up time is to go straight, so I went at the jump like an arrow. I didn't give myself enough room on the landing and had to scramble to make the next two turns, and I knew that all I was going to do was survive. I skied aggressively through the next three turns, skied smoothly around a big basketball turn, dove onto the next pitch and skied it cleanly, got some nice air off the last jump, and worked the terrain as much as I could on the bottom. I had regained a lot of time, but it wasn't enough. I crossed the finish line in fourth place. "Damn it!" I shouted. I knew I had given the race away.

Then I thought, *I'm glad I didn't fall; I made it down; I've got one medal; it's over; I get to go see Mom.* I ended up getting bumped to sixth, only thirteen-hundredths of a second away from a bronze. Considering how the day had gone, I felt it was a good result.

The best part of my day was that Pilla finally got an Olympic medal in the downhill. She got the silver, Florence Masnada of France got the bronze, and Katja, my old rival, got the gold. She had finished sixth in the Super G, so we'd switched our results. They were all my friends, and I was happy for them.

As I walked to Cookie's ski room with Brad, Tim Layden of *Sports Illustrated* approached me and asked for an interview. We talked as we walked, and I gave him the truth about that night and the truth about why I hadn't won the downhill. But he chose to write the juicier version he'd heard from Dad: that J.J. had gotten into a shoving match in the bar and I'd been so upset and distracted that I'd finished sixth in an event I was favored to win. J.J. ended up looking bad, when he had been the one holding all of us together. The article was called "Street Fighting," and it asked the question, "Did unrest in Street's camp hinder her quest for another medal?" After all I'd been through just to get to Nagano, the idea that I could get derailed by fights with my boyfriend and my dad was laughable. The real reason was a lot less sexy: I didn't want to get hurt again.

AFTER THE INTERVIEW WITH TIM LAYDEN, BRAD AND I WERE WALKING TO Log Haven. He wanted to relay a request from Rossignol. But I'll need to give a little background first.

After a skier places in the top three, some sleight of hand takes place in the finish corral. The athlete's skis may be several years old, so a representative for the athlete's ski sponsor takes the skis the athlete raced on and hands him or her a different pair—the new skis the sponsor wants to promote in the marketplace. A medalist ends up in endless photo ops, which in effect are free advertising. And at a high-profile event like the Olympics, this advertising can be invaluable.

On the day I won the Super G, a Rossignol rep should have been there to take my Olys and hand me a pair of Dualtecs. But the Rossignol team was spread a little thin that day, and they were so convinced I wouldn't contend they didn't bother to send anyone to the Super G. So the skis you see in the photos are the ones I actually skied on.

Apparently, Rossignol was upset at the missed opportunity. They were angry at Cookie because they felt he should have been prepared to make the switch. Now they wanted to make up for the oversight.

After the downhill, as I was heading back to Log Haven to pack and go to Hawaii, Brad said, "By the way, Rossignol would like us to make time to do a photo shoot." He said they wanted to photograph me for an ad, wearing my gold medal and holding the Dualtecs. And they wanted to do it that day.

I looked at him and said, "No."

Before Brad could argue, I went on, "I'm not telling everybody out there that Dualtecs won a gold medal."

The idea of advertising a pair of skis I hadn't competed on struck me as unethical. If Cookie had handed the Dualtecs to me, I don't believe I would have taken them. I didn't want the world to think the Dualtecs were working for me. Besides, I just wanted to pack and get to Maui. I didn't have time to hang around and do a photo shoot.

That night we all packed our bags and drove to Nagano. We spent the night there, and the next day we took a bullet train to Tokyo, a bus to Narita, and a plane to Hawaii. We were in Maui by the afternoon.

THERE'S A FLIP SIDE TO REACHING YOUR DREAM, A SIDE PEOPLE DON'T talk about much. After the initial high wore off, after the joyful hugs and the tears of disbelief, I was left feeling a little empty, as if there was a vacant room where my aspirations had once lived.

In Maui we celebrated and toasted my success, and I indulged in the pleasures I'd denied myself for the past year. I ate whatever Mom cooked, I slept a lot, I imbibed a little, and I watched TV shows I'd been missing. But when I was alone, I felt unfamiliar questions floating to the surface: Now that I have the gold medal, what dream will take its place? What will satisfy me now? What star do I wish on next? Where do I go from here?

I would go back to the World Cup. There were two races left, one in Morzine, France, and the World Cup finals in Crans-Montana, Switzerland. The thought was comforting in a way. Ski racing was more familiar than what I was experiencing emotionally. I could be, for two more races at least, the person I knew myself to be: a competitor, no matter what. I wanted to finish strong to solidify my ranking for the next season, so I could pick my start numbers and guarantee myself good start positions.

On February 19 David Letterman told a joke about me: "Earlier today, Picabo Street held a press conference to announce that she is donating money to build a new wing for her hometown hospital. It will be called the Picabo ICU."

Did Letterman know something I didn't?

On the last day of February we flew back to the mainland. My parents took most of my luggage to Portland, and I stayed in Los Angeles to do "The Tonight Show" with Jay Leno. My dressing room was filled with congratulatory banners and jars of red, white, and blue M&M's. When I walked onto the set, the audience gave me a standing ovation, and Jay said, "Thanks for making us all proud." I showed him my medal, and we talked about how heavy it was. Then he asked me how I got my name (of course), about my fall in Åre, Sweden, and the difference between the downhill and the Super G. I described the call from President Clinton, but when I said he was "such an amazing man," Jay made fun of me because the Monica Lewinsky scandal was all over the news.

"His sport's a little different from your sport," Jay quipped.

After that I stopped in Vegas to make a quick appearance at the annual ski industry trade show. From there I went to Portland and packed for Europe. J.J. and I decided he would stay behind since it was such a short trip. Nadia would come with me to handle all the requests that kept pouring in.

I told Mom I'd come home safe. "I promise."

The snow was bad in Morzine, and after five days the downhill was canceled. Cookie had brought a new batch of Dualtecs for me to try. Even though I'd refused to pretend I'd won the Olympics on them, I still wanted to make the skis work for me. Cookie and I had agreed to work with Rossignol after the World Cup finals and try to develop skis I liked. In the meantime, they wanted to be able to say I'd actually competed on them, so I agreed to train on them in Morzine.

Another bad sign. I was cruising along a flat, easy course on a pair of Super G skis when I got lazy and dropped my hip too far. My ski shot out from under me, and I crashed hard, bonking my head. *That was really odd*, I thought as I got up. My head hurt, yet I hadn't hit it very hard. I was wearing my ram helmet, and I wondered if there was something wrong with it. I called Mom and asked her to FedEx me a new one.

Gnarly had seen me fall. "What was that?" he said, skiing up to me.

Later at the hotel, the team doctor examined me and said I had a mild concussion. "You need to go home, Peek," Gnarly said. "Your season's over. Two concussions in a season isn't good."

I said, "Yeah, you know, I'm getting the same kind of vibe. I'm not sure. I'm going to ride it out a little bit longer and see what happens."

There was a war waging inside me. My guides, my instincts, were telling me to pay attention to the signs. *It's over*, they whispered. *Go home. You know you want to.* The knucklehead competitor inside was telling me to tough it out. *You're not a quitter!* she shouted. *If there's a race happening, you have to be in it!*

By the time we got to Crans-Montana, I was deeply ambivalent about whether to race or not. Herwig had heard I'd been considering leaving, and at dinner the night before the race, he said, "I'd like to talk to you later."

I went to my room to pack because we were supposed to leave the next day after the race. I was feeling on edge, reluctant to ski, wanting to go home. I expected Herwig to come to my room, but when he hadn't shown by ten-thirty, I went looking for him. I found him and Gnarly in the hotel bar, nursing drinks and looking tense.

"You never came to find me," I said.

"I'm not going to come chasing after you," Herwig replied curtly. "I've got enough going on; I don't need to deal with this, too. I've got to find a replacement for Andreas."

That was how I found out that Gnarly had resigned. I couldn't believe it. He'd never let on he was thinking about quitting the team.

"Is that true?"

Gnarly nodded guiltily. "I'll explain it to you later."

Then Gnarly left the bar, and Herwig and I sat at a table and hashed out our differences. "Picabo," he said, "if you want to go home, go home. If you don't want to go home, I want you to be here 110 percent."

I think Herwig was trying to push me over the edge. He thought the news about Gnarly would break me and I'd throw in the towel and we'd all go home. Instead I gave him a look. "Is that it?"

"Yeah. Make a decision tonight: it's on or it's off."

At that I marched out. I made my decision right then and there: it was on. I was going to have a good race for Gnarly because it would be our last. I was going to prove Herwig wrong one more time. And I was going to prove to everyone else that my Olympic medal was legit.

The next morning at the start Cookie handed me a pair of Dualtec downhill skis. I had agreed to race on them. I'd taken a couple training runs on them and felt okay. Between that and my training in Morzine, I decided I could make them work in a race. I didn't have much of a choice. Rossignol was going to stop making my old-school boards. If I wanted to keep ski racing for Rossi, I'd have to make the Dualtecs work.

What the hell? I have nothing to lose.

11

WHEN YOU'RE HURT, YOU'RE DIRT

Friday, March 13, 1998

Sion, Switzerland

Long-stemmed roses in a large, dark room: they were the first thing I saw when I emerged from the anesthesia. The roses were yellow and white, a cheery note in the gloom, and I wondered who'd sent them. I looked around the private room and realized how alone I was. I had to call J.J. and tell him what happened. What did happen? Suddenly it all rushed back: A high-speed crash into a safety fence. My left leg crumpling like paper. Feeling the end of my femur trying to poke through my skin. Screams of pain and fear. Being hoisted into the helicopter and airlifted to the hospital. The snap of a surgical glove in the operating room. I remembered it all. And then I tried my best to ignore it.

My left thigh was wrapped in nothing but a soft bandage. This shocked me. It seemed like so little protection, considering what the Swiss surgeons had done: sliced my thigh open lengthwise like a Wienerschnitzel and screwed the pieces of my femur together with an eight-inch steel plate. I had lost a great amount of blood. Dr. Bob Scheinberg, the ski team physician who helped me on the mountain and assisted at the surgery, told me later that when my thigh was cut open, a ribbon of blood arced clear across the operating room.

The femoral block was still inserted into my groin for pain relief. But I could tell there was something seriously wrong with my right knee, too. When I asked Bob, "So, what's up with the knee?" he hemmed and hawed. He didn't want to make me more upset than I already was.

"I blew it out, didn't I?"

"We'll make that determination once we get back to Vail," he answered. But I knew what a ruptured ACL felt like. I remembered the oath I'd made to myself last year: three ruptured ACLs and I'd quit. Did I mean it?

My condition was stable, but Bob worried that I might have suffered damage to the artery that supplies blood to the lower leg. For some reason the Swiss doctors refused to give me clot socks, tight spandex booties that help prevent blood clots from forming in the legs. Bob wanted to get me to the Steadman Hawkins Clinic in Vail as soon as possible. I was all for that. I don't do well in hospitals, especially foreign ones.

The nurses at Hospital de Champsec in Sion flew in and out of my room like birds. They poked and pricked my body and left, chirping to each other in French. I didn't understand a word they said. There was one nurse who was nice and who spoke good English, but she was gone after the first shift change. I was upset that I didn't have the clot socks, and when the nurses flew in, I'd growl, "I don't need a sponge bath. I need *protection*." Then they'd fly out, forgetting to take the bedpan with them.

For the two days I was in that hospital, Nadia stayed by my side, leaving only to field phone calls from the press. "Our plan is to fly her home Sunday," she told the Associated Press on Saturday, March 14. "We are trying to make the special arrangements needed to get her out of Sion tomorrow, but it's not easy."

Bob wanted me on a Medivac flight, but it was expensive—around forty thousand dollars. Nadia left my room to make a phone call and later came back with some bad news.

"The ski team's insurance won't pay for the flight," she said. "They say you're in stable condition and your knee isn't an emergency. They want you to wait a couple of days and fly commercial."

"Nadia, call Steve."

"Really?"

"Yes. Even if we don't use the plane, he'll be really pleased that I thought of him."

Nadia left again, and I fell asleep. She called Steve Wynn, Las Vegas billionaire, ski racing fan, and owner of a dolphin named Picabo. She got his secretary, Cindy, on the phone, and Cindy put Nadia on hold while she called Steve. A few minutes later she got back on with Nadia and told her that Steve was sending his plane right away. "She's in Sion, correct?" Cindy asked. Nadia asked her to hold off for an hour while she tried to make the Medivac flight happen. Cindy said, "If you call us back and give us the word, the pilot will be airborne in ten minutes."

Nadia's next call was to the ski team. It was time to twist the screws. "I think it would be in your best interest to fly Picabo home on Sunday morning," she said. "A friend of hers is going to send his private plane to come get her. And I don't think you guys want your gold medal athlete saying that her team wouldn't cough up the bucks to come pick her up."

At 6:00 a.m. on Sunday, my door banged open, and the nurses fluttered in.

"Good morning," I said drowsily. "What's happening?"

"You have a flight to catch," one nurse chirped in passable English. "We've got to get you up and out of here."

I was ecstatic. "All right, you can poke me; you can prick me; you can do whatever you want to me—I'm outta here!"

Then the nurses changed my bandage, and I saw the wound for the first time. It was a fierce incision about ten inches long, held together with thirty-seven metal staples. My skin was pinched and puckered between each staple, like a poorly sewn curtain, and the whole area was caked with dried blood. I knew what kind of scar that incision would leave. Each hole from each staple would leave its own mark. It would look as if a crocodile had tried to take a big bite out of my thigh. I would bear the scar of this trauma for the rest of my life.

One of the nurses asked me a question, and when I didn't answer, she looked down and saw that I was holding my face in my hands and bawling uncontrollably. "Oh, chérie," the nurses clucked, showing more concern in that moment than they had in two days.

The Medivac flight from Switzerland to Colorado took twelve hours. Sion is situated in a box canyon, and a full fuel tank would have made the plane too heavy to clear the mountains. So we had to stop twice to refuel, once in Ireland and once at a place called Forbisher's Bay near the North Pole. By the time we landed at Denver International Airport, where we cleared customs, I had run out of pain medication, though for some reason I didn't feel any pain at all. I was just glad to be back on American soil. We landed at Eagle County Airport near Vail at 4:30 P.M. and had to wait another hour for the ambulance. By 6:30 P.M., I was in my room at the Vail Valley Medical Center, getting briefed on all the tests I'd have to endure the next day to gauge the extent and nature of my various injuries.

Mom and J.J. flew to Vail. Unfortunately, Mom came down with such a bad case of altitude sickness that she had to go to the emergency room. I felt terrible for her. She had come out to support me, and here she was needing to be taken care of. J.J. slept on a cot by my bed and carried me to the bathroom in the middle of the night. My room filled with flowers from well-wishers, so many bouquets they gave me a headache. Soon every room on my floor had flowers.

Dr. Richard Steadman and Dr. William Sterret, the clinic's fracture specialist, told me that the Swiss doctors had done an excellent job inserting the metal plate. It was eight and three-quarter inches long, half an inch wide, and three-quarters of an inch thick. When Steadman stuck the X ray up on the light box, it looked like a giant shoehorn had been stuck in my leg.

My fracture was the worst Steadman had seen in twenty-seven years of treating major ski injuries. Almost ten centimeters of bone were fractured. The bone was sheared in half, and there were two main fragments, the big shaft and a lower part, which connected to the knee. In between were many pieces of crushed bone, too many to count. If one of the larger fragments had punctured my femoral artery, I could have bled to death on the mountain. As it was, the news was not all good. An MRA (magnetic resonance arteriogram) revealed a narrowing in the artery. The less-sophisticated arteriogram at the Swiss hospital had missed the fact that a bone fragment had bruised the artery wall, and now, four days later, a hematoma was impeding the blood flow.

The doctors elected to watch the injury for a few days. If my feet turned blue or went numb, it meant that a clot was cutting off the circulation to my lower legs. In that case the doctors would have to cut the back of my thigh open and repair the artery. I spent two days looking at my feet, praying they wouldn't change color. They didn't, and the doctors told me that the artery would eventually heal itself.

An MRI of my right knee revealed what was called a "bucket handle tear of the meniscus cartilage." The meniscus, which is usually on the back of the joint, had flipped to the front. Not only that, my right ACL had been completely ruptured, just as I suspected.

Steadman decided to postpone the surgery on my right knee. I couldn't put any weight on the broken leg, and if he operated on the right, both my legs would be useless for up to two months.

"I don't want to be in a wheelchair, Richard."

We agreed I'd go home to Portland to rest and heal, and return in a month for the knee surgery, after my femur was stronger. Using a brace, I'd be able to get around on my right knee, but sparingly.

"When can I ski again?" I asked him.

"Barring any complications, next spring."

By this time the press was speculating on how long I'd be out, or whether I'd come back at all. The word "retirement" was floated like a trial balloon. Brad Hunt urged me not to give any interviews until I knew what I was going to do. Steadman and I knew that a lot of skiers would call it quits after suffering injuries like mine. His philosophy was to never discuss such things when you didn't know what the outcome would be. He also knew that ultimately it was my decision, not his.

Over the next year, I would make the round-trip from Portland to Vail at least a dozen times for medical reasons. Flying commercial was expensive, and besides, I couldn't bear to let the public see me in this condition. So Steve Wynn generously donated the use of his private plane.

When I got home, I saw Dad for the first time since leaving for Europe a month earlier. We hugged and cried. Dad was blown away by how quickly my fortune had shifted. We had reached the dream we'd worked so hard for all those years. We'd been on such a high, yet hadn't been allowed to stay up there and enjoy it. He was as devastated as I was.

A couple days after I got home, Dad and I were sitting in the living room. He looked over at me and said, "If you never ski again, I don't care. If you ski again and win, I don't care. I just want you to become a healthy, whole woman again. That's all I care about."

I broke down into sobs. I knew how tough that in itself was going to be. I knew that this recovery would make what I went through in 1996–97 look like playing patty-cake. "Healthy" seemed so far away, like a distant country for which I had no passport, no itinerary, no way of knowing how long it would take to get there.

"HORRIFIC." THAT WAS THE ADJECTIVE THE PRESS USED AGAIN AND AGAIN to describe the accident. Every night, I relived the horror in my dreams. I'd be tumbling toward the fence, and just as I was about to hit it, I'd wake up, drenched in sweat and gasping for air. Night after night, for three weeks, the same dream.

The month before my knee surgery creaked by. I was physically and emotionally drained. My knee didn't work very well. I wasn't supposed to spend too much time on it. I couldn't put any weight on the left leg at all.

Mom bought some supplies to make my life easier: a stool, so I could sit in the shower, and a lift for the toilet seat, so I didn't have to squat as low. She made a special seat for me in the kitchen, a big comfy chair with another chair facing it, piled with pillows where I could rest my legs. Steadman believes that keeping an injured knee moving speeds the healing process and helps prevent the buildup of scar tissue, so Mom went to a medical supply company and rented something called a "continuous passive motion machine." I'd sit down, strap my right foot in, and watch my foot go, around and around. Steadman doesn't believe in plaster casts because they can accelerate the atrophy process, so my left leg was encased in a stiff brace.

My parents did everything they could to cheer me up. Mom held more "viewings," this time with the gold medal. We talked about the Olympics and what a thrill my victory had been, and all the good memories lifted my spirits. I came to accept the situation. *All right*, I thought. *I've done this before. I'll do it again.*

On April 3 I gave my first interview. I told the *Rocky Mountain News* that I was going to skip the next season and possibly even the following one. "I'm going to wait until I'm absolutely 100 percent sharp and have been training for a long time," I said. "I have to return. I really don't want to finish this way."

On April 3 we also celebrated my twenty-seventh birthday. It was a small, quiet gathering, just my parents, J.J., and my friends Jeff and Susan Livick. Jeff was a ski patroller we'd met at Mount Hood during a photo shoot. I tried my best to be upbeat, soldiering on, hiding the pain as I'd always done. As I prepared to leave for the airport on April 6, I went through the motions, packing, talking on the phone. Steve Wynn's pilot flew me back to Vail.

My surgery was scheduled for April 7. That morning a nurse wheeled me into pre-op on a gurney. I was given a sponge and a packet of Betadyne, an orange antiseptic liquid, and instructed to scrub my right knee for two minutes.

As I was about to start scrubbing, I was struck by the beauty of my right knee. The skin was smooth and pale and lightly freckled, completely pure and unmarred, like a snow-covered meadow before a bunch of kids tromp through it. I was hoping never to hurt this leg, never to have it cut open. Steadman posted photos of his clients—famous athletes like Martina Navritalova and Dan Marino—on the walls of his clinic, a gallery of champions with knees brutalized by their sports. The first time I went to Steadman's clinic at seventeen, I had looked at those photos and sworn that my knees would never look like theirs.

Fuck, I now thought. *I'm going to have both legs scarred up. I'm not going to make it through my career without looking like some of the people up on those walls.*

I scrubbed my nice-looking knee and felt a deep sadness creeping over me. It was the first sign of trouble ahead.

Steadman put my meniscus cartilage back where it belonged, but he decided against operating on the ACL because the surgeries required completely different rehabilitative regimens. Instead he drilled tiny holes into the base of my right femur so that they would leak bone marrow, rich with red blood cells, onto the ligament and promote healing. He told me there was a 60 percent chance at most that this would work.

Post-op was the worst. I couldn't move. I couldn't do anything. I had no leverage point whatsoever. I couldn't use my left leg. I couldn't use my right leg. This was as close as I'd come to being paralyzed, and I had an all-new appreciation for what Muffy Davis had gone through.

My stay in Vail was brief. I spent it being wheeled around on gurneys, lifted from bed to bed. After two days, Steve Wynn's pilot flew me home.

THIS IS WHAT IT TOOK TO GET OUT OF BED.

First, I'd slide my legs slowly, inch by inch, to the side of my bed. Then I'd grab my crutches—they were the kind that cupped your forearm—which I kept beside the nightstand, leaning against the wall. I'd extend the crutches out in front of me and lift my upper body up, like a diver in a pike position; put my crutches on the floor; and hoist myself up. Because I wasn't allowed to put any weight on my legs, I had to drag them behind me, crutching arduously from one arm to the other, like one of those cartoons where a lost soul is dragging himself through the desert toward water.

Mom did everything she could to help me. She cooked and brought me my meals on a TV tray. But she was having problems with her own knees. Her arthritis had almost crippled her, and she hobbled slowly around the house. It hurt me to watch her. We didn't have one good leg between the two of us. I hated to ask her to get me anything; I couldn't lean on her when I got out of bed, so if I wanted a glass of water, I either had to drag myself out of bed to get it or just lie there. It was easier to just lie there.

Dad wasn't good around people who needed help. His dad had been a navy nurse whose attitude was, if you're sick, you'd better be in a hospital. So Dad made grocery runs and kept the hot tub clean and tried to pretend there was nothing wrong with me. Baba came every few weeks, but Lauren was pregnant with their first child, and he needed to be with her back in Ketchum.

J.J. didn't fly up very often. I could feel him pulling away. Was it the crutches? The scars? Did my weakness repulse him? I wasn't the woman he'd fallen in love with, the vital skier with a gold-plated mission. He wanted Sister Slope, not the Bride of Frankenstein. I worried I was losing him, which made me feel even worse.

Two weeks after the knee surgery, I was lying in my bed, my legs elevated on a pillow. I flipped my comforter back, and what I saw sent me spinning. I saw a scar like an angry zipper running the length of my left thigh. I could see every staple, every single hole made by each staple. Ribbons of bloody tissue hung off the wounds. I saw my right knee, swollen and red, the incisions still fresh and oozing. Both legs scarred, ruined. I could see my muscles already starting to wither, a sign that atrophy was setting in.

This wasn't supposed to happen to me. When I was young, I was too much of a badass to think I could get badly hurt. *I won't blow apart*, I'd tell myself. *I'm tougher than that.* I was invincible, the girl of steel. Fall down; get up: I excelled at it. As long as I could hide my pain I could keep going. Scars were advertisements for weakness, proof of my frailty. Besides, they were unfeminine and ugly. Women weren't supposed to have scars like this.

I felt myself falling into a black hole. In the past I would go into a funk after losing a race, but no matter how upset or angry I was I could flip a happy switch and become the smiling, sunny, irrepressible girl the media loved so much. Now I didn't know where to find that girl. The girl that had taken her place cried a lot. She sat and cried and worried.

Will my legs ever be the same? What will happen to my body? Will I ever be able to ski again? Do I have enough money to stop? What will I do if I stop?

I can't do it again. The rehab, the training, the anxiety. I'm not standing in the on-deck circle, waiting to bat for two years.

On top if it, I hadn't accepted winning the gold. Reporters called, but I knew I was getting the attention because I was hurt, not because I'd won a gold medal. Victory canceled out by tragedy: that had become my story, and it wasn't the one I wanted to tell.

I felt like a dirt bag. I stayed in my room and cried and shook my fist at the unfairness of it all. I didn't want to see anyone or talk to anyone. If someone called, I asked Mom to take a message. I didn't want to hear the question: "Picabo, will you compete again?" because I didn't know the answer.

I lay around the house, watching stupid stuff on television. Every few days, I changed locations. I'd spend three days holed up in my room, make my way out to the living room and spend three days there, then go back to my room for three days—back and forth like that, for six weeks. Sometimes, for variety, I lay on a chaise lounge on the porch.

I began to reevaluate my theory on karma. What had I done to deserve this? I had to have been the Boston Strangler in a previous life to carry all this bad karma into my current lifetime. Maybe there was another explanation, a master plan that some higher power, whether it was God or some other entity, had created for me. Maybe this plan was put together in advance, the way a pilot creates a flight plan before taking off. I envisioned my spirit sitting down with some sort of cosmic counselor and saying, "All right, these are the lessons I'm going to learn in this lifetime, and this is how I'm going to do it." We scripted it out, and then I came down here and did it.

On the other hand, maybe it wasn't scripted at all. Maybe my spirit had met with the higher power and said, "Okay, these are the lessons I want to learn in this lifetime. Build me physically, mentally, and emotionally to handle them." And then I came down and just improvised.

All I knew was that there was a master plan and I didn't have much control over it; I was just along for the ride. I accepted that there were lessons I was meant to learn from my suffering and that I needed to open up and let them flow into me.

Mom spent a lot of time talking me through that dark period, and one piece of advice has stuck with me. "This is a time when you're supposed to think about what you've accomplished," she told me. "That's why you've been put in this situation: to force yourself to think about where you've been and where you're going."

I didn't want to think about where I'd been. I tried not to think about skiing at all. After a month, the nightmares stopped. If I had any dreams, I couldn't remember them at all.

WHEN I WAS GROWING UP, MOTHER'S DAY WAS ALWAYS A BIG DAY IN OUR house. I'd bounce out of bed in the morning, all smiles, and run into the kitchen and give Mom a hug. Dad would make her a big, beautiful breakfast. It was her special day.

Mother's Day came around that May, as usual. After all Mom had done for me, the least I could do was to tell her I loved her in person, just as I always had. But I was too depressed to get out of bed. My body felt heavy, immobile, as if the steel plate in my left leg had spread to occupy every bone in my body.

I picked up the phone and dialed J.J.'s number in San Francisco. He didn't visit much, but he could still support me from a distance. We talked for four hours. He reminded me of all the things I had accomplished and how great the totality of my life had been. He tried to point out the simple lessons that I was too emotional to see. "You needed a break," he said. "Some higher power is telling you to rest."

Finally, some higher power told me to get out of bed, so I dragged myself to my feet and dragged myself into the kitchen. It was late afternoon already. It had taken me the entire day to get from my bedroom to the kitchen.

Mom was there, wiping the counters. She turned and saw me standing in the doorway, leaning on my crutches. I could sense she was surprised to see me, but she tried to pretend it was just another day.

"Tired of eating someone else's cooking, are you?" she wisecracked. "Come to make your own?"

"No," I said softly. "I came to wish you happy Mother's Day." I crutched the length of the kitchen and collapsed in her arms. We both dissolved into tears, but she couldn't hold me up so I had to sit down. I eased myself into my special chair, and she made me my favorite breakfast, bacon and scrambled eggs. It had made Mom happy to see me standing there, willing to make an effort. And seeing Mom happy made me happy, if only for a moment.

If you asked me what brought me out of my depression, I'd be hard-pressed to come up with a single revelatory moment. As an athlete, my mood was hitched to my physical well-being, and as that started to improve, the darkness lifted gradually, like a sky lightening at dawn. I needed a goal, a time line, a plan of attack, no matter how hypothetical or far-fetched. My goal before the accident was to compete and win at the 1999 World Alpine Ski Championships in Vail and then retire. My new goal became simply to ski in them. Whether I ultimately returned to ski racing or not, I had something to shoot for, and that's all that mattered.

In late May, Steve Wynn's pilot flew me to Vail for my six-week post-op checkup. Steadman examined my knee and said the meniscus was healing nicely. I told him about my plan to ski that winter. He said I could try skiing with a knee brace. If it didn't work, he'd fix the ACL in the spring of 1999, after the Worlds.

"How long will the plate have to stay in?" I asked.

"Most people leave it in all their lives," he answered. "But you're probably going to want to take it out. We'll keep it in there for a year, until next spring. I know that's bad timing, but . . ."

"Then I'm going to have to try and ski with it in. See if it works. If it does, then I'll go with it and have it taken out when my career's over," I replied.

"That would be the best-case scenario. The only problem I have with that is that the plate is going to create a stress point on your bone. And if you crash again, that's where your bone will break, on top of that plate," he cautioned.

Before I could ski I had to be able to walk. And for that I needed Cheryl Kosta, the same physical therapist who had helped me in 1997. Every day I hoisted myself into my car and drove to Cheryl's office. This rehab program was much more complex because each leg required a different type of exercise. The repaired cartilage in my right knee needed to be coddled, moved very gently and precisely. My left leg had to be moved more aggressively, and that's the one she spent more time on. Cheryl started with one leg, then the other. This doubled the length of each session, but I had nothing else to do.

Cheryl was instrumental in getting me moving. She wanted me to heal as quickly as possible, and she would call Richard and ask him what else she could do to move things along. Cheryl's attitude was contagious, and eventually I began to ask myself, "What more can you do?" I began to see results in July, and in August Richard gave me the okay to start working with Matty again. All those years of training without an injury to my right knee helped the muscles bounce back quickly. Soon I was down to one crutch, and by the end of the summer I could hobble around without that one too. I felt as if I was walking on a set of stork legs, but at least I was walking. My parents would drag me out into the world, even if it was just to the mall. I tried not to panic about how long my recovery was taking. I just steadied on, believing in my program, sticking with it.

As I felt my legs get stronger, my mood started to brighten. The 2002 Olympics were three and a half years away. The lure of competing at the Games in my own country was irresistible. I had three and a half years to get back to the skier I once was, if that was possible. I knew that my legs would eventually heal; the thing I worried about most was my psyche. The mountain is like a shark: if it smells fear on you, it will bite. I wondered if I'd ever be able to shake the fear I'd felt on that mountainside in Crans; the fear I felt when I woke up from another dream, my heart racing; the fear I felt when I just *thought* about going eighty miles an hour downhill, something I used to do without a second thought.

I had started to see warning signs. Little, no-brainer things I used to do, like jumping the last two steps in a stairwell, had become scary. Walking itself was dangerous; my muscles were so weak that one misstep could reinjure my knee, and I found myself wary and hesitant, second-guessing every move, every step. Before I had a relationship with fear, I never felt as if I was going fast enough. Now that fear and I were on a first-name basis, everything seemed accelerated. I found myself poking along in the slow lane on the freeway on the way to Cheryl's, casting nervous glances in the rearview mirror.

By now, my dream had changed. In my dreams I'd find myself at the top of a run, trying to decide which section I could ski. If a section was too difficult, I went around it. Eventually the dream evolved to where I attempted it, but my legs would be so tired toward the bottom that I could barely go on.

I knew that the only way to stop being haunted by the crash was to face it head-on. I had a copy on videotape, and one day I got brave enough to watch it. Jeff and Susan were visiting, and I popped the tape into the VCR. At the part where I started screaming, Susan started to cry softly, and I felt my femur throb with sympathetic pain. "Look," I said to my friends, "I'm alive. It could be worse."

One day my old coach came to visit. After the Olympics, Herwig had resigned as head women's coach and gone to work for the Salt Lake Organizing Committee as director of the 2002 Olympic Alpine skiing venues.

Herwig and I had stayed in touch, and in September he flew up to Portland to see me. Despite our fight the night before my accident, there was no bad blood between us. Herwig had left the decision to ski to me. I had held my fate in my own two hands.

I was caught between desire and fear. Some days I woke up eager to go for a comeback; other days I just wanted to throw in the towel, call it a career. I explained all this to Herwig when he came to visit. As he saw it, I had three options.

"Picabo," he said, "you've accomplished a lot. You can quit now and move on. No one would be angry or blame you if you did.

"The other thing you can do is train and be part of the team again. When you get back into racing, you can feel if it's good or not. If you don't like it, you can say, 'I tried it; I'm afraid of going fast; I'm not going to do it anymore.' No one's going to blame you for that because everyone will see that you tried.

"Third, you can go full program. Join the team and give it your best shot. Don't give up. It won't be fun in the beginning. The first year, you have to be patient. And the second year, if you're in good shape and you've trained enough, then you can go for the kill again."

Go for the kill again. Did I have it in me?

I knew in my heart that option three was the only way to go. I don't walk out the door on a challenge. My style is to meet it head-on.

When I was twelve, one of our Triumph neighbors, Carl Massaro, had a horse named Solero. Mom remembers him as a mangy desert mustang, but to me, he was the most beautiful damn thing I'd ever seen, a charcoal gray Arabian with a diamond on his chest and a white spot on his forehead. A previous owner had beaten Solero, leaving him jumpy and unpredictable. I spent every minute I could with that horse. I cleaned and treated his hooves and helped Carl reshoe him, being careful not to get stepped on. I braided his mane with ribbons, as if he were a doll, and fed him carrots, his favorite. When I brushed Solero's coat, I would look into his wet, wild eyes and feel his hide twitch and shiver. "Carl, can I ride Solero?" I'd ask, and Carl always said no. He knew that Solero and I were a match made in hell. It's true; Solero scared the bejesus out of me. But I knew that the only way to conquer that fear was to ride him someday.

That's how I was with ski racing. I knew I would get back on that horse. The only question was how fast I'd be willing to let it run.

IF GIVEN THE CHOICE BETWEEN TEARING UP MY KNEE AND BREAKING A bone, I would choose breaking a bone, every time. Bones mend. Ligaments and cartilage refuse to heal. They flare up and shift around and basically screw you over.

All I did was step out of a car. On October 3, 1998, I drove into downtown Sun Valley to have breakfast with my parents, Baba, and Lauren. I parked and went to exit my car. When I put weight on my right foot, my meniscus cartilage popped out of place again. It hurt like hell, and I knew immediately what had happened. I broke into tears. Five days later I was back in Vail, having my third surgery in seven months.

Steadman said one reason the cartilage had retorn was that the ACL hadn't been there to hold it in place. He couldn't put off repairing the ACL any longer. He reconstructed the ligament, just as he had my left ACL in December 1996. I was facing another winter on crutches and countless more trips to Cheryl's office. My goal of skiing at the Worlds, skiing at all that winter, was gone.

For eight months, I practically vanished from the public eye. Months I should have spent racking up new endorsement deals and promoting my various product lines were spent sequestered in my house and undergoing endless rehab. The media checked in with me once in a while, especially those papers like *USA Today* and the *Rocky Mountain News* that had followed my career closely for years. Otherwise, I kept a low profile. I didn't want to parade my injuries in public, and besides, there wasn't a lot of demand for a wrecked ski racer with a big question mark on her forehead.

One of my few public appearances at that time was a formal fund-raiser for the U.S. Ski Team called the Ski Ball. A New York Ski Ball was held every November, and on November 10, Nadia and I flew out for it. I did an interview with the Associated Press, my crutches parked nearby, and uttered a sentence I never thought I would hear myself say: "I have a strong feeling that I am going to be too afraid to run downhill again. And if I'm afraid to run downhill, I would be afraid to run Super G."

I told the reporter my long-term goal was competing at the 2002 Olympics, but that I planned to switch to the slalom or GS. They were slower. Safer.

In November, I began to ease myself back into the ski team. I went to its annual Colorado training camp, where my old teammates greeted me warmly. I spent ten days clapping and cheering everyone on and cringing when anyone crashed. I was beginning to see my position on the team: the veteran who could share her experience with the young ones, just as Tamara McKinney had once done with me.

As usual, we received our new uniforms for the season at that fall camp. I got one too, even though I wouldn't be competing. I sat on the bed in my hotel room, checking out all the pieces of my new uniform as I'd done every fall for the past twelve years. Over the years I'd come to take the ritual for granted, but that night I felt some of the old thrill I had when I was fifteen and trying it on for the first time. My only regret was that I wouldn't be racing in it.

At that moment, Sarah Schleper, a promising nineteen-year-old racer from Vail, came into my room to chat. She had beaten her teammates by two seconds during training in October yet finished sixtieth at the first World Cup of the season in Austria. Sarah was a rising star on the technical team, but she didn't have the confidence to embrace her promise. Having been there myself once, I knew the diagnosis.

"Sarah," I said, "you're afraid to be the best."

Her eyes got big and she said, "What do you mean?"

"Everybody on the team sees you as the one to beat already, so you don't have anything to worry about. Why don't you just get it?"

I needed some advice on how to deal with my own fears, and for that I turned to Sean McCann, head of the U.S. Olympic Committee's sports psychology department. Sean had traveled with the women's ski team since 1993, counseling us on everything from performance anxiety to family problems. Sean had helped me when I was under such pressure to make it to Nagano, and a year later, in Beaver Creek, I turned to him again. I told him I was afraid of so many things: of hurting myself again, of not being able to ski like I used to. Could I get over this fear, and if so, when?

Sean had always been impressed by my confidence and energy. But he could see there was something different about me, a vulnerability that hadn't been there before. He said it wasn't unusual for an athlete who's experienced a traumatic injury like mine to feel an overwhelming, paralyzing anxiety. There were two separate kinds of fears: those related to the injury and those that resulted from the injury. The first step toward getting past my fears was to identify and categorize them into those I could control and those I couldn't. I could spend all day mulling over my various insecurities and doubts, and that would drain energy from the job I had to do: get better. I needed to be disciplined about walling off the unhelpful thoughts, and focusing my famous energy on the positive things that would help me return to skiing, such as rehab.

"Just keep categorizing it all for yourself," he said. "Just remember you can go all day on the good stuff and put a time limit on the bad stuff. As you need to, rely on me, but I'll trust you'll put it together for yourself as you usually do."

A month later, at the 1998 U.S. Olympic Committee Athlete of the Year banquet in Indianapolis, I met an athlete who embodied the power of positive thinking. I was one of three finalists in the women's category, with tennis player Lindsay Davenport and track star Marion Jones. The men's finalists were cyclist Lance Armstrong, swimmer Lenny Krayzelburg, and mogul skier Jonny Moseley. The event is sort of like the Oscars; all the nominees show up to find out who won. I had won the USOC honor in 1995, and I felt honored when I won again in 1998. And I also enjoyed being able to walk up and accept the award without crutches.

But what really stood out about that night was meeting Lance Armstrong. Lance had battled back from testicular cancer and was reclaiming his title as the world's best road cyclist. He had overcome the ultimate adversity; he had been to the doors of heaven and back. Lance seemed almost weightless, as if he had gone into a confessional chamber, been forgiven for all his sins, and walked out purified. I remember being pulled into a dark corner to do an interview and seeing Lance and his wife, Kristin, float through the room. I was so moved by their power. They seemed so light and free. I was envious because I felt heavy, stuck in the doldrums. At the time no one could have predicted that Lance would go on to win three consecutive Tour de France titles, an amazing achievement for anyone, but especially for a cancer survivor. All I wanted that night was to shake Lance's hand, to feel some of his healing energy flow into me. And I did.

BY JANUARY 1999, I COULD WALK DOWN A FLIGHT OF STAIRS WITHOUT holding the handrail. Every morning I woke up stiff and hurting. Each leg hurt in a different way: the right knee with a dull, throbbing ache, the left thigh with a sharp, metallic tang. Some days it felt like I had the body of an old woman.

I also had a new job: director of skiing at Park City, Utah. My job was to ski with customers (once I could ski again), appear in advertisements, and promote the resort at travel conferences and trade shows. Since Park City was set to host the GS events at the 2002 Winter Olympics, I had yet another reason to want to ski there. That the resort's CEO, John Cummings, wanted me to represent the place was a huge boost to my self-esteem at a time when I really needed it.

I was contractually obligated to live in Park City, so I moved into a condo at the bottom of a mountain nicknamed the Crash Pad. My parents stayed behind in Portland. I spent a good part of January and February hobbling around the base area. Each leg seemed to have its own agenda— the left felt better straight, the right bent. Sometimes it was hard to walk in a straight line. I was limping badly, too proud to use a cane. I hated it when people stared at me, questioning my future with their eyes. It made me want to yell at them, "I won't be a gimp for the rest of my life!"

I was hoping to ski the following season, and that winter I started to train more seriously. I'd lost so much leg muscle I was wearing a size 8 in pants (I wear a size 12 when I'm at my fighting weight), and it was time to start building it back up. Matt James faxed me workouts I could follow at my new gym in Park City. Keeping my balance on the snowy slopes was actually good therapy for my legs. Sometimes I put on a U.S. Ski Team jacket and signed autographs and smiled for pictures. Other times I walked anonymously among the tourists, just another skier trying to figure out the sport.

Now that my shield of invincibility had been cracked, I felt more human, more compassionate. My pace in life had slowed dramatically, giving me more time to pay attention to someone other than myself. In airports I used to blow by the people who were traveling slowly and needed a hand here and there. *Slowpoke*, I'd think. Now *I* was that slowpoke, the one who needed a hand.

My new job at Park City happened to coincide with one of the biggest news stories of the year. Every reporter in every interview asked me the same question: "What did I, an Olympic gold medalist, think about the Olympic bribery scandal?"

In late 1998, allegations surfaced that members of the Salt Lake Organizing Committee (SLOC) had bribed IOC board members to win the 2002 Winter Games. Marc Hodler, a member of the IOC executive board, told the press just before he retired that corruption was entrenched in the Olympic bid process. The IOC began an investigation into the Salt Lake bid process, and in the winter of 1999 a new allegation of greed came out practically every day. There was the charge that in 1995 SLOC helped pay the college tuition for one IOC member, and that a Salt Lake backer carried fifty thousand dollars in cash to the same IOC conference in Budapest that I'd attended. Earl Holding, the owner of Sun Valley Resort and an SLOC board member, came under scrutiny. He was building a huge hotel in downtown Salt Lake City called Little America, and people started saying it was improper for a board member to profit from the bid process.

The scandal hit close to home. I had cut my teeth on the Olympic dream. I had practiced "The Star-Spangled Banner" and fantasized about standing on that podium. I had flown on Earl's plane to Budapest. Marc Hodler, the whistle-blower, had put the silver medal around my neck at the 1993 World Alpine Ski Championships in Morioka. The whole thing left me disappointed and confused. Disappointed because I'd played a role in getting the Games to Salt Lake. Confused because I had been looking for corruption, for the white envelope under the table. How had I missed it?

When two bid-committee executives, Tom Welch and Dave Johnson, got most of the blame, I got mad. I had watched them work their butts off to get the Games to Salt Lake. Tom spent a lot of his own money, and Dave worked himself until he was bug-eyed with exhaustion. They ended up wearing the brown helmet for the whole thing when they had just been playing the game, and the game was played to win. In a sense, all they did was play by the rules, even the rules that were unwritten.

The athletes weren't shocked. We just started realizing how much money was flying around our scene and how little of it we were getting. Where was all the money to train the athletes? The U.S. Ski Team had teetered on the verge of bankruptcy for years and had to cut money for development and travel. Where was our fair share? Weren't the athletes the whole reason for the Olympics?

The irony is, I felt as if we could have gotten the Games without selling out. We could have taken a stand against corruption and changed the system that way. Instead, we'll end up changing the system by getting busted. If that's what it takes to clean up the system, fine. The United States can handle it. "There are many people in the Olympic movement who truly want to see it get clean and pure," I told *Newsweek* in February 1999. "This is our chance—and our responsibility—to pounce and get it turned in the right direction."

I pray we can. I am a case study of how aspiring to the Olympics can change your life, and I refuse to believe that dream will die for future generations.

IN SPORTS, THOSE WHO CAN'T COMPETE, COMMENTATE. IN FEBRUARY 1999, NBC hired me to do color commentary at the Worlds in Vail. It was great to see all my old Euro friends again. I made my old friend Tamara McKinney, who was living in Tahoe, come and ski down the slalom course wearing a tiny camera on her helmet. And I helped Meisi through a difficult time. She'd become the best woman ski racer in Austria, and her teammates were jealous. She was leading the World Cup overall coming into the Worlds and was under a lot of pressure to win a gold medal. I spent a lot of time with Meisi in her room, talking her off the ledge. So when she won the Super G, I felt as if I'd helped. A few days later, she won the GS, too. The Austrians cleaned up that year; the United States didn't win a single medal.

I ended up getting good reviews for my commentating, but the whole experience was frustrating. I didn't want to be sitting there talking about it; I wanted to be doing it. Being there brought all the old warrior emotions to the surface. Instead of feeling sad and depressed, I felt competitive and pissed.

The Associated Press took a photo of J.J. and me with my arm around him, watching the races. We seem happy, but in reality we were struggling. Life with me was a roller-coaster ride; I was up one day, down the next.

J.J. was getting tired of being my cheerleader. I visited him in San Francisco a couple times, but it wasn't the same. He had dedicated his life to supporting me in the year before the Olympics, but now that I had nothing but time to give to him, he didn't seem to want it.

While I was in Vail I went to see Dr. Steadman. He caught me wincing when I crossed my legs, and I confessed that the plate had been causing me a lot of pain. Richard had worried that it would be dangerous for me to ski with the plate in, so the decision was clear. "Let's take it out," he said.

On March 15, a year and two days after my fall in Crans, the plate came out. Bill Sterret, the fracture specialist, unscrewed it from my leg and packed the screw holes full of pulverized cadaver bone. I was awake during the procedure, and I remember wanting so badly to see my leg slit wide open. I kept trying to peek over the sheet that shielded me from the gory details. "Bill," I said, "I really want to see my leg. Can you come up with a way to do that?" Bill asked someone to fetch his digital camera, and a nurse sterilized it and brought it into the operating room. I still have that photo of my leg cut open. You can see the bone, which has healed nicely. It's gory, but I'm proud of it. Showing people that photo is my way of embracing and accepting what happened to me. I still have the metal plate, too. I'm thinking about using it as a door knocker.

The metal plate had made taking an MRI of my left knee impossible since the MRI works on a magnetic field. While my leg was open, Richard checked out my left knee arthroscopically and saw that the cartilage under the kneecap was damaged as well, probably from the fall a year earlier. He did a procedure called a microfracture, in which tiny cracks are made in the bone so that marrow can leak out and stimulate the formation of new cartilage.

My femur was weaker without the plate, so I had to go back on two crutches for six weeks. That felt like a huge setback, and it pushed me back into a dark state of mind. Right after the surgery, I went to Las Vegas with J.J. for the annual ski industry trade show. Steve Wynn put us up at the Mirage in one of his best rooms, a lanai suite. It was humiliating to crutch around the Las Vegas Convention Center, seeing business associates and other racers and feeling like a polio victim. I couldn't wait to go back to my room and hide.

While I was in Vegas, I got a call from Brad. He said Nike had this great idea for a new commercial. I would be the star. There was only one catch: I'd be in a wheelchair.

"You've got to be kidding me." I was completely insulted. Nike wanted to make fun of my legs? It was the stupidest idea I'd ever heard. "No way," I told Brad.

The thought of doing the commercial made me even more miserable than I already was. *A wheelchair, huh?* I'd show them. *I'm going to start using just one crutch—one crutch, just to keep me from putting weight on my leg.* I was ready.

The lanai rooms were at the far corner of the hotel, through a set of locked doors and down a long hallway. One afternoon, J.J. and I were returning to our room when we got into a fight, a real knock-down-drag-out. I don't remember what it was about; we were fighting a lot by that time. I was trying to unlock the door to the hallway so I could get to our room and go to the bathroom. I was on some medications that made my bladder feel as if it was about to explode.

I struggled with the key for a few seconds and finally managed to open the door. I started crutching like a maniac down the hallway to our room. By the time I reached the lanai I was about to pee my pants. To get to the bathroom, I had to maneuver down two steps into the living room and around the corner to the bathroom. I started going down the stairs when I lost my balance and fell down them instead. I crashed to the floor with a thud.

It was the worst fall I had ever taken—worse than Vail, worse than Bormio, worse than Åre. A year's worth of pain, frustration, and fear welled to the surface, and I went berserk.

I got back to my feet in a blind rage. I took my crutch and smashed it into the wall. It hit the doorjamb, bent in half, and broke. I flung my ruined crutch across the room and kicked the stereo with my left foot, ripping the unit off the wall. I couldn't believe what I'd done, but I couldn't stop, either. I picked up an ashtray and hurled it across the room. It exploded in a shower of broken glass. *Boom!*

The noise snapped me out of it. I stood there, panting, surveying the wreckage. Finally I said to myself, *I gotta pee.* And I went to the bathroom.

The damage was minor; still, I felt bad about it after all Steve had done for me. All I can say is I was under a lot of stress that spring. My body was rebelling. My relationship was crumbling. And I was about to go to court.

There's a saying in the ski industry, "When you're hurt, you're dirt." It means that an injured skier is damaged goods, worth about as much to his or her sponsors as a Confederate dollar. A lot of people doubted whether I would ever race again, or if I did, whether I could approach my former greatness. All my existing sponsors kept the faith—all but one.

My relationship with Rossignol had been rocky since I refused to do the photo shoot in Nagano. The company sent me flowers after the accident, but after my second surgery in April 1998, they told Brad they wanted to exercise an injury clause in my contract that would cut my salary by more than half. Rossignol claimed I had lost my "value" as a sponsored athlete, yet they were still using my image in ads, and my signature ski, the Peak, was still on the market.

"Do everything," I told Brad. "Exhaust every option. If I have to walk away from this deal, I want to know that I tried everything to make it work."

The negotiations went nowhere. Finally Brad said, "I recommend arbitration."

"Take it to 'em," I answered.

The arbitration hearing took place in Salt Lake City in April 1999. It was like a trial without a jury. I took the witness stand and testified about the events of the past year. Rossignol's lawyer cross-examined me, and I became very emotional on the stand. The judge was an older man named Carman Kipp. He was also a ski racing fan, and he ruled that Rossignol had to pay what they owed me. I had prevailed, but the victory was bittersweet.

That wasn't my only legal battle that year. Apparently the Sun Valley Co. thought my name still had value, because in the fall of 1999 the company used it in some of its promotional materials. On December 16, my lawyers filed a complaint with the U.S. District Court in Boise, claiming the resort had used my name without permission and owed me compensation. It felt strange to be suing the ski resort I'd grown up with, the mountain that had shaped me into a champion. But my lawyers told me I had no choice. My contract with Park City gave that resort exclusive rights to use my name and likeness for promotional purposes, and if I didn't stop Sun Valley from violating that right I was opening the door for other resorts to do the same thing.

Some people thought I was suing Sun Valley for the money. To prove otherwise, I pledged to donate any money I made, after paying my legal fees, to the Hailey and Sun Valley ski teams. The case was settled fairly quickly, and I'd made my point. "Picabo Street" wasn't just a memorable name anymore. It was a brand, and I had to protect it.

Two months after the arbitration with Rossignol, J.J. and I called it quits. We agreed we'd come together for one purpose, to win the gold medal at Nagano. That mission was over, and so were we. Contrary to what Sapphire had said, even eight lifetimes hadn't been enough.

It took seven conversations with Brad and several script rewrites before I agreed to do the wheelchair commercial. I'd finally decided that making light of my situation might somehow help me feel better about it. Wieden & Kennedy, Nike's ad agency, kept sending me little storyboards so I could see how the commercial would look. This was the concept: I'm stuck in a hospital. I'm jonesing so badly to go fast that I whip around the hospital in my wheelchair, wreaking havoc. Little did I know that commercial would play a big part in rebuilding my self-confidence.

That summer, I flew to L.A. to shoot the commercial in a vacant wing of a hospital. I had a blast. I hung out in a hospital gown for a day and a half, eating sushi and watching TV in a room while the crew set up each shot. I had a stunt double whom they used to rehearse the scenes, but I insisted on doing all my own stunts. I'd come out of my room, shoot my scene, and go back in again while they set up the next one. There was one scene where I had to bomb down a stairwell in the chair. I remember putting on my game face, just as I would in the starting gate, and rattling down the steps. In another scene I barreled past a nursery in the maternity ward. One crewmember would push me, I'd fly by the window where you view the newborns, they'd take the video, and another crewmember would catch me. Sometimes they'd just send me into these mats. I must have gone barreling into the mats fifty times that day. My left leg was jacked up in a stiff brace, sticking straight out. I had to lean forward and stop myself with my hand before my foot hit the wall.

For the last scene, I was supposed to come flying through the waiting room and across the finish line, pull my brake, spin around, fly backward out the doors, and get run over by an ambulance (that last bit takes place off camera). The crew poured about forty cans of WD-40 on the floor to make it slippery. Everyone was very careful with me, but after I left, seven people slipped and fell. Three of them got hurt.

There was one stunt I took a pass on. I was supposed to charge down a hallway, skid hard around a corner, knock over a tray piled high with metal bedpans, and then haul ass down the hallway. The wheelchair was rigged with two cables. A crewmember stood at one end and pulled the wheelchair straight toward the bedpans and spun it in the other direction, at which point another crewmember pulled the wheelchair down the hallway. It took them a couple tries to perfect the timing, and on the first rehearsal my stunt double went crashing into the wall. She had this big knob on her elbow, and her head was dinged. I mean, she went *in*.

I stuck my head out the door to see what was going on, took one look at the wreckage, and said, "Let me know when you guys get a little closer on that one, okay?" Then I closed the door. I let the stunt double handle that one.

Shooting that commercial was the equivalent of taking the first fall of the season: I proved to myself that I could take a physical risk and walk away from it. I pushed my limits in a controlled environment and wasn't afraid to put my body on the line. Not only that, it was nice to be treated like a star again.

My next small-screen adventure was an extreme sports show called "Danger Zone" for the Outdoor Life Network. I was the host. I learned thirteen new sports, one for each episode, ranging from street luge to rock climbing. Taping the show was fun and stimulating, and a great way to break my body back in. I didn't have to do anything too outrageous. Each episode had people who were experts at the sports, so the dangerous stuff was left to them. I just got to dabble.

We started filming in June 1999, as soon as I got off crutches. For two months, the crew and I traveled all around the country: Oregon, Colorado,

North Carolina. The coolest thing I did was learn how to hang glide in Nags Head, North Carolina, not far from where the Wright brothers took that first flight in 1903. I started by sailing off sand dunes, and later I got towed behind an airplane. Once I got some speed, it let me go and I flew on my own. I loved the feeling of flying high above the earth, suspended in my harness. I steered the hang glider with my upper body, and for once my legs weren't holding me back; they were just along for the ride.

Around that time I shot one last commercial for Nike. It was a montage of athletes who had been disfigured by their sports. The soundtrack was Joe Cocker's "You Are So Beautiful." A bull rider who'd lost an eye. A football player with an amputated pinky. A wrestler with a cauliflower ear. A runner with mangled feet. And me. My scene is toward the end. I'm doing rehab when the camera catches me looking at my terrible scar. When I notice that the camera is on me, I stand up and push my chest out and look straight at it with a defiant expression that says, *Yeah? What about it?* I did that commercial to prove I wasn't ashamed of my scar.

IN AUGUST 1999, MY PARENTS AND I DECIDED TO REASSESS OUR LIVING arrangements. I was twenty-eight and still living with my mom and dad. Sure, the house was mine, but they took care of it—kept the refrigerator stocked, the plants watered, the dog fed. During the two years I'd been injured we had spent a great deal of time together, and I had begun to feel like a visitor who had overstayed her welcome. Dad and I had such similar energies. If he felt bad, I did, too. We'd send each other on emotional roller-coaster rides, and it got to be too much. I'd grown up quite a bit in those two years, and I wanted to see if I was grown up enough to live on my own. I needed to know that. Mom and Dad had stayed together, and I was proud that, by asking them to live with me, I had helped make that happen. Now I knew it was time to break off on my own, to regain my freedom and to give them theirs.

Mom and Dad moved back to Idaho to be closer to their grandson, Cade Christopher, who had been born the previous December. I bought them a house in the middle of an alfalfa field south of Hailey, in horse country, and left Duggan with them. I put the Portland house on the market. We'd had a lot of ups and downs in that place—too many. I bought a new house in the hills outside of Park City. From my window I could see the ski trails across a valley and a new freeway going in for the Olympics. The Sun Valley area was only five hours away—a trip around the block for me—and I could drive up there whenever I liked.

I wasn't ready to live completely alone. Jess, my friend from Maui, moved to Park City to be my roommate and work as my personal assistant. She and Steven had separated and she was yearning for a change. I'd had girlfriends in the past, but I'd never lived with one of them. We had a blast. We decorated the house together and did girly things like sitting on the floor cross-legged, playing cards and drinking red wine. When I was getting dressed up for an appearance she'd be straight-out honest with me. "No, no, no," she'd say, walking into my bedroom. "You are way too bloated to wear that." Or she'd exclaim, "You look fabulous!" Jess and I lived together for nine months, and it was the first time I truly bonded with a woman other than my mother. (You know how much trouble I've had with my teammates.) I was a constant witness to a total sweetheart. She was sweet on the phone to everyone she spoke to, sweet to everyone who came to the house. She was sweet even when she was telling someone to fuck off. Like me, she was an Aries, a fire sign, yet she had so much more control over her anger. I'd say to her, "How can you tell someone to go fuck themselves with a big fat smile on your face?"

She'd just shrug and flash her pretty smile and say, "Practice, I guess."

Growing up I couldn't show my vulnerabilities. Not with my dad, not with my gang, and certainly not on the racecourse. If I did, I'd get my ass kicked. Jess helped me tap into a sweetness I'd been suppressing for years. She showed me that I could get what I wanted without being abrasive or aggressive. And I, in turn, showed her how to stand up for herself a little more, to say no and not to let her friends take advantage of her good nature. I toughened her up, and she softened me up.

Something else impressed me about Jess. She had big blue eyes, but one of them didn't work. She'd lost the sight in her left eye, the result of a childhood infection. That bad eye moved with the good one, but the pigmentation was slightly different. Despite that, she'd been a ski racer and lived a normal life. Sometimes I spent a day doing everything with one eye closed, trying to see the world as Jess did. The more I ran into things the more I respected what she had accomplished. Like Muffy, she hadn't let her disability slow her down or make her bitter.

Jess and I decided to spend that Christmas alone, just the two of us. We were Santa's little helpers. We wrapped presents wearing Santa hats and elf slippers. We drank eggnog and listened to Christmas carols and giggled hysterically amidst heaps of wrapping paper. I laughed more with Jess than I had at any period in my whole life. Life felt darn close to normal.

But I knew that life would be completely normal only when I was competing again. I was still serious about becoming a technical skier, but the downhill was beginning to exert its pull. It was the horse that had bucked me off, and I wanted to get back on, to prove I could ride it. The Olympics were a little over two years away. It wasn't about winning a medal anymore (though I thought a bronze would go nicely with my silver and gold). My victory would be just getting there.

On December 27, 1999, one year, nine months, and fourteen days after the fall in Crans, I buckled on my ski boots, stepped into my bindings, and went skiing.

The ski trail I chose for my first run in almost two years was Payday, the same trail where I'd skied my first big downhill when I was twelve. I was a twenty-eight-year-old woman in an expensive red suit from the Picabo collection by Spyder, but I tried to channel the energy of that teenage girl in the handmade blue suit who had loved nothing more than speed.

The day was very cold, the sky gray, the trees coated with rime. I cried the whole way up the chairlift. As I pushed off at the top of the run I made a few easy turns, nice and mellow, just another skier getting her ski legs back. I went slowly, relishing the feel of the snow under my skis and the wind in my face. I got up a little more speed. I was surprised at how strong my legs felt and how my body remembered what to do. As I went down I could feel the grin spread across my face and the tears streaming down my cheeks. The run flattened out toward the bottom, and I dropped in my tuck to see if my legs could take it. They could. I didn't go much faster than forty miles an hour that day, but it was probably the most important run of my life. It was everything that I'd dreamed it would be: fresh and raw and vivid and life affirming.

After I got home, Jess and I were in my bedroom, talking about the run. I was rummaging through a stack of clothes on the couch, looking for a shirt to change into. Suddenly a rush of emotion overtook me. I began to shake and sweat. I entered a sort of trance state. I blacked out, and when I came out of it, I was in a fetal position on the couch with my shirt off, though I didn't remember removing it.

"Are you okay? What's up?" Jess asked worriedly.

"Did you take my shirt off?" I demanded.

"No, you took your own shirt off! Where did you go? Where were you?"

That was a good question. I had been knocked out before, but I'd never simply lost consciousness like that. In retrospect I believe that I was releasing two years of pent-up stress and anxiety about skiing. That run on Payday showed me that I had nothing to be afraid of, and the volcano just blew. Afterward I felt completely calm and relaxed. I knew everything was going to be all right.

In the winter of 2000 I skied as many days as possible at Park City. When I wasn't signing helmets or posing for photos with tourists, I bopped around the mountain. People could meet me at an appointed time for a "ski with Picabo Street" session. They'd often ask me to give them pointers. I saw some very coordinated and athletic people put on skis for the first time and turn into fumbling rookies. It reminded me of how hard it is to ski, how afraid I had been my first time. I gained an appreciation for what I'd been able to accomplish, and it started to give me confidence.

Sometimes Jess would come with me. She had seen me ski on TV, but the first time she saw me ski in person she exclaimed, "Oh my god, you're so good! You're such a beautiful skier!" At the time, Jess's praise was just what I needed.

My confidence grew with every run. As the winter went on I challenged myself on harder and harder terrain: longer, steeper, bumpier. There was a ski camp at Mammoth Mountain, California, in May 2000, and I wanted to be ready. I ended every day, no matter the conditions, with a last run on Silver King. This was my idea of endurance training. By the end of the day the snow could be brutal, all chopped up and lumpy and thick. There were days when it required a total survival mode and I had to do whatever it took to get down. I'd pull off to the side of the trail, breathing hard, my legs burning, glowing with accomplishment. I'd look back up the trail and think, *Gotcha*. And ski off.

In March 2000, Jess left Park City. She wanted to go back to Maui to try to make her marriage work. I cried for days after she left, but I knew she had to go. It was time for me to stand on my own two feet.

You MIGHT BE WONDERING IF I EVER RODE SOLERO. IT TOOK A FEW YEARS, but I finally did it. I was fifteen, and my family had moved back to Hailey from Salt Lake City. Carl Massaro was buying our property in Triumph, so we drove out there to talk to him about it.

When we got to Carl's house I could see Solero prancing around in his corral.

"You know what?" I said to Carl. "I'm going to ride that damn horse."

"Okay," he answered. "You're big enough now."

As we put on Solero's bridle and saddle, I thought to myself, *I've cleaned your hooves and helped to shoe you and brushed every inch of you and braided your mane and petted and scratched you where you liked it. I've paid my dues, put in my time. Now it's my turn.*

Carl warned me that Solero would do everything he could to throw me off. "You have to establish your dominance, prove to him that you're running the show, that you're going to go where *you* want to go, not where *he* wants to go."

I swung up into the saddle. Solero threw back his head and I yanked on the reins with all my might. Then I dug my heels into his flanks and off we went down East Fork Road, toward a stretch of evergreen forest in the distance. We started at a trot, which became a canter, which turned into a full gallop. Over the next hour and a half Solero did everything he could to throw me: he ducked under low hanging branches, he stopped short, he reared a couple of times, Lone Ranger style. That ride was wild and thrilling and slightly out of control. It was the most exhilarating experience of my life, second only to the downhill. I knew I wouldn't have been able to handle that horse any sooner, and I was proud of myself for accepting Carl's advice to wait.

When I got back to Carl's place, he helped me dismount Solero and asked, "How was it?"

"Worth the wait."

12

ROOKIE WITH BAGGAGE

I PARACHUTED BACK INTO THE WORLD CUP CIRCUIT WITH A HEART FULL of hope and a head full of fear, wearing borrowed clothes. In half a lifetime of traveling to Europe, I had never lost a piece of luggage. In December 2000, on my way to Val d'Isère, France, for my first international ski race in thirty-three months, the bag with all my gear went astray. I had no speed suit, no helmet, no gloves. All I had was my boots. I had to borrow an entire speed wardrobe from my teammates. I slapped a piece of duct tape on the front of the helmet and wrote "Park City" on it in black marker. In a way, it was fitting that I skied that first race in other people's clothes, considering how little like my old self I felt.

The two years I spent recovering from my injuries changed me in subtle ways. I emerged from that time a calmer, more mature, more compassionate human being. My life had gotten so much simpler, and I realized I liked it. I didn't need to command the room anymore. I didn't want to thrive in chaos. My needs were simple: to resume my place on the team and prove to myself and the world that I had what it took to get to the Olympics in 2002. A simple goal, yet infinitely complicated, too. I was new, but not entirely improved: the fearless Picabo, the one brimming with confidence, was lying low. I had a long way to go, physically and mentally, to become world-class again.

In May 2000, when I showed up at my first on-snow training camp in two years, I understood what Rip Van Winkle must have felt like when he woke up out of his lengthy nap. A lot of things and people had changed. Cookie was still there—we greeted each other with a hug hard enough to crush walnuts—though now he worked for the U.S. Ski Team, not Rossignol. Jim Tracy was still the head speed coach, but Marjan Cernigoj had been promoted to take Herwig's place as head women's coach. As for my teammates, I recognized some faces: Megan Gerety, Kirsten Clark, Katie Monahan, Sarah Schleper, and Jonna Mendes, all of whom I'd raced with before my accident. But I didn't know the junior team: Julia Mancuso, Lindsey Kildow, Hilary McCloy, and Libby Ludlow. They were all strangers, and they knew me only by reputation. I hadn't expected the ski team to stay frozen in time during my absence, but the changes took some getting used to. And people had to get used to me. I got a lot of different reactions. Some people walked around me and gave me my space. Others came up and told me how great they thought I was. A few people simply left me alone. I knew what many of them were thinking: *Why is she doing this? She's accomplished everything a ski racer can. Why not just quit?*

My answer is this: I couldn't control that crash in Crans, but I could control the way I left the sport. I would not allow kissing a fence at sixty miles per hour to be my last hurrah. That's not how I wanted it to end, so I chose to keep going.

Athletes will call their first season back from an injury a "rebuilding year." I'd started rebuilding in January 2000, skiing hard at Park City. My legs got stronger with every run, and so did my confidence, but I knew the true test of my mental state would be in real race conditions. Sean McCann had told me I needed to get back into a competitive environment. If I could get close to my old self, I could go on autopilot and let instinct and habit take over. I hoped that the old confidence could kick in gradually, with every race. But first I had to build a good, strong physical foundation.

Every so often Jim Tracy, my speed coach, would call and leave an encouraging message on my answering machine. "Strong body, strong mind," he'd say. "Happy training."

I really started hitting it hard in the gym that winter. I followed workouts that Matty faxed me from Portland. He came to Park City to train me for two weeks, and I went to Portland to see him. I wanted to race at the U.S. National Alpine Championships in late March, but my knee wasn't 100 percent. I know I said I wasn't a particularly superstitious person, but my crash in Crans and its aftermath caused me to reconsider a lot of things. I had broken my leg at Crans on a Friday the 13th, and that was enough to put me off the number thirteen. Now I refused to ride a chairlift with the number thirteen on it. And when a reporter pointed out it was my thirteenth year on the team, I got the willies. The last thing I wanted to do was push my luck.

Instead, I went to the races as a commentator for NBC. That's where I saw some of the hot, young up-and-comers, like Caroline Lalive, a four-event skier who represented the ski team's next generation. The day of the slalom, I was on the hill early with an NBC crew, checking out the course, when Caroline showed up, the first girl on the hill. "Caroline impressed me this morning," I told the camera later. "She came out here wanting to do well and she's going to."

Attitude was everything, but the right skis were a close second. With my Rossignol contract over, I needed a new ski sponsor. Cookie rounded up a big selection of skis, and I tried every brand out there at Mammoth in May. I decided on a German ski called Völkl. Hilary and Katja had skied on them, so I'd been curious about them. The head of the North American division was a friend. I knew he would get me the skis I needed, when I needed them.

I was in for a big change here, too. In the two years I'd been gone, ski technology had changed dramatically. Skis were shorter, had a more exaggerated hourglass shape, and required a totally different technique—you generated power through the turn, not with the hips as much, but more with the core of the body. I used to muscle the ski through the turn; now all I had to do was tip it on edge and roll my knees into the turn. I generated more speed with less effort, and I felt behind all the time, as if I was trying to play catch-up with my own skis. It was like going from wooden to aluminum tennis racquets, and I struggled mightily at first. I still haven't quite got it right, but that spring and summer I felt as if I was learning to ski all over again.

The new skis and my concerns about going fast conspired to ding my confidence. I used to just barrel down a run and hit the fall line and gulp down the speed juice. Now I found myself standing at the top, dissecting every inch of snow, second-guessing my every move. *The snow is inconsistent over there. There are bumps over there. And down there, it's not groomed at all!* I'd pick my way down the mountain the same way I walked—before putting my left foot down I looked at the ground to see exactly where my foot was going and what it was landing on. I carried that habit onto the hill with me. I was nervous and tentative, my eyes on the ground. It blew my teammates away. I wasn't the Picabo they knew.

"PICABO, ARE YOU READY?"

I stood high on a mountainside in Portillo, Chile, watching the clouds shuttle back and forth across the sun. When the sun was shining, the course below me stood out in high relief, every bump and rut visible. When the clouds won, the light went flat and swallowed every potential pitfall. *I hate flat light.* I stood there and watched the sky nervously, waiting for my moment.

Speed and I were getting to know each other again, like a couple reconciling after a long separation. This was my third ski camp of the year but my first day of downhill training. I spent the first week in Portillo training GS and tooling around on long downhill boards, tucking once in a while to get the feel of them. They felt good, and I told my coaches I was ready to jump into speed training. We started the first run halfway down the course, the second two-thirds up. I took it mellow and slow, wearing my warm-up clothes, which slowed me down. Nothing serious. I was focusing on technique, not speed.

For the last run the coaches moved the start all the way to the top. Jim and the other coaches were parked along the course, waiting for me to go. Once in a while I heard Jim's voice crackle over Sheri's radio. Sheri Woroschuk was the physical therapist for the women's speed team. She was in the start with us every day, working on our bodies up to the last second.

"Picabo," she repeated, "are you ready?"

"No, not yet." I backed out of the start. "I think I'll wait for that cloud to clear the sun."

I let a couple of skiers go ahead of me. Finally the sun came out and the light on the course brightened. *Okay, I can see now.* I pushed out of the gate. It was a tricky start. I made a sharp left, pushed hard across a side hill, and then rolled into my first big turn. Four turns into it I was at full speed and in the thick of it, hanging on. The run felt good, and I knew I was smiling because I could feel the wind on my teeth. Every few seconds a thought, a small ping of emotion, would flash across my brain: *Oh, this is fun. Oh, I'm going fast. Oh, I remember this, this feels good, this is me, I can do this again.* By the time I got to the bottom I was so excited I wanted to yell out how great that was. But no one was around to hear me. So I grabbed onto my pole straps and swung my poles around in a circle—*woo woo woo!*—like a little kid swinging a lariat, all the way to the chairlift. I rode back up with a big shit-eating grin on my face. "That was great," Jim said. "It looked fun. How was it?"

"Okay, next?" I said, laughing.

The next day I was back on the mountain, stripped down to my speed suit, ready to go full bore. No more taking it easy. This was it, the real deal. The pitch was very steep. The coaches had dug a new start out of the snow, a few yards above yesterday's start, and I found it odd that they hadn't filled the old hole in.

The men's start was about four turns above the women's. Chad Fleischer, a member of the men's team, was up there waiting for me to go. I was about to push out of the gate when I got a funny feeling, as if an inner voice was telling me not to go, not yet.

"You can go; you're clear," said Sheri, who was standing by the start wand.

"No, let's let Chad go."

I watched Chad push out of the start, and as soon as he got on course, the weird vibe struck again. "Sheri," I said, "get into the start hole with me." She backed into the start and we crouched together like soldiers in a foxhole. I wanted to make sure if Chad hit something, it was my helmet, not Sheri's head.

Chad made a turn above us, and I could see him leaning too far in, bouncing around, on the edge of control. "Oh, God," I said out loud, "he's going to fall."

Chad cleared us, but as he laid into his next turn, his skis went out from underneath him and he wiped out right below us. He went sliding toward the old start hole, and to avoid going into it he tried to stand up, spinning around and crashing badly.

That should have been my run, I thought. *I should have been the one who fell.*

I said to Sheri, "You know what? I think I'm going to take a break." I skied down to Chad and asked him if he was okay. He reassured me that he was fine; it just felt like he'd tweaked something a little bit. (In fact, Chad had hurt his knee and was flown home the next day.) I skied down to Jim, shaking and crying, completely blown away.

"Get the hell off the mountain," he said.

"Excuse me?"

"If this freaked you out that much, then go. You need to take a break and get over it."

Jim and I are friends, but he's very emotional for a guy—sort of the anti-Ernst. He is just as passionate as I am about doing well. I know how much he believes in me, how much he wanted me out there. He wasn't being unsympathetic; he was just disappointed.

Knowing this didn't make me any less pissed. Suddenly my old competitiveness was unleashed and my stubborn nature took over. *Screw you. I'm proving to myself and everybody else that I can do this.*

"You know what, Jim? *I* will decide when I'm ready to leave the mountain." And with that I skied over to the lift, got on, rode to the top, and skied that run top to bottom without hesitating. I was a downhiller again.

That was a big day. I proved to everyone that I was ready to turn it up. Later Jim came up to me and said, "I'm really proud of what you did today. I didn't expect you to stay out there."

"I didn't expect you to do it." The more I heard that phrase, the more I wanted to defy expectations, just as I always had.

Portillo was a milestone in more ways than one. You know how I said before that I ski better when I'm not in love? That summer I met a man who changed that.

I'd first met John Mulligan at Mammoth in May. Like Cookie, he was a waxing technician, only he was in charge of preparing the skis for the junior speed team. John was my age, twenty-nine, quiet and sort of shy. He spoke with his eyes, which were the color of a high-mountain lake. I was attracted to John from the moment I saw him, but I tried to block it out. At Hood I went out of my way to avoid him. If we spoke, I made a point of looking down at the ground, because I knew if I looked in his eyes

I was a goner. All my emotional resources were being poured into my mission. I had to learn to ski again and get over my fear and keep on training. *No way*, I thought. *No way am I taking the time out of my life right now to start up another relationship and have it end up like the one with J.J. Forget it. I'm not even going to think about it.*

By the time the team got to Chile, there was no avoiding the attraction. John and I were thrown together on the first day. We found ourselves in the back of a truck, unloading ski bags. Without speaking, we'd automatically grab the same bag and move it, silently in synch. It was amazing. Finally I let myself stand up and look at him. John did the same, and when I looked into his eyes, I fell in love with him immediately. It was scary how quick and intense it was. *I can't believe how much I like this person already. I'm not supposed to. I shouldn't.* Being in love again was like skiing again: alternately scary and fun. At times I wanted to control my feelings, other times just go with them and allow myself to get completely swept away.

Before we left Portillo, John suggested I stop over and see him in Tampa, Florida, where he lived. I said no, then regretted it immediately. When I got home to Park City, we talked on the phone for three days straight. "I'd like to come see you," he said. "Okay," I replied. He was in Park City the next day. We spent most of September together, and in October I flew to Florida for a few weeks.

By early November, I had my heart set on racing the GS at the World Cup season opener in Park City on November 16–18. The first speed World Cup was a Super G at Aspen on November 24–25, followed by two downhills and a Super G at Lake Louise at the end of the month. My goal was to ski them all and then head to France for the European World Cup kickoff in Val d'Isère.

Our final tune-up for the season was our traditional early November ski camp in Colorado. I went into it lighter than usual. I'd been watching my diet like a hawk. I hadn't been able to train, so I had cut back on my caloric intake. I figured my new style of skiing didn't require as much power as it used to so I didn't need to be as big. I thought I could be little and still win. In addition, I thought that weighing less would put less stress on my knees. I showed up at camp and everyone cried, "Oh my God, you're so skinny!" We were training at fourteen thousand feet for two weeks and I was only eating eighteen hundred calories a day. "I never want to see it below two grand," Sue Robeson, our sports science specialist, admonished me. "If you don't eat enough, your body's going to starve and store fat. And then you're working against me, and against yourself."

We were staying at Beaver Creek, a posh ski resort near Vail, but training at Copper Mountain, another twenty minutes up I-70. I was feeling very strong in the gates, and when Marjan told me my times were good enough to earn me a spot on the GS team for Park City, I was ecstatic. "You deserve the second spot, if you want it." I told him I definitely did.

The drive from Beaver Creek to the freeway took me past Dr. Steadman's clinic in Vail. Richard was keeping close tabs on my right knee, so at the end of a day of running gates I'd swing by his clinic and say, "Here's what I look like after training today." If necessary, Richard would aspirate the fluid from my right knee. It was an ugly procedure. He stuck this big, nasty needle into the knee joint, found a pocket of fluid, and started drawing it out into a big vial.

After my third day of GS training, Richard pulled forty-four ccs of fluid out of my knee and changed vials six times. The effusion was a red flag signaling more cartilage damage.

Richard scheduled an MRI for the next day, November 12. It showed that I'd re-torn the meniscus. He scheduled surgery for four days later. As for the GS and slalom, he said, "You can't do it. It's too hard on your knees."

That pronouncement killed my GS dream. Having the decision made for me made it easier to accept. If I was going to ski in the World Cup, it would have to be in speed.

I embraced the opportunity. I stayed in Colorado and trained downhill during the days before the surgery. Richard had to do one more aspiration to get me through them. Those downhill days were my saving grace. The conditions were perfect, with snow so silky, groomed, and easy to ski it's called "hero snow" because you can do no wrong on it. A handful of Euros—the Austrian team, the Russians, a couple Norwegians—had come to train at Copper for the first downhill in Lake Louise, and I beat them in training runs by a second and a half.

The surgery wasn't a big deal, just a quick arthroscopic cleanup, and the recovery was only a few weeks. I added ten minutes of rehab with Sheri to the end of my workouts. But Lake Louise was out of the question, too. As I told the Associated Press, "Being able to walk without a limp for the rest of my life is more important." My World Cup return would be a Super G in Val d'Isère, France, the same course where I'd made my comeback in 1997. I had finished tenth that day. All I wanted to do this time was finish, period.

I LOST MY GEAR BAG EN ROUTE TO FRANCE (I CHANGED PLANES IN LONdon, but the bag didn't). My emotional baggage, on the other hand, definitely arrived with me. I was carrying the weight of the past into that race. I had been the most dominant skier in the world, the Olympic gold medalist, a monstrous presence on the circuit. Now that I was back, people expected me to be the same fiery, tempestuous downhill diva as before. But I wasn't. I felt soft and vulnerable and way, way behind.

Skiers who hadn't even been in contention three years earlier, particularly Renate Goetschl of Austria and Regine Cavagnoud of France, were now cleaning up. They had finished first and third, respectively, in the World Cup overall the previous season. Micki Dorfmeister was second, and Isolde Kostner, my Italian buddy, finished fourth in the overall and third in the downhill. Pilla and Meisi were still there, but they were coming back from knee injuries as well. Katja Seizinger was gone. She had blown out both knees in 1998 and called it a career. I ached for her presence on the World Cup. I could have used the old rivalry to fire me up.

I represented the old guard. The hot ones had been rookies five years ago, when I was the World Cup royalty. Now I had returned from exile, humbled, but my younger peers expected me to be the same imperious queen. I'd walk up to someone and try to engage him or her in conversation, and that person would look at me as if thinking, *You're the best. You're not supposed to be talking to me.* But I wasn't the best, not anymore. So I stuck close to the people who knew who I really was: Cookie, Sheri, Meisi, and my coaches.

But inevitably I collided with my past.

One day during training, I was sliding into the start. The race chief looked vaguely familiar. Then he spoke to me, and I placed him immediately.

"Oh, my friend," he said in a thick French accent, "just don't hit me this time."

A scene from my former life as a diva: January 1996, Val d'Isère, France. Katja had run before me, and after she went some course workers had skied onto the course and started smoothing it out with their skis. This was totally taboo. I got furious and started screaming, "Get off the track! Get off the track!" But no one did anything. The race official was turned away from me, and to get his attention I whacked him on the arm with my ski pole. He turned to me and I yelled, "Get them off the track!" He said nothing, simply turned back around, and called the course workers off the course. Then the race official looked at me, as if expecting an apology, but I was too furious to oblige. During my run I ended up making a big mistake, dragging my hand on a crucial roundhouse turn and finishing sixth to Katja.

Four years later, when that race official recognized me, I tried to make up for past omissions.

"I'm so sorry," I said, feeling my face flush.

"I understand," he answered. "You were right. Those workers shouldn't have been there. But hitting me with your pole . . ."

"I'm sorry. It was an extension of my arm. It was my only way to get your attention."

He just laughed some more. My past let me off easy that time, but I was pretty hard on myself. The whole week I kept my head low and didn't say much. I didn't hang out with my teammates, and Jonna got mad at me for being so distant. At twenty-three, she was young and carefree, the way I used to be. "I have really bad energy right now," I told her. "I don't want it to affect you." She said I was underestimating her as a teammate, and she was right. We broke through a barrier, and I knew I could rely on her when I needed to.

My start number on race day was thirty-four. I tried to remember the last time I'd started that far back, even in the Super G. I think it was 1994.

I had to wait a long time to race. I didn't recognize any of the skiers back in the pack with me. I felt anxious, unable to rein in my focus. As my start time approached, the conditions worsened; the light was flat, the course was deteriorating, and a storm was coming in. *I hate flat light.* Anxiety started washing over me in waves. "God, I'm nervous!" I said to Cookie and Sheri, as if verbalizing it would cut the tension. It didn't work.

Cookie and I tried to create the same prerace vibe, the same chemistry, the same old feeling of, "Let's fire it up; let's get it going." I did my warm-up, I clicked into my skis, and Cookie wiped the bases, just like the old days. As I entered the start, I looked down at my skis and saw a message scribbled on masking tape: "Remember, you're the best."

I did remember; that was the problem. If only I could be that fearless skier again, just for this run. I stood in the start, a knot in my throat, my chest in a vise, tears accumulating in my goggles. I had felt moments of fear in the past but had been able to work through them. The fear I was feeling at this moment was all encompassing. I couldn't control it. I didn't even know exactly *why* I was crying. I wasn't afraid of falling per se. Maybe I was afraid that my focus wasn't tight enough to enable me to ski as well as I knew I could. Maybe I was afraid I was going to hold back in some way and was crying in advance for my shortcomings. Maybe I knew that I still wasn't used to my new skis. It didn't matter. There was no turning back, no excuses. The countdown commenced. *Picabo, are you ready?* Ready or not, I had to go.

Sean had told me that ski racing was like riding a bike: it was something you didn't forget. As I got on course, I could almost feel my muscles remembering what to do. I could feel that old sensation, that old love for speed, spark up a bit, as if someone was blowing on a glowing ember to coax a fire back to life. But I skied with hesitation. I didn't attack the course; I waited for it to come to me. In the Super G that makes all the difference. "Welcome back Picabo Street!" the announcer said as I crossed the finish line. The crowd roared, and their approval warmed my soul. Meisi and Pilla were there and wrapped me in a hug. I had crossed the line in twenty-eighth place but finished the day where I'd started, in thirty-fourth, two and a half seconds behind the winner, Regine Cavagnoud. At least I had finished. Still, my result was something of a shock. I hadn't finished that far back since I was a scrub filler in my late teens.

At the bottom of the course I was mobbed by reporters with notepads and microphones. All I wanted to do was find a private corner and cry to release all the anxiety and anticipation of the day. But they all wanted me to give myself to them, so I thought, *Fine. All I want to do is go away and cry. You guys won't let me do it, so I'm going to cry right here in your faces while I'm talking to you.* I turned around and cried for twenty minutes, through six interviews.

Later, at the hotel, I sat down with Paul Robbins, the ski team's chief correspondent, and described the run to him: "I raced with my head, not my heart. I didn't have it in me that you need to risk to win. There were so many distractions. I had so many feelings it was hard to focus on my game. I totally skied with my head. I stood up more than I usually do. I just wanted to see where I was going."

He asked me to describe myself at that moment with one word.

"'Rookie.' Or maybe 'rookie with baggage.' Yeah, maybe 'rookie' because of the uncertainty and focus. I'm glad it's over. I'm looking forward to getting my luggage."

My bag showed up by the time I reached St. Moritz in mid-December. The Swiss resort was wall-to-wall fur coats and expensive cars. I'd never competed there, so I had a new course to learn, which only complicated my comeback.

Fortunately, the weather was sunny, and the light was good, and I felt much calmer in the start. My goal was to finish in the top twenty in the downhill. I attacked the course and crossed the finish line in nineteenth place, which made me happy. But then the day went sour. Alison Powers, a young hot one we called "Powie," ended up in seventh, and I ended up getting knocked out of the top twenty. Missing my goal really pissed me off. Our hotel was about a half mile from the bottom of the course; after the race Sheri waited for me to give me a ride. But somewhere our communication broke down, and I ended up walking off the mountain to the hotel. By the time I got there, my knees hurt so badly I was in tears. Everyone had been there for a while and had eaten lunch. Just something that small, missing lunch with the team, sent my emotions spinning out of control. It was almost a sign: maybe I didn't belong here after all.

In the next day's Super G, I tried harder and felt as if I skied more aggressively, but my time was slower. I finished forty-sixth. I was so frustrated. I cried until it was time to leave the hill. I felt as if I were wearing a backpack that kept getting loaded with more and more weight. My past was my baggage, and I couldn't get rid of it. The heavier it got, the more tired I became. I was exhausted all the time. I slept a lot. I was sad and spent a lot of time alone. I kept trying and failing, trying and failing. I felt humiliated, demoralized. My teammates helped me as much as they could, involving me in activities like shopping trips and giving me pep talks on the chairlift. But some of them didn't know what to say. Clarkie and Jonna and Powie were young and had never been hurt. Injuries had forced me off skis for almost three years of my life. They didn't understand. Megan Gerety had missed the previous season because of bad knees, so she could relate—almost too much. We just seemed to remind each other of our former selves. We'd never been particularly close, and now we steered clear of each other entirely.

I missed John, too. He was traveling with the junior team. But he stayed hands-on, even at a distance. He watched my races on TV and then he'd call and we'd talk about them, or he'd comfort me when I felt down—which was often.

Dad and I had fallen back into our routine of talking after every race. The day after the downhill at St. Moritz, I didn't call. I was in my room packing when the phone rang. I picked it up, sobbing. It was Dad.

"Are you okay?"

"Physically, I'm fine. But I'm a fucking emotional wreck, and I think I'm coming home."

I told him I was going to think about it over Christmas and decide whether to come back in January.

Later the phone rang again. It was Baba. "How's it going?"

"I'm having a really hard time, man," I said. "I keep trying and it doesn't work. I'm scared and my knees hurt. It's something different that stops me every day, and it's really bumming me out. Maybe this wasn't a good idea."

"Think about this," Baba said. "If you had come back to the sport and been able to just whoop everybody's ass after two years away, you wouldn't have any respect for yourself or your sport. You'd have no way to gauge what a good athlete you are and how much you've accomplished. Now you're getting to see it. You're getting to eat your humble pie, and having these troubles will make it that much sweeter when you get back. And if you never get back, who cares? You're still there. You're still competing. You're not in the front, but you're not in the back, either. You're in the middle. At least you're not scrub. But you're gaining respect for yourself and your sport right now. You need to look at it that way; otherwise, it's going to eat you up."

Baba's words were food for thought, and I had ten days to chew on them. The next day Pilla and I hugged good-bye. She was struggling, too, and we embraced and threw on our glasses to hide our tears. I said, "I'll see you when I see you." And we both left for Christmas break, not knowing if we'd see each other in January.

AFTER THE COLD, GRAY DECEMBER IN EUROPE, CHRISTMAS IN TAMPA WAS a balm. I met John's mother, and we spent lazy hours fishing on his boat and working on our tans. Ironically, I'd felt nervous about going. I equated Florida with margaritas and Jimmy Buffett songs and laziness. I didn't want R&R right now. I wanted to figure out how to ski faster. I felt ravished for speed, starved for it. But a complete and utter lack of snow turned out to be just what I needed. Out of sight, out of mind. The weather was sunny, the people were happy, and the food was yummy. One day John and I motored across the bay to eat at a little shrimp joint and had to make our way back by the glow of a flashlight. His laid-back personality balanced out my antsy energy. A quiet guy who liked simple pleasures. I could get used it.

I'd been careful about my diet in Europe, but in Florida I let myself go. Being light didn't seem to be helping my skiing. "Aw, screw it," I said, and I started to eat.

I returned to Utah for New Year's with John feeling reenergized and looking forward to two days of training with the team on the Olympic downhill course at Snowbasin. The course is called Wildflower, but don't let the flower-power name fool you. It's technically difficult, not a glider's course, but I felt an immediate affinity for it. It was love at first ski, and as I barreled down, I was reminded that this swatch of American soil was the reason I was torturing myself. I had a mission, and I had to keep going, my eyes on the horizon, not at my feet. My short-term prospects weren't all that rosy, anyway. The 2001 World Alpine Ski Championships were in St. Anton, Austria, January 29–February 10, and I knew I might not make the team.

"I've accepted it's going to be a tough year," I told *The Salt Lake Tribune*. "That's okay. I didn't come back to the sport for this season. I came back for next year."

The next big race was at Cortina in mid-January. Pilla showed up with a different look in her eyes, and so did I. We were ready to step it up. I loved Cortina, and I went in there with a good attitude. That course and I were old friends, and I knew I'd be able to attack it and work on the things I needed to work on.

The night before the race I got my start number: fifty. The back of the pack. *Jesus Christ,* I thought, *I didn't start this far back in my first World Cup year. I'm starting all over again. I'm really, really starting all over.*

I went into the start gate at Cortina feeling neutral—not aggressive or competitive or angry. My mind was a clean slate, and I could write whatever story on it I wanted. Good, bad, or indifferent. It was up to me.

The fog bank that morning was almost as thick as the cigarette smoke in an Italian disco. As I entered the start, I literally could not see the first gate. When I pushed out, it was as if I was dropping into an abyss. If I hadn't known that course like the back of my hand, I would have been in trouble. As it was, I skied the top of the course by braille, my skis like fingers, feeling their way along every inch of terrain. As I approached the steepest pitch, I left the fog bank behind, and Marjan told me later that by the way I shot out of that fog he knew that everything was going to be okay. I had my hands forward and my shoulders rolled and I wanted it. It didn't matter that I couldn't see. I wanted the speed. I wanted to go fast.

The old guard acquitted itself well that day. Megan got fifth, her best result in three years, with a time of 1:33:62. I skied out of fiftieth place and finished in fifteenth, with a time of 1:34:43. It was my first top-twenty result since my comeback. Jonna and Caroline tied for nineteenth, and Clarkie tied for twenty-third.

But it wasn't enough to get me a spot on the downhill team at the Worlds. I still had one shot: the next day's Super G. "You could qualify tomorrow if you got a top fifteen for sure," Marjan told me. "But in downhill, we've got our team."

I started number sixty-one the next day—scrub!—and finished out of the top fifty. Everyone on the women's A team was going to the Worlds: Clarkie, Jonna, Megan, Sarah, Caroline, Kristina Koznick. Everyone but me.

I put on a brave face in interviews. I told reporters I knew I wasn't ready to race at the Worlds. I would have wanted to medal and would have pushed myself too hard. I would race a couple Europa Cups in France, where the pressure wasn't as high. I hadn't skied a Europa Cup since 1993. Not only had my forward progress stalled, I was actually going *backward*.

The team couldn't believe they were going without me. And I couldn't believe that a World Championship team existed without me. Cookie was helping Chip move the cargo van out of the bottom parking lot, and he took off and forgot to say good-bye. The whole thing was odd.

The next day, Jim drove me to Innsbruck, where I would meet up with the junior team. I cried as I left Cortina.

NOW I'M REALLY SLUMMING IT, I THOUGHT. ON THE EUROPA CUP YOU drive long hours, stay in lame hotels, eat lousy food. But I was willing to put up with it for two weeks. That's how determined I was to make it back to the top.

The only good thing about skiing the Europa Cup was seeing John. But, frankly, I worried about traveling with him. It was like being coworkers in the same office, and I wasn't sure our relationship would thrive on it.

From Innsbruck we flew to Milan and drove to Abetone, Italy. The race was a GS so I didn't compete. I just sat and watched it rain. We nicknamed the resort Raintone.

My new teammates were teenagers. There were five of us: Hilary McCloy, sixteen, from Vermont; Julia Mancuso, fifteen, from Lake Tahoe; Lindsey Kildow, fifteen, from Vail; and Courtney Colise, nineteen, from New Hampshire. And me. Picabo Street, twenty-nine. Some of them were newborns my first year on the team. At dinner I'd think, *I'm sitting across the table from a high school junior.* And they were probably thinking, *She's practically thirty!*

From Abetone we drove several hours to Pra-Loup, France. That was the same place where Hilary Lindh and I had finally called a truce back in 1995. I had been on top of the world then. It was almost surreal to be going back to Pra-Loup, starting over. The kids rode in the team van. I rode with John, who was driving the cargo van. We didn't try to hide our relationship because we knew we were going to be together forever.

I felt sort of like the chaperone at a high school slumber party. When the girls and I were together as a group, I refused to regress. At meals I'd engage the physical therapist, a woman in her thirties named Sue, in conversations about her adventures as a medical volunteer in third-world countries. Afterward, Courtney and Hilary would go to their hotel room and surf the Web on their laptops. I could hear them in their room, giggling.

Each of the girls was going through a personal drama. Courtney was struggling with a chronic groin injury, trying to ski through until the spring, when she was scheduled to have surgery. She trained in Pra-Loup and then flew home. Tatum Skoglund, an eighteen-year-old from Washington State, took her place. On January 2, Tatum had found her brother dead in his bed; he had died of a rare gastrointestinal hemorrhage. Yet here she was a month later, gearing up to race in the World Junior Alpine Championships on February 2. Lindsey was fighting with her dad a lot. Hilary had had a blood disease the year before and was still recovering. She had days of fatigue, but overall she skied well and struggled through some tough conditions. I admired her guts and I gave her helpful hints on things like how to kill time before the start. I tried to be supportive, a buddy. I would stop by their rooms regularly to check up on them. I had been there once myself. I wondered how many of them would hang with it.

I worked hard to get along with Julia Mancuso. She talked too much and flirted with John and didn't give me much respect. I think she felt insecure in my presence and competitive with me. She'd been shuttling from the World Cup to the Europa Cup, and by Pra-Loup she was worn down. I beat her by five and a half seconds in training, and she ended up pulling out of the race and leaving, complaining of burnout. Lindsey wanted to leave, but later I found out that her father had said to her something along the lines of, "If you walk away from this weekend and don't race against that woman [meaning me], you're an absolute fool. Because she has so much to teach you." Lindsey stayed.

I didn't want to lose in Pra-Loup, and to this day I don't know why I did. I skied with power and control. I made better turns and flowed more smoothly from one section of the course to another. I was no longer standing up before a jump. I was getting bigger air, making bigger turns. I wasn't afraid to go fast. Yet I finished third and fifth. I had felt in control and skied awesome. Now I was getting really pissed off. I felt as if the higher power was saying, "You skied well enough to beat everybody, but I'm not going to let it happen. I'm going to slow you down and keep punishing you and make you keep banging your head against the wall."

John reminded me of the little things that had gone right that week. "You seemed more connected to your skis," he said. "You skied more aggressively. You took your skiing to a whole other level."

I went home to Park City for a few days of rest. I knew I probably wasn't going to qualify for the World Cup finals in Åre, March 7–11, either. That left one last World Cup, a downhill in Lenzerheide, Switzerland. I had clinched my first downhill title there in 1995. I flew back to Europe one last time.

The United States had done well at the Worlds. Daron Rahlves won the men's Super G in superb fashion, and Megan took fourth in the women's downhill. Jonna was ninth, and Clarkie tied for eighteenth. She would have gone faster if she hadn't hooked a gate with her arm.

Meanwhile, the media was calling my comeback "less than memorable" and my results "uninspired." But I was starting to feel more like my old self. I had more confidence, and I was getting my skis under control. "If I can get in the top ten here, it will be another big step," I told the Associated Press the day before the race.

It was a great day. I got seventh, Megan got eighth, and Clarkie won the race, giving the U.S. team its first World Cup win that season. After the race the team was gathered in the lunchroom, and when Clarkie walked in, Jonna said, "Let's give her a standing O." And everyone stood up and clapped for Clarkie, and she blushed and looked like she was going to cry. We were genuinely happy for her, and it made me think back to when my teammates would walk away when I mounted the podium. I thought, *I hope I can win a race soon. Maybe my team will stand up for me.*

The best news was that everyone finished in the top twenty-five in the world in downhill. Almost everyone—I missed the cut by two points. I didn't qualify for the World Cup finals, but in a way I didn't mind. I had hurt myself three years ago in the finals. While the rest of the team went to Sweden, I flew to Canada and met up with John and the junior team again. There were four Nor-Am races at Whistler, British Columbia, two downhills and two Super Gs. Skiing the Nor-Am circuit was another step backward, but in reality it was the best step I could have taken.

On February 28, 2001, I won my first race of the season. On March 1, I won my second. On March 2, I won my third. On March 3, I won my fourth. Four races, four wins. I was also ten pounds heavier by this time. Coincidence? Who cares. I was winning.

Granted, I should have won, since I was racing against teenagers. But then the Canadian national team blew in for the Super Gs, and I kicked their asses by more than a second and a half in the last race. I also drew confidence from knowing that being in love with John seemed to help my skiing. Maybe it was the care with which he prepared my skis. (Ladies, you haven't lived until you've had your bases waxed by the man you love.) Or maybe it was simply the fact that he loved to ski so much. On the days when I was dragging or being a punk, I'd just look at him and think, *He would give anything to be in my shoes, to be able to race and be good like me. I'd better enjoy this.*

And I did. Every day I skied faster, nailed more turns, worked on my technique. My confidence stepped up another notch, and the backpack seemed to lighten. Just in time for the last race of the season. One last shot to prove myself to the world.

NORMALLY A NOR-AM RACE IN UTAH IN MID-MARCH WOULDN'T ATTRACT much of a field. But this wasn't any old race. The 2002 Winter Olympics were in less than a year, and this was the first competition on the women's Olympic downhill course. And so the entire women's World Cup dragged their tired asses to Ogden, Utah.

The best part was I lived only an hour way, in Park City. John and I stayed home until the night before the first training run and then drove to Ogden. We checked into the Best Western, and the next morning we went to a restaurant called Jeremiah's for breakfast. All the Euros were there, jet-lagged and haggard, looking like they'd gone ten rounds with the sandman. Their eyes were puffy and they were nodding off into their coffee cups. This is what I was thinking, what my former self would have said out loud, before I went and got all compassionate: *How you guys feeling? Shitty? Well, you'd better figure out how to not feel so shitty next year when you get here in midseason, because it's not going to be any differ-*

*ent. It's at the same time of year. I've been doing it for fifteen years, three
times a year in your countries. So guess what? No sympathy.*

The new Picabo said hi to the racers and wished them a good week.

I had another advantage on the field. I'd just won four straight races and
was on a tear. And because they were Nor-Am races, I had a lot of points,
which put me in the top seed. Racers with Nor-Am points took precedence.
For the first time that season, I picked my start number every day, anywhere in the top thirty. Cavagnoud, Dorfmeister, Kostner: all the hot girls
with all the good World Cup points got thrown in the back of the pot to
wherever they got drawn.

The weather was stormy and the race was postponed several times. I
was training well, finishing in the top three every day. On March 13, at
breakfast, I looked at my Rolex and saw the date. Three years exactly since
my crash in Crans. That thirteen thing again. No matter. I had a job to do.
I ended up with the second fastest time that day. Herwig was there in his
role as director of the Olympic Alpine skiing venues, and one day we rode
up the chairlift together. I think he was a little surprised that of the three
options he had stated that day in Portland, I had gone for number three,
the hardest.

"Picabo," he said, "if you go all the way, you can prove me wrong."

"What do you mean?"

"I told everyone that you're not going to make it again."

"Well, up yours!"

"I'll tell you one thing: if you get back on that Olympic podium, you
will rewrite history."

I'm not sure what Herwig meant. Maybe he meant that no skier had
ever come back from such serious injuries to win an Olympic medal. Or
that no one had ever won an Alpine skiing medal in three consecutive Winter Olympic Games. I'll have to ask him someday.

All I knew for sure was how badly I wanted to win at Wildflower.

There's a strategy that takes place at a pre-Olympic race. A competitor
who does well becomes a favorite going into the Games, and the pressure
can be paralyzing. So a racer will hold back so as not to tip his or her hand,
and to keep the element of surprise going into the Games.

One day Jim said, "Let's talk about it. Are we going to show our cards
or hold back a bit?"

I looked at him and said, "I don't give a shit. I can deal with the pressure of next year if I win here. I'm fine with it. I'm skiing my heart out here. If I can beat these girls here, I'm stoked."

"All right, fine. You go get it. You do your thing."

The race happened abruptly. There was a brief break in the weather, so a training run was changed to the actual race. Baba and Lauren had driven from Sun Valley to watch the race, and a couple of my aunts from Salt Lake were going to come as well. But they missed it. I was on my own, and somehow it felt right.

The top of Wildflower begins slowly, with a gradual, mellow pitch that rolls into a long, gentle side hill. I dropped off the side hill and made one, two, three quick turns above the first pitch, a fourth and a fifth turn on the pitch, a sixth turn as I came off the pitch, and then a big right-footed seventh turn onto the first jump. By the time I hit that jump I was shifting to third gear; as I landed I shifted to fourth gear and went ripping through the next section. I dropped to the right, dropped to the left, dropped again to the right, went uphill briefly, made a quick zigzag, and two turns later flew off another jump. I landed underneath the gondola and rattled through three big open turns, holding my tuck the entire time, and by the time I got through a series of gates I'd shifted into fifth gear and was hauling official ass. I flew back underneath the gondola, caught flight off a side hill, and landed on the bottom pitch. Then I tucked straight to the finish for one hundred yards—a good football field—and by the time I crossed the finish line I was hitting max velocity and had to screech to a halt before I hit the end of the finish area. At no point did I slow down or check my speed; I kept shifting and shifting and going and going, sticking with it, going faster, faster, and faster still.

I crossed the finish line with a time of 1:41:57. Micki Dorfmeister, who had won the World Cup downhill title that season, was second, half a second slower than me. Hilde Gerg of Germany was third.

The win was almost anticlimactic. The whole thing just felt surreal. My Euro friends were happy for me. Hilde made some excuse about her new skis not being able to turn, but I just smiled. I had proven myself to the Euros in a way I never had before. My love of the sport, my drive, my will—there was no doubt how much I wanted it. And I wanted more. I was probably the only woman out there who wished the season could keep going, one race after another. I left the season hungry, and humble pie was not on the menu.

Later Sean McCann, my sports psychologist, came up to congratulate me. "Picabo," he said, "what I saw you do this year, the way you pulled yourself together mentally and got past the fear and anxiety, was a great, great victory. In ways, it was a bigger accomplishment than winning an Olympic medal. I'm more proud of you for this than for anything you've ever done."

John had to stay at the hill to work, so after the race I drove home by myself. I decided to make a call. I dialed Matt James's number in Portland; his voice mail picked up.

"Matty!" I yelled. "I'm just calling to tell you that, well, I did it. I won on the Olympic downhill course. I'm psyched; I've got my confidence back. But I know if I'd been stronger I could have skied it even better. So let's do it, man. Let's shock the world again."

EPILOGUE

ONE LAST STORY ABOUT GOING FAST.

A couple years ago, I appeared in an air force training video about knee injuries and rehabilitation. Afterward the air force guys asked me what they could do to thank me besides giving me a T-shirt. I answered, "F-16, baby. Thunderbirds."

For years I'd been compared to a jet fighter pilot on skis, and I'd dreamed of flying in a jet. That would be the ultimate rush. No lurking cops with speeding-ticket quotas to fill. Just the wild, blue yonder and all the speed I could handle. It took a while to make that flight happen, but on June 19, 2001, it finally did. As I was strapped into that rear cockpit at Hill Air Force Base near Ogden, I knew I was in for the ride of my life.

I was dressed just like a real pilot, in a G suit and an oxygen mask. When that F-16 took off straight up twelve thousand feet at four hundred miles an hour, I screamed and hollered with delight. We did barrel rolls to the right and the left, two or three of them in a row, pretending we were dodging bullets. We did nose-overs, where the plane flies straight up and does a back flip. (You can't do a forward flip because the blood could run to your head and pop your eyeballs out and make your brain explode.) This was the supercharged version of that plane ride back when I was eight, and I felt like a kid again, loving every second.

The G forces generated by a jet fighter are different from those on a downhill course. In the jet there was no third directional tug, no feeling of being pulled into the center of the earth. In the air it was a pressure that started in my eyeballs and grew until it was like having an elephant on my lap. I wanted to pull as many Gs as possible. At four Gs I could still breathe. At six Gs the G suit started puffing like an adder on my stomach and legs, pushing the blood into my brain so I didn't "G lock," or pass out. The tight suit and the mask triggered in me a claustrophobic feeling and I had to fight to stay calm. Seven Gs. "How are you doing back there?" my pilot, Captain Korey Amundson, asked. His call sign was Beef. "Great! More!" Eight Gs. Nine Gs, the maximum the jet could do. "Faster!" I yelled.

Suddenly I felt the plane surge as though through a wind tunnel and a loud *boom!* like the sky splitting in half. "We just broke the sound barrier!" Beef announced. Eight hundred miles an hour. I had gone as fast as I would ever go, almost as fast as the human body could go without exploding. Now I'm a member of the Nine G Club. That's my call name: Nueve.

The flight lasted an hour. The last thing we did was buzz Snowbasin twice and scope out the Olympic downhill course. When the 2002 Winter Games roll around, no one else in the field will have seen Wildflower from a thousand feet in the air. The snow had melted and I could see the bones of the course, every twist and turn and rocky drop-off. I could see the fluorescent-green face of the giant scoreboard tucked into the trees. In less than a year that scoreboard would be flashing the medal-winning times. Maybe mine will be one of them; maybe it won't. All I know is I'll be the underdog once again, just the way I like it.

And then what? I'll be almost thirty-one after the 2002 Winter Olympics. When it's time to walk away from ski racing, I'll know it. I've seen too many athletes prolong their retirements and exit in less than glorious fashion. I'm not quite ready to quit, but the day is coming, and when it arrives, I'll recognize it. I'll be ready for it.

What will make me happy afterward? I struggle with that question a lot. It's funny, but having a mission and accomplishing it make me feel satisfied and complete, but not happy. Happiness and fulfillment are not necessarily the same thing for me.

Trying to have a normal life will make me happy. I know with a name like mine, I can never be completely normal. My unique name is a blessing and a curse. I can't escape it. Let's face it; you hear someone call out the name "Picabo," and there's pretty much only one person he or she could be referring to. A few years ago I adopted a new middle name, a secret alias, in effect. It's a very normal name; a million other women have it. It's the name I use when I don't want to be Picabo for a little while.

I want to explore normalcy, a life away from being Picabo. I want all those things I've been holding at arm's length all these years, the things that get in the way of being a warrior, like marriage and kids. I want to put down roots. I have just the spot: a piece of land about an hour from Jackson Hole, Wyoming. Look to the east at dawn and you can see the Teton Range rising out of the mist. It's so far from everything. Sometimes, when I want to slow life down, I turn off my cell phone, and John and I drive out there with a trailer and camp for several days.

I'd like to do all the things I haven't been able to because I haven't had the time or because they were too risky physically. I want to go to the Super Bowl. I want to ride my ATV and my snowmobile. Go water skiing and winter camping. And skiing, of course, but just for fun, making lazy, casual turns in the snow. I want to stay active, but at a lower intensity. I don't want to be in pain anymore. My nephew, Cade, calls my scars "Auntie Peek's owies." I'll have to learn to live with them. I can tell you this much: I don't plan on adding to my collection.

Wherever I go, whatever I end up doing, I'll always be the girl from Triumph doing her best to make it happen. I don't go back to Triumph very often; I want to remember the place as it was. But last spring I drove to Triumph. A film crew had come to shoot a short documentary about my life, and they wanted to shoot some footage of me at the place where it all started.

I'll admit I was curious. I hadn't been back in three years, and I wondered how the old place looked. John drove and the film crew followed us in another car. After we passed the old iron bridge, I said, "Go right here," and we turned off Highway 75 onto East Fork Road.

John and I passed the boardinghouse (exterior painted, windows intact) and the ruined mill, which is beyond saving. We passed our old house, which has been spruced up with a new roof and windows. The pavement still stops at Triumph, but there are new homes tucked into the hills. Now it's the kind of place where people go jogging with their dogs. The old red pickup we used to haul Tom the mule in sits back in the hills, full of bullet holes where people have used it for target practice.

The land is holding out as best it can. Porfrey Peak is still there, of course; Baba owns the quarry business now, and four or five times a week he makes the gear-grinding drive up that road and comes back down with a big load of rock. That rock is still used for new buildings all around the Sun Valley area, and beyond: it's being used for the new buildings going up at Snowbasin for the Olympics. Talk about things coming full circle. Dad, who couldn't stay retired, works for Baba as a mason, and at night he still comes home and washes the rock dust off his hands. Mom still plays the piano every chance she gets. She's still the musician, still the glue that holds us together.

Going back to Triumph made me want to be a little girl again, to run and play as I used to. Maybe that's why what was done with the black sand bothered me so much. As part of its cleanup efforts, the state had come in with bulldozers and spread out the piles of black sand, then put dirt over the top so they looked like fields of dirt instead of lead deposits. The state also filled in the marshes and covered them with topsoil and planted foliage. I think it's sort of deceitful. People who drive out there five years from now won't know what lies underneath those new plants. But I'll know. Hiding the black sand detracts from the authenticity of the community and what it represents to me and the people who lived there in my era.

Most of them are gone. Billy and Jamie's parents still live there, as well as a few people who were mean to us as kids. Otherwise, all the people are different. That day I drove out with John and the film crew, I didn't see anyone I knew. The only people I saw were a pack of eight kids running down the road.

After a couple seconds I started yelling at John to stop the car. "Stop, stop, oh my God, stop!" He braked hard and I opened the car door and jumped out. My jaw dropped like Sebastian the crab in *The Little Mermaid*. Those kids looked just like my gang had twenty years earlier, feet flapping on the pavement, hair flying in the wind. Only there was one big difference: it was seven girls and one boy, trying his best to keep up.

"It's completely flip-flopped!" I said out loud.

I couldn't believe it. I knew that little boy was going to turn out to be someone special, because those little girls were going to work him over, all day, every day. I watched them run down the street and thought, *I would have given anything for that to have been the scenario when I grew up here. For it to have been all girls. How sweet would that have been?* Of course, then I wouldn't have turned out to be the person that I did. The Tiger. The champion who fell down and refused to stay down. The woman standing in the middle of a road, watching eight kids race the wind and wanting with all her heart to take off after them.